SAINSBURY'S
GOOD SOUP BOOK

LINDSEY BAREHAM

Published exclusively for J Sainsbury plc
Stamford House   Stamford Street
London   SE1 9LL
by Martin Books
Simon & Schuster Consumer Group
Grafton House   64 Maids Causeway
Cambridge   CB5 8DD

ISBN 0 85941 870 7

First published 1995

Pictured on the front cover:
Roasted Red Pepper and Tomato Soup with Basil Cream and Olive Croûtes (page 36)
Pictured on the back cover:
Cod Chowder with Puy Lentils and Salsa Verde (page 59);
Borscht (page 55) and Cabbage Soup with Dumplings (page 58)

Design: Green Moore Lowenhoff
Cover illustration: Sally Swabey
Photography: Steve Baxter
Author photograph: Catherine Shakespeare Lane
Food preparation: Jane Stevenson
Styling: Marian Price
Typesetting: Stylize
Printed in Italy by Printer Trento

Contents

The Author

Lindsey Bareham is a restaurant critic turned food writer, who has eaten out on behalf of *Time Out, The Good Food Guide*, the *Daily Telegraph*, the *Sunday Telegraph*, the *Sunday Express*, and the *Gault Millau Guide to London*.

Twenty years of reviewing the best and many of the worst restaurants in London and the rest of the country provides Lindsey with a unique background for cookery-writing. She used her experience of cuisines from around the world to write two classic cookery books, *In Praise of the Potato* (1989, republished 1995), and *A Celebration of Soup* (1993). In 1994 she co-wrote *Roast Chicken and Other Stories*, a cookbook with Simon Hopkinson the chef and co-proprietor of Sir Terance Conran's Bibendum restaurant.

Lindsey's passion for seasonal British produce and understanding of unusual and imported ingredients give her cooking an international flavour. She's a great believer in making good food accessible to everyone and her recipes can be followed by the most inexperienced cook – including her teenage sons.

Lindsey writes regular columns for *Homes and Gardens* and *She*, broadcasts regularly on London Radio and BBC Radio, and is food advisor to *Pie In The Sky*, the television series starring Richard Griffiths as the chef-detective Henry Crabbe.

Black-bean Soup with
Tomato and Avocado Relish

Spring Potato Soup
with Herbs and
Chive Cream

Soda Bread

Pumpkin Soup with Coriander and Chilli Gnocchi

Gazpacho

Introduction

A steaming bowl of hot soup is one of the most soothing, delicious and easily digested foods that it's possible to eat. Soup can mean so many things and be flavoured in so many different ways. It can be simple, elaborate or anywhere in between. It can be hot or cold, thick or thin, classic or innovative, carefully contrived or a mélange of leftovers. It can be a comforting dish with a creamy texture, a heart-warming broth, an elegant, crystal-clear consommé, or a meal in itself.

I love the versatility of soup, and the endless possibilities that it presents for the home cook.

Stock- and soup-making have been the focus of my attention for the past three years. Out of the blue, an old flatmate turned up on my doorstep with a novel eating disorder – she was recovering from a broken jaw and was restricted to a liquid diet. Her food cravings and a new acute appreciation of multi-faceted flavours became my challenge. From being a keen soup-maker, I became obsessive. I learnt to 'build' stocks, particularly vegetable combinations, and soup took over as the mainstay of my family's diet. The more soups I cooked, the more I wanted to cook.

We moved with the seasons, from wintry vegetable and pulse purées to delicate consommés and chilled summer gazpacho. To satisfy my family, I began experimenting with things to add to soup. Dumplings, croûtons, meat-balls, sauces and salsas and other garnishes accompanied all those creamy purées. As my friend recovered, we moved on to stewy soups; and when I entertained I cooked soup-suppers, offering a choice of several soups with various complementary garnishes and accompaniments.

Soup is an open-ended gastronomic journey and can be sampled in every country's cuisine. It's widely regarded as man's oldest food; for centuries, soup was the daily fare of the ordinary people of the ancient empires of Egypt, Greece and Rome.

Soup in the nineties has made a dramatic comeback. Healthy, fast and economical, it's the ideal food for our times. Part of the reason for this is that

Recipe Notes

All recipes in this book give ingredients in both metric (g, ml, etc.) and Imperial (oz, pints, etc.) measures. Use either set of quantities, but not a mixture of both, in any one recipe.

All teaspoons and tablespoons are level, unless otherwise stated.

1 teaspoon = a 5 ml spoon;

1 tablespoon = a 15 ml spoon.

Egg size is medium (size 3), unless otherwise stated.

Vegetables and fruit are medium-size unless otherwise stated.

Freshly ground black pepper should be used throughout.

old-fashioned thickening ingredients like flour are no longer necessary. Soups can be given extra body with potato, onions and garlic, or breadcrumbs, and avocado, among other things. The wide range of produce now available means that the possibilities for soup-making are endless. I'm an unashamed enthusiast.

Soup-making Equipment

Very few utensils or pieces of equipment are essential for soup-making, and most of them are in general use anyway.

Vital, however, is at least one **cook's knife**. Cooks are always going on about the importance of a decent knife in the kitchen and it really is worth buying the best you can afford, and building up a set of knives. Look after them and they will last a lifetime. Always wash cook's knives immediately after use, and sharpen them little and often with a professional **steel**. I've never got the knack of using a traditional steel, but I highly recommend the kind of **knife sharpener** that incorporates two miniature spring-loaded steels through which you run the knife; foolproof *and* effortless!

I find a 9 cm (3½-inch) **paring knife**, and a 15 cm (6-inch) **cook's knife** invaluable for trimming and slicing vegetables. And I wouldn't be without my Japanese **cleaver/chopper**, which is surprisingly versatile and ideal for bruising and pounding garlic. I'd also recommend either an 8 cm (3-inch) or a 13 cm (5-inch), thin, **curved boning knife**, which makes light work of preparing meat.

Preparation and Cooking Times
Preparation and cooking times are included at the head of the recipes as a general guide; preparation times, especially, are approximate and timings are usually rounded to the nearest 5 minutes.

Preparation times include the time taken to prepare ingredients in the list, but not to make any 'basic' recipe, such as a stock.

The cooking times given at the heads of the recipes denote cooking periods when the dish can be left largely unattended, e.g. baking, and not the total amount of cooking for the recipe. Always read and follow the timings given for the steps of the recipe in the method.

A user-friendly **vegetable peeler** will save time, and a pair of razor-sharp **scissors** will come in very handy. At least one decent wood or plastic **chopping board** is vital.

Many of the recipes in this book specify the use of a **liquidiser** or **food processor**. Either can be used for most of the operations in this book, since there is usually plenty of liquid. One of these is useful but not essential and speeds up jobs that can be done by hand. Although it's not so fast (or such a pain to wash up), I often use my **hand-held blender** for liquidising jobs. Alternatively, a really useful and inexpensive gadget for soup-makers is a large

mouli-légumes food press. It's really a sophisticated sieve-cum-masher and comes with three different-size metal discs for puréeing. Its relative the **mouli-julienne** comes with five blades of varying sizes for slicing and grating.

Puréed soups that are made from fibrous vegetables, or that contain pips and skins, need to be sieved. I use a 15 cm (6-inch) steel **sieve** for all my sieving jobs and use a wooden spoon to push the purée through. I never seem to have enough **wooden spoons** and would also recommend owning at least two **rubber spatulas** and two **wire balloon whisks**. I find a **zester** useful but not essential.

A **perforated skimmer** or **spoon** is useful for all sorts of jobs and a **bulb baster** is handy for skimming the fat from the surface of stock. This is a plastic or glass tube with a rubber bulb on the end: squeezing the bulb causes liquid to be sucked up. A **measuring jug** is more useful than a set of **scales**.

The best pan for cooking stock is tall and narrow, to avoid unnecessary evaporation, and with side-handles for easy transportation. I've recently bought a proper heavy-bottomed **stock-pot** but any saucepan will do.

I used to make all my soups in various-sized, vitreous-enamelled cast-iron **casserole dishes** but these days I prefer non-stick lidded **saucepans**. When soups need to be left to simmer for any length of time I use a **simmer mat**, to prevent the food from burning.

Stocks and Stock-making

For many people, stock remains the stumbling block to soup-making. Not all soups rely on stock and many are overwhelmed by it, but it's true that stock is often the body and soul of a soup.

There is no mystery about stock-making. The basic method, whether you use vegetables, poultry, meat or fish, is always the same. It requires no particular skills, and, once a few undemanding preparations have been made, it cooks itself. At its most basic, it's the liquid you've cooked the vegetables in. At its most complex it's a crystal-clear, intensely flavoured, gelatinous consommé.

Stock can be satisfactorily stored in the fridge for three days. It also freezes well and keeps in near-perfect condition for up to three months. Freeze stock in small quantities, so you can just defrost what you need. Concentrated stock takes up less freezer space.

If you don't want to bother with making your own stock there are alternatives. I keep a few tubs of ready-made fresh stock in the freezer – the range currently includes vegetable, chicken, beef, lamb and fish – and several cans of chicken and beef consommé in the cupboard. For certain soups I use stock-cubes, but I like to dilute them with more liquid than usual. I also use vegetable cooking-water instead of plain water, adding a splash of wine if I have some.

Don't forget that many soups – particularly thick vegetable purées, soups made with dried beans and pulses, and minestrone-style soups – are best made with water.

Stock-pot Guidelines

- Always use fresh, top-quality ingredients.
- To avoid evaporation, choose a tall pan rather than a shallow one.
- Put the bones and/or vegetables into cold water and bring the water to the boil. Lower the heat immediately and let the stock simmer very gently.
- Skim any froth that rises to the surface.
- Never cover the pan, or the stock will boil too fast and fat will boil back into the stock, making it cloudy.
- Do not stir the pot during cooking: stirring redistributes the fat, again making the stock cloudy.
- Strain the liquid, let it cool and then chill it overnight.
- Remove the fat that will rise to the surface.
- Freeze chicken carcases and bones, for example, after you cook roast chicken, so that you always have the ingredients for a good stock to hand.
- When you've cooked your stock, you can concentrate the flavour by simmering the skimmed stock until it has reduced by at least a third.

Brown Chicken Stock

Preparation time: 40 minutes + 2 hours cooking
Makes about 1.2 litres (2 pints)

This recipe makes a full-bodied stock with a rich, dark-brown colour. It can be diluted with water for recipes that require a light chicken stock.

1 kg (2 lb) chicken winglets, carcases or giblets (not the livers), or a combination, chopped
125 g (4 oz) each onion, carrot and celery, chopped
2 tomatoes, chopped
2 garlic cloves, crushed
300 ml (1/2 pint) boiling water
1 litre (1³/4 pints) cold water
6 peppercorns
a generous pinch of salt
a bouquet garni made with a small bunch of parsley, 2 branches of thyme and a bay leaf

Preheat the oven to Gas Mark 6/200°C/400°F. Spread the bones out in a roasting pan and roast them for 15 minutes. Add the vegetables and roast everything for a further 5 minutes.

Transfer the bones and vegetables to a medium-size pan. Pour the boiling water into the roasting pan, scrape up any bits left behind and then pour the water into the saucepan, over the bones and vegetables. Add the cold water and slowly bring the stock to the boil. Reduce the heat to a simmer. Skim away the froth that rises to the surface, add the peppercorns, salt and bouquet garni and continue cooking for 2 hours.

Strain the stock into a bowl, let it cool and then refrigerate it. Remove the layer of fat that forms on the surface before using the stock.

Light Chicken Stock

Preparation time: 30 minutes + 2 hours cooking
Makes about 1.75 litres (3 pints)

This is the stock I use all the time; it's an inevitable consequence of roast chicken.

1 cooked chicken carcase, winglets, bones, giblets and any skin, meat and jelly
1 onion, chopped
green part of 4 leeks, chopped
2 carrots, chopped
1 garlic clove, crushed with the flat of a knife

1 bay leaf
a small bunch of parsley
2 branches of thyme
6 peppercorns
a generous pinch of salt
about 2 litres (3¹/2 pints) cold water

Put all the ingredients in a large pan, cover with the water and bring the water slowly to the boil. Turn down the heat and let the stock simmer gently, uncovered, for 2 hours.

Strain the stock into a bowl, let it cool and then refrigerate it. Remove the layer of fat that forms on the surface before using the stock.

Vegetable Stock

Preparation and cooking time: 30 minutes + 15 minutes cooking
Makes about 900 ml (1½ pints)

Many people are flummoxed by the prospect of making vegetable stock. This is a shame, because vegetable stock is quick to make and will appeal to resourceful cooks. The cooking water from most vegetables and from pulses is a useful base for a vegetable stock, but different ingredients become building blocks of flavour.

Garlic adds a mellow sweetness, lemon grass lends a pungent, delicate lemon flavour, and aubergines, lentils and mushrooms give a 'meaty' savour. Tomatoes add acidity and colour, and carrots add a mellow sweetness.

To get maximum flavour quickly, vegetables and trimmings should be chopped small; it's often quicker to do so by hand than in a food processor. Sautéing the vegetables first intensifies their flavour. Always use clean, fresh vegetables.

This recipe should be regarded as a guide: adapt it, depending on what vegetables you have to hand.

25 g (1 oz) butter

1 large onion, chopped

1 large carrot, chopped

1 celery stick, with leaves, chopped

trimmings from any of the following: mushrooms, leeks, fennel, green beans, lettuce, asparagus, broccoli

a small bunch of parsley, with stalks

2 branches of thyme

900 ml (1½ pints) cold water

salt and pepper

Melt the butter in a medium-size pan and stir in the vegetables and trimmings. Sweat the vegetables, covered, over a low heat, for 10 minutes. Add the parsley, thyme, and a pinch each of salt and pepper. Cover with the water. Bring to the boil, turn down the heat and let the stock simmer for 15 minutes. Strain the stock and adjust the seasoning.

Fish Stock

Preparation time: 10 minutes + 20 minutes cooking
Makes about 1.2 litres (2 pints)

Most of the goodness and flavour in fish stock comes from the bones and trimmings of fish. Fish-heads are particularly good. All white fish and most crustaceans make satisfactory fish stocks, but avoid oily fish, such as mackerel, herring, sprat and sardine.

Different combinations of fish and shellfish can give marked differences in flavour, but the best combination is sole, turbot, cod or halibut bones, heads and tails, with any trimmings of flesh. Shrimp and prawn heads and tails give a surprising amount of flavour.

Because fish stocks cook quickly, any flavouring vegetables must be finely chopped. Onion, carrot, leek and fennel bulb, with parsley, thyme and half a bay leaf, are the usual choice.

Fish stock is never as clear as meat and vegetable stocks and shouldn't be clarified. The flavour of fish stock will deteriorate if you cook it for longer than specified: once you have strained it, you can strengthen its flavour by reduction in the normal way, if necessary.

500–750 g (1–1½ lb) bones, heads, tails and trimmings from non-oily fish

1 onion or leek, chopped finely

1 carrot, chopped

a bouquet garni made with a small bunch of parsley, a layer of fennel and a branch of thyme

4 peppercorns

a pinch of salt

about 1.5 litres (2½ pints) cold water

Rinse the bones, etc., under cold running water, carefully removing gills, blood, and viscera. Chop the bones into 5 cm (2-inch) pieces. Pack all the ingredients in a stock-pot and cover with the water. Bring the water slowly to the boil, turn down the heat and let the stock simmer for 20 minutes, skimming any grey bubbles that rise to the surface. Strain the stock.

To Clarify Stock

Stocks made with raw bones produce scum. If the scum isn't removed it will cloud and spoil the finished stock. Stocks that are prepared following the basic guidelines (page 9) will be relatively clear. Most soups in this book don't require crystal-clear stock, which is only important for consommés and other clear soups. For these soups, the stock has to be clarified after it has been strained and the fat has been removed.

Clarification involves a second cooking with other ingredients, which trap the impurities that cloud the liquid. White of egg is the most effective clarifying agent; it's usually mixed with other ingredients, to introduce new flavours or to concentrate the original flavour. Clarification is a relatively straightforward process that gives impressive results. This recipe produces a fortified stock that could be served as a consommé.

To clarify the stock without flavouring it, whisk together two egg whites and two tablespoons of iced water or crushed ice. Follow the procedure below.

2 egg whites

250 g (8 oz) mixed chopped leeks, carrots
    and onions

125 g (4 oz) minced meat or diced chicken

2 tablespoons iced water or crushed ice

1.75 litres (3 pints) chicken or meat stock,
    chilled and skimmed of fat

Place the egg whites, vegetables, meat and iced water or crushed ice in the bowl of a food processor. Process them until they're thoroughly combined. Whisk the mixture into a tall pan containing the chilled stock. Continue to whisk as you bring the liquid up to the boil. At boiling point, the ingredients will form a white crust. Turn down the heat and leave to simmer very gently for 30 minutes. Do not stir. The egg white will puff and turn a murky grey as it catches the tiny particles suspended in the stock.

Wring out a large piece of muslin in cold water. Use it to line a sieve placed over a bowl. Remove the stock from the heat. Crack a hole in the middle of the crust and ladle the glossy clear stock through the hole into the sieve.

To concentrate the stock further, reduce it by one-third.

Spring Soups

Spring is full of promise for soup-making. The first little courgettes can be quickly cooked with mint and puréed into a speckled green nectar. Tender, young broad beans can be turned into bright-green cream and served with bacon. And early new potatoes can be cooked with fresh herbs.

With the first herbs of the season making an appearance in the shops, now is the time to make herbs a feature of soup.

Cream of Potato, Leek and Onion Soup with Buttered Onions

Preparation and cooking time: 30 minutes
Serves 4–5

Soups made with the combination of leek, onion and potato, as this one is, can't fail to be delicious, whatever the proportions and final finish. In this version, when almost equal quantities of potato, leek and onion are simmered until soft and then puréed, the leeks give the soup a silky and creamy finish. The addition of buttery strands of soft onion stirred into the soup just before serving adds a surprising 'garnish'.

2 large onions
1 large leek, chopped
500 g (1 lb) potatoes, peeled and chopped
a small bunch of parsley
1.2 litres (2 pints) water
25 g (1 oz) butter
100 ml (3¹/₂ fl oz) double cream
1 tablespoon finely chopped fresh flat-leaf parsley or snipped fresh chives
salt and pepper

Chop one of the onions and put it in a medium-size saucepan with the leek, potatoes and the small bunch of parsley. Cover the vegetables with the water, and season generously with salt and pepper. Bring the water to the boil and simmer for approximately 15 minutes, or until the vegetables are tender. Pour the soup into the bowl of a blender or food processor and liquidise it. Pour it through a sieve into a clean pan, adjust the seasoning, and reheat.

While the vegetables are cooking, halve the remaining onion and slice it very finely. Heat the butter in a small pan and gently soften the onion until it's floppy and golden. Tip the contents of the pan into the liquidised soup and simmer it very gently for 5 minutes.

Just before serving, bring the cream to boiling point and pour it in a pattern on top of the soup. Serve garnished with parsley or chives.

Broad-bean Soup with Bacon

Preparation and cooking time: 1 hour
Serves 4–6

At the start of the short broad-bean season, the small, young beans are tender enough to eat whole. Later, as the pods grow, the beans inside develop a thick sheath that has an almost plastic texture when cooked. Inside that dull grey-green cover is a bright green bean with a sweet, delicate flavour.

Since I made this discovery, I always take the trouble to shell broad beans after cooking. For this soup it isn't essential, but if you do, the flavour and colour of the soup is greatly improved and sieving is unnecessary.

I've made a very successful version of this soup with frozen beans; in which case blanch the beans for 30 seconds in the hot soup water before adding them to the onions.

1 tablespoon vegetable oil

40 g (1½ oz) diced bacon

1 onion, chopped

1 garlic clove, chopped

1 potato, cubed

1 tablespoon (15 g/½ oz) butter (optional)

750 g (1½ lb) whole young broad beans or
750 g (1½ lb) podded broad beans

4 tablespoons chopped fresh mint

1 litre (1¾ pints) hot water

salt and pepper

4–6 tablespoons crème fraîche, to garnish

Heat the oil in a small frying-pan. Add the bacon and cook it until most of its fat has run out and it's evenly crisp and golden. Remove the bacon with a slotted spoon and set it aside on kitchen paper.

Drain the bacon oil into a medium-size pan, leaving behind any sediment. Stir in the onion, garlic and potato and season generously with salt and pepper, adding a tablespoon of butter if the mixture seems too dry. Cover the pan and let the vegetables sweat gently for 10 minutes. Add the beans and half the mint. Cook, uncovered, for 5 minutes.

Add the hot water, bringing it up to the boil and let it simmer for 10 minutes. If removing individual bean 'shells', do so now. Pour everything into a liquidiser or food processor and whizz at top speed for 2 minutes. Pour the soup into a clean pan, through a sieve if you haven't shelled the beans. Stir in half the remaining mint, taste and adjust the seasoning with salt. Reheat the soup and serve with a spoonful of crème fraîche, a few of the crisp bacon dice and a sprinkling of the remaining mint.

Broad-bean Soup with Bacon

Sweet Potato Soup with Tomatoes

Mushroom Soup with Mushroom
Gremolata

Mushroom Soup with Mushroom Gremolata

Preparation and cooking time: 45 minutes

Serves 6–8

You can use any mushrooms for this elegant soup: the important thing is to use plenty of them. It's thickened with brown breadcrumbs, instead of flour, which give the soup a light and velvety texture.

Gremolata is usually made with lemon zest, parsley and garlic, but here mushrooms are used instead of lemon zest. A small amount is spooned over cream to add a flavour-boost and colour-contrast.

For the soup:

50 g (2 oz) stale brown bread, crusts
    removed

2–3 tablespoons milk

50 g (2 oz) butter

3 shallots or small onions, chopped

1 garlic clove, chopped finely

750 g (1½ lb) mixed mushrooms, chopped

1 tablespoon finely chopped fresh parsley

a generous pinch of nutmeg

1.2 litres (2 pints) light chicken stock
    (page 10)

142 ml (5 fl oz) carton of double cream

juice of half a lemon

salt and pepper

For the gremolata:

15 g (½ oz) butter

125 g (4 oz) large flat mushrooms,
    chopped very finely

2 garlic cloves or 1 shallot, chopped finely

1 tablespoon finely chopped fresh parsley

1 tablespoon finely chopped fresh parsley,
    to garnish

Moisten the bread with the milk and leave it to soak. Melt the butter in a medium-size saucepan and soften the shallots or onions and garlic in it. Stir in the mushrooms and cook them gently for 5 minutes, stirring occasionally.

Squeeze the surplus milk from the bread and tear the bread into pieces. Stir the bread into the mushrooms and then add the parsley, nutmeg and chicken stock. Bring the soup to the boil, turn down the heat and let the soup simmer gently for 10 minutes.

Meanwhile, make the gremolata. Melt the butter in a small frying-pan. Gently sauté the mushrooms, garlic or shallot and parsley for about 10 minutes, until the juices evaporate and the mushrooms are black.

When the soup is ready, whizz it in a food processor or liquidiser and return it to a clean pan. Reserve 6–8 tablespoons of cream and add the rest to the soup. Re-heat and adjust the seasoning with salt, pepper and lemon juice.

Serve the soup with a swirl of cream topped with a dessertspoon of gremolata and a sprinkling of parsley.

Sweet-potato Soup with Tomatoes

Preparation and cooking time: 30 minutes
Serves 4

This is a Brazilian recipe that I discovered while I was writing A Celebration of Soup.
*The short ingredients list belies its subtlety and interest, and my family have become
addicted to it. It's a useful soup to know about, because sweet potatoes keep for ages.
I've made it very successfully with a 400 g can of tomatoes and 1¹/2 beef stock-cubes.*

500 g (1 lb) sweet potatoes, peeled and
   sliced thickly
50 g (2 oz) butter
1 onion, chopped finely
4 plum tomatoes, peeled, de-seeded and
   chopped
900 ml (1¹/2 pints) beef stock
salt and pepper

Cook the sweet potatoes in salted
water until tender, about 10 minutes.
While the potatoes are cooking,
heat the butter in a small pan and
gently sauté the onion until soft.
Squash in the tomatoes, stir them
around and boil the soup hard for
5 minutes. Tip the cooked sweet
potatoes, tomato mixture and stock
into a liquidiser or food processor and
purée it.

Pour the soup through a sieve into
a pan and re-heat it. Season with salt
and pepper and serve at once.

Courgette and Mint Soup with Mint and Courgette Cream

Preparation and cooking time: 25 minutes
Serves 4–6

*Mint and courgette were made for each other. In this soup, the quick cooking of the
courgette and the last-minute addition of the mint and parsley give the soup a sharp,
fresh flavour. It's a very pretty pale green, with darker green flecks.*

50 g (2 oz) butter
a bunch of spring onions, sliced finely
1 kg (2 lb) courgettes, chopped
1 cooked potato, cubed
1.5 litres (2¹/2 pints) hot light chicken stock
   (page 10)
4 tablespoons chopped fresh mint
2 tablespoons chopped fresh flat-leaf
   parsley
salt and pepper

For the garnish:
1 small courgette, cubed and blanched for
   30 seconds
4–6 tablespoons crème fraîche

Heat the butter in a large pan and gently sweat the spring onions in it until
they are soft but not coloured. Stir in
the courgettes and potato, and season
generously. Pour on the hot stock and
bring it to the boil. Turn down the

heat and simmer for 5 minutes.
Pour the soup into a food processor or
liquidiser, add 3 tablespoons of mint
and the flat-leaf parsley and liquidise
it. Return the soup to a clean pan,
reheat it, and taste it for seasoning.

While the soup is heating up, make
the garnish by mixing the remaining
mint and the courgette into the crème
fraîche. Serve the soup with a spoonful of the garnish in each bowl.

Roasted Tomato Soup with Green Dumplings

Preparation and cooking time: 1 hour
Serves 4–6

This is an intensely flavoured yet light and elegant soup, which is simplicity itself to make.
All the ingredients are roasted together and then puréed with a light stock. Because no fat
or oil is used, it's low in calories and it can be served hot or cold.

For the soup:
2 onions, halved, roots trimmed, unpeeled
1 kg (2 lb) plum tomatoes
4 fat garlic cloves, crushed with the flat of
   a knife
2 carrots, split lengthways
900 ml (1^1/$_2$ pints) vegetable or light
   chicken stock (page 10 or 11)
salt and pepper
For the dumplings:
125 g (4 oz) soft goat's cheese
50 g (2 oz) fresh breadcrumbs
1 tablespoon each finely chopped fresh
   mint, parsley, basil, and chives
1 large egg (size 1–2), beaten

Preheat the oven to Gas Mark
6/200°C/400°F. Place the onion halves
cut-side down on a heavy baking tray.
Stand the tomatoes on their core ends,
and tuck the garlic and carrots around
them. Bake for 40 minutes.

Meanwhile, make the dumplings.
Put the goat's cheese in a bowl and
mash it well with a fork. Mix in the
breadcrumbs and herbs and season
with salt and pepper. Mix the beaten
egg into the cheese mixture. Take a
teaspoon of the mixture and with a
second teaspoon, mould it into little
dumplings. Continue until all the
mixture is used up.

When the vegetables are cooked,
allow them to cool slightly and then
remove their skins. Place them, and
any juices, in a liquidiser or food
processor and add the stock. Liquidise
the soup. Pour it through a sieve into
a saucepan.

Reheat the soup until it's simmering gently and then check the seasoning. Add the dumplings and poach
them for 3–4 minutes or until they're
firm. Serve immediately.

Greek Fish Soup with Cheat's Rouille
Roasted Tomato Soup with Green Dumplings

Greek Fish Soup with Cheat's Rouille

Preparation time: 25 minutes + 25 minutes cooking
Serves 6

In Greece, this soup is called kakavia *and it's very similar to* bouillabaisse, *the saffron-flavoured fish soup from the South of France. It's quick and easy to prepare, and makes a meal in itself. It can be made with any firm-textured fish, and it's all the better for being made with a mixture of fish. Oily fish, such as herring, mackerel, sardine and tuna, aren't suitable.*

I like to serve this with a garlicky, Tabasco-spiked rouille in the bouillabaisse *tradition, but that's an optional extra.*

2 onions, sliced finely

500 g (1 lb) ripe tomatoes, peeled and
    chopped

1 kg (2 lb) waxy new potatoes, scraped,
    sliced and rinsed

1 teaspoon dried oregano

a handful of celery leaves, chopped

6 tablespoons olive oil

1.75 litres (3 pints) fish stock (page 12)

1 kg (2 lb) mixed fish, such as hake, monk-
    fish, red or grey mullet, cod, haddock,
    bream, brill and weever, skinned and
    cut into similarly sized chunks

juice of 1 lemon

salt and pepper

For the rouille:

200 g (7 oz) canned or bottled pimientos,
    drained

1 large garlic clove

1 tablespoon olive oil

a generous pinch of salt

about 6 drops of Tabasco sauce

To serve:

1 lemon, cut into 6 wedges

12 wafer-thin stale baguette slices, toasted

Spread out the onions and tomatoes in a large pan and cover them with the potato slices. Season generously with salt and pepper, and sprinkle over the oregano and half the celery leaves. Pour on the olive oil and cover with the fish stock.

Bring the liquid quickly to the boil and then boil it hard for 15 minutes, until the potatoes are cooked. Add the pieces of fish, tucking them under the liquid. Cook for a further 5 minutes.

Make the rouille by liquidising all the ingredients together.

Squeeze over the lemon juice and check the seasoning. Garnish with the remaining celery leaves and serve with the lemon wedges, rouille and croûtes.

Spring Potato Soup with Herbs and Chive Cream

Preparation and cooking time: 35 minutes + 4 hours chilling (optional)
Serves 4

Every year as spring approaches and new-season herbs start appearing, I eagerly await the arrival of the first Jersey Royal potatoes. This soup, made when the season is under way and prices have dropped, is a favourite way of enjoying their delicious flavour. Use whatever herbs you can get: a mixture of leafy herbs such as watercress, parsley, coriander, basil, mint and chervil, work very well. The soup can be served hot or cold.

25 g (1 oz) butter

a bunch of spring onions, sliced

500 g (1 lb) Jersey Royal potatoes, scraped and chopped

900 ml (1¹/₂ pints) light chicken stock

6 tablespoons finely chopped mixed fresh herbs, e.g., watercress, parsley, basil, mint and chervil

salt and pepper

For the chive cream:

1 tablespoon snipped fresh chives

4 tablespoons crème fraîche or fresh soured cream

salt and pepper

Melt the butter in a large saucepan and sweat the spring onions in it until they are softened. Add the potatoes and pour on the stock. Bring to the boil and then cover the pan and let the soup simmer for 15 minutes or until the potatoes are completely tender.

Purée the soup in a liquidiser or food processor and season it to taste.

Just before serving, stir in the mixed herbs. To make the chive cream, mix the chives into the cream, and season with salt and pepper.

Serve the soup with a spoonful of the chive cream in each bowl.

If you plan to serve the soup cold, chill it for at least 4 hours after liquidising it. Stir in the herbs just before serving; the chive cream is appropriate for the cold soup too.

Avgolemono Soup with Chicken and Parsley Meatballs

Preparation and cooking time: 1¹/₄ hours

Serves 4–6

Avgolemono means 'egg and lemon': a combination that is popular throughout the Middle East in soups and sauces. Avgolemono is also the name of a classic Greek soup, made by simmering rice in fish or chicken stock, and whisking in egg yolks and lemon juice at the end. It's sometimes served with meatballs, as here, and has a distinctive creamy and tangy flavour.

For the soup:

1.5 litres (2¹/₂ pints) chicken stock

125 g (4 oz) long-grain rice, washed

1 boneless, skinless chicken thigh,
    trimmed of fat

2 egg yolks

juice of 1 lemon

salt and pepper

For the chicken meatballs:

1 garlic clove, crushed with a scant
    teaspoon of salt

1 onion, grated

1 tablespoon finely chopped fresh mint

1 egg yolk, beaten

40 g (1¹/₂ oz) fresh breadcrumbs

4 tablespoons finely chopped fresh
    flat-leaf parsley

Place the stock, rice and chicken thigh in a medium-size pan, season generously and bring the liquid up to the boil. Turn down the heat and let it simmer gently for 15 minutes. Remove the chicken thigh from the pan and set it aside. Using a slotted spoon, remove about half the rice and add it to a bowl containing the garlic,

onion and mint. Mince the chicken meat and add it to the bowl. Blend the ingredients thoroughly and add the beaten egg yolk to bind them. Using a wooden spoon, gradually incorporate the breadcrumbs to make a dry mixture.

Scatter the chopped parsley over a tray or work surface. Form the chicken mixture into marble-sized balls – you will be able to make at least 26 – and gently roll them in the parsley until they are completely covered.

Bring the soup back to simmering and lower the meatballs into the broth. Maintain a simmer and let them cook for 10 minutes. Some of the parsley will come off, but most of it should stick to the meatballs.

Carefully transfer the meatballs to a soup tureen or a large bowl. Whisk the two egg yolks and the lemon juice together and then whisk them into the soup. Continue to whisk, without allowing the soup to boil, for 30 seconds. Pour the soup over the chicken rissoles and serve immediately.

**Avgolemono Soup with Chicken
and Parsley Meatballs**

Summer Soups

Cool, refreshing, light and nutritious, summer soups are much underrated. Hot, Mediterranean countries are very good at summer soups: Gazpacho, the famous salad soup of Spain; Vichyssoise, the chilled leek and potato soup of France; and Pappa al Pomodoro, the ambrosial bread and tomato soup from Italy, are all simple to prepare and amongst the finest soups it's possible to eat.

Not all summer soups are served chilled. During the summer, when tomatoes are at their tastiest, is the time to make tomato soups that can be served hot, warm or chilled. And the perfect start to a salad meal is a compote of lightly cooked, seasonal vegetables – such as courgettes, peas and green beans – served with shredded rocket and some dainty Melba toast. Summer is also a great time for potato soups, made with delicious new-season potatoes – try serving them with a garnish of chopped tomato, cucumber and mint.

Compote of Summer Vegetables with Watercress

Preparation and cooking time: 15 minutes
Serves 4

This light, fresh soup is made with a mixture of quickly cooked, young, new-season vegetables. It's thickened and seasoned with egg yolks, lemon juice and watercress. You can vary the quantities and mixture of vegetables, depending on what's available. Cauliflower and broccoli florets, sliced runner beans, sweetcorn and diced new potatoes would all be suitable.

900 ml (1¹/₂ pints) vegetable or light
   chicken stock (page 10 or 11)
¹/₂ teaspoon salt
75 g (3 oz) carrots, peeled
175 g (6 oz) courgettes
125 g (4 oz) green beans
a bunch of spring onions, sliced finely
250 g (8 oz) shelled peas
2 egg yolks
juice of 1 lemon
leaves from a bunch of watercress,
   chopped finely

Bring the stock to a steady simmer with the salt. Meanwhile, chop the carrots and courgettes into 5 mm (¹/₄-inch) cubes, and slice the beans into 5 mm (¹/₄-inch) lengths. Add the spring onions to the stock, followed 30 seconds later by the carrots. After 1 minute add the peas and 30 seconds later add the beans and then the courgettes. Turn the heat down very low. Whisk the egg yolks and lemon juice together. Add them to the soup and simmer very gently for 1 minute, taking care not to let the soup boil. Stir in the watercress and serve at once.

Chilled Curried Apple Soup

Preparation and cooking time: 1 hour + 2 hours chilling
Serves 6

Unlikely though this might sound, the combination of apples and curry works surprisingly well. Don't be alarmed by the quantity of curry powder: its effect is softened by cream and lemon juice and reduced by the chilling process.

15 g (¹/₂ oz) butter
1 onion, chopped
1 tablespoon medium-hot curry powder
1 kg (2 lb) dessert apples, peeled, cored and chopped
900 ml (1¹/₂ pints) light chicken stock (page 10)
juice of 1 lemon
142 ml (5 fl oz) carton of single cream
salt and pepper
a few leaves of mint, to garnish

Melt the butter in a medium-size pan and soften the onion in it. Stir in the curry powder and let it cook for 1 minute. Add the apples, stock and a generous seasoning of salt and pepper. Bring the soup up to the boil, turn down the heat and cover the pan. Simmer gently for 20 minutes.

Liquidise the soup. Pour it through a sieve into a glass or china bowl, let it cool and then chill the soup for at least 2 hours.

Add the lemon juice and cream, garnish with the mint leaves and serve at once.

Lettuce and Pea Soup with Chervil Cream

Preparation and cooking time: 25 minutes
Serves 4

This is a quick and delicate summer soup that can be served hot or cold. Later in the year, the lettuce could be replaced with leaves from three big bunches of watercress.

2 round lettuces, shredded
750 g (1¹/₂ lb) shelled peas
2 cooked potatoes, cubed
900 ml (1¹/₂ pints) boiling vegetable or light chicken stock (page 10 or 11)
142 ml (5 fl oz) carton of whipping cream
1 tablespoon chopped fresh chervil
salt and pepper

Place the peas, lettuce (or watercress if using), and potato in a medium-size pan. Season generously with salt, add the hot stock and simmer for 4 minutes or until the peas are tender. Pour the soup into the bowl of a food processor or blender and liquidise it. Pour it through a sieve into a clean pan and reheat it gently.

While the soup is re-heating, whip the cream and stir in the chervil. Taste the soup and adjust the seasoning as necessary. Serve each helping with a spoonful of the chervil cream.

**Compote of Summer Vegetables
with Watercress**

**Lettuce and Pea Soup
with Chervil Cream**

Chilled Curried Apple Soup

Minted Cucumber and Yogurt Soup

Preparation and cooking time: 15 minutes + 5 hours infusing + chilling
Serves 6

Cucumber with yogurt is a refreshing combination that's popular throughout Eastern Europe, the Middle East and Asia. With mint added it's served as a salad in India (raita), Turkey (caçik), and Greece (tzatziki) but goes well with garlic, dill, tarragon, coriander, and chopped tomato.

This soup combines most of those flavours and is perked up with Tabasco sauce. It's an effortless soup that's become a great family favourite.

2 cucumbers, peeled, de-seeded and cubed
1 tablespoon salt
250 g (8 oz) carton of Greek-style yogurt
275 ml (9 fl oz) tomato juice
900 ml (1¹/₂ pints) stock, made with 1¹/₂ chicken stock-cubes
2 tablespoons finely chopped fresh mint
1 teaspoon chopped fresh coriander
about 6 drops of Tabasco sauce

Place the cucumber in a colander and strew it with the salt. Leave it to drain for 30 minutes.

Meanwhile, thoroughly mix together the yogurt, tomato juice, stock and 1 tablespoon of mint. Leave to infuse for 20 minutes.

Strain the infusion through a fine sieve into a clean bowl.

Rinse the salt off the cucumber and pat the cucumber dry with absorbent kitchen paper. Add the cucumber to the yogurt mixture and stir in the remaining mint, the coriander and the Tabasco sauce. Leave to infuse for 30 minutes.

Taste the soup, adding more salt and Tabasco if you think it needs it. Chill for 4 hours before serving.

Cream of Asparagus Soup

Preparation and cooking time: 30 minutes
Serves 4–6

For me, the arrival of asparagus in early summer is a real highlight, and in the height of the season I recommend that you treat yourself to a big bunch to make this recipe.

This soup could be called 'essence of asparagus': it tastes just like liquid asparagus. Serve it for a special occasion, with thin slices of buttered brown bread.

50 g (2 oz) butter
250 g (8 oz) white part of leek, chopped
150 g (5 oz) new potato, cubed and rinsed
750 ml (1¹/₄ pints) cold water
750 g (1¹/₂ lb) asparagus, woody stems discarded

¹/₂ teaspoon salt
up to 125 ml (4 fl oz) double cream (optional)

Melt the butter in a pan (not an aluminium one: asparagus, like spinach, reacts with aluminium and the flavour will be spoiled). Stir in the leeks, coating them thoroughly with butter. Cover the pan and let the leeks stew gently for 5 minutes until they are soft but not browned. Add the potato and water. Bring up to the boil and let the soup simmer for 10 minutes. Add the asparagus, cut in half if necessary. Turn up the heat and boil vigorously for 5 minutes.

Pour the asparagus mixture into the bowl of a liquidiser or food processor and whizz it for a couple of minutes to make a smooth purée. Pass the soup through a fine sieve and use the back of a wooden spoon to help push the purée through. Return to a clean pan; taste the soup and adjust the seasoning.

Serve the soup hot or cold with a swirl of cream, if you like. To make an even creamier soup, add 125 ml (4 fl oz) cream after sieving.

Rocket and Potato Soup

Preparation and cooking time: 45 minutes
Serves 4

I first came across this simple Italian peasant soup six years ago, when I was writing In Praise of the Potato; *it has become a great favourite. Filling, and thick with bread and diced potatoes, it's the peppery, bitter tang of the rocket that transforms this soup into something special. When it's made with water it's good, but I like to add half a stock-cube to give it a bit more body.*

750 g (1¹/₂ lb) new potatoes, scrubbed and diced

1.2 litres (2 pints) water

¹/₂ chicken or vegetable stock-cube

¹/₂ teaspoon salt

two 30 g bags of rocket leaves, rinsed

125 g (4 oz) stale ciabatta or french bread, crusts removed, cut up roughly

5 tablespoons olive oil

salt and pepper

Place the potatoes in a medium-size pan with the water, stock-cube and salt. Boil for 10 minutes. Add the rocket and simmer for 10 minutes. Stir in the bread, turn off the heat and cover the pan. Leave to stand for 10 minutes. Stir in the olive oil, taste and adjust the seasoning with salt and pepper. Serve immediately.

Pappa al Pomodoro

Preparation and cooking time: 30 minutes + 1 hour standing

Serves 6

This is an ambrosial soup that comes from Tuscany. It's a traditional peasant dish, made with yesterday's bread and tomatoes from the garden. It relies on perfectly ripe tomatoes that are full of flavour, and it's worth using really good olive oil for the garnish.

It can be eaten hot, warm or cold but is at its best, I think, served warm for an al fresco meal on a hot summer day.

5 tablespoons olive oil

3 garlic cloves, crushed with ½ teaspoon salt

750 g (1½ lb) very ripe tomatoes, peeled, de-seeded and chopped

10 basil leaves, chopped

1 litre (1¾ pints) light chicken stock (page 10)

1 very stale wholemeal loaf, weighing about 500 g (1 lb), crusts removed, torn into small pieces

salt and pepper

To serve:

extra-virgin olive oil

grated parmesan cheese

Heat the olive oil in a medium-size pan and sauté the garlic for a minute without browning it. Add the tomatoes and basil and let the soup boil for 4–10 minutes. Pour on the stock, season with salt and pepper, and, when the soup is boiling, stir in the bread. Cook for a few minutes until the bread flops and merges with the tomatoes. Cover and leave to stand for an hour.

Mix the soup well, check the seasoning, and serve each helping with a swirl of olive oil and some freshly grated parmesan cheese.

Pappa al Pomodoro
Rocket and Potato Soup

Vichyssoise

Preparation and cooking time: 50 minutes + 4 hours chilling

Serves 6

Louis Diat, the great chef of New York's Ritz-Carlton hotel in the twenties, invented this refinement of potage bonne femme, the everyday fare of thousands of households all over France.

He remembered his mother chilling the soup with milk, when he was a child growing up in Vichy; hence the name Vichyssoise. The classic version is made with milk and double cream, but you can use all milk if you prefer.

It's the simplest of soups to make, soothing, refreshing and filling, and everybody seems to like it.

1 kg (2 lb) white part of leeks, sliced

1.2 litres (2 pints) light chicken stock
    (page 10)

500 g (1 lb) potatoes, peeled and diced

1/2 teaspoon salt

300 ml (1/2 pint) milk

284 ml (10 fl oz) carton of double cream

a small bunch of fresh chives, snipped

pepper

Simmer the leeks in the chicken stock for 20 minutes. Add the potatoes and salt and cook for a further 15 minutes, or until the potatoes are tender.

Liquidise the soup and then pass it through a fine sieve into a bowl. Push the soft vegetables through with the back of a wooden spoon; the sieve will catch any fibrous bits of leek. Allow to cool.

When the soup is cold, add the milk and cream and correct the seasoning. Chill the soup for at least 4 hours.

Serve the soup in ice-cold bowls and garnish it with the chives.

Gazpacho

Preparation time: 30 minutes + 4 hours chilling
Serves 6–8

This is my version of the famous cold salad soup from Andalusia. It can be made with whatever is ripe and to hand, but it usually has a tomato base, enriched and seasoned with olive oil and vinegar and thickened with bread. The raw garlic gives it a kick.

Gazpacho is served iced, with ice-cubes, and a selection of garnishes such as croûtons, black olives, and finely chopped tomato, cucumber, red or yellow pepper and hard-boiled egg. These can be stirred into the soup just before serving; or place them in little bowls, to be added at the table.

For the soup:

900 g (2 lb) ripe plum tomatoes, peeled and chopped, or a 550 g jar of passata (sieved tomatoes)

250 g (8 oz) white breadcrumbs

1 cucumber, peeled and chopped

$1/2$ a Spanish onion or the white part of 8 spring onions, chopped

2 garlic cloves, chopped (optional)

2 red peppers, de-seeded and chopped

3 tablespoons sherry, red-wine or white-wine vinegar

5 tablespoons of olive oil

900 ml (1$1/2$ pints) iced water

salt

For the garnishes:

2 slices of white bread, cubed

olive oil

1 red onion, chopped finely

1 red pepper, de-seeded and chopped finely

3 plum tomatoes, peeled, cored, de-seeded and chopped finely

$1/2$ cucumber, cubed

Place all the soup ingredients in the bowl of a food processor and liquidise them; it may be necessary to do this in batches, with a proportion of the water. Pour the soup through a sieve – to catch any pips and skin – into a glass or china bowl. Cover with cling film and refrigerate for at least 4 hours.

To make the croûtons, fry the bread cubes in the olive oil.

Serve with the garnishes in little bowls for people to help themselves or stir the garnishes into the soup just before serving.

Roasted Red Pepper and Tomato Soup with Basil Cream and Olive Croûtes

Preparation and cooking time: 1 hour roasting + 30 minutes
Serves 4–6

This soup is simplicity itself to make, and the end result is a fat-free, glossy, fresh-tasting, tomato-red purée. I like to serve it hot with a dollop of crème fraîche and basil, but the cream is optional.

This soup is also delicious cold. Chill it for several hours; then garnish it with basil and, if you like, a swirl of really good olive oil; omit the cream.

Roasting red peppers and tomatoes intensifies their flavour and gives them an added richness. Roasted onion and garlic become mellow and sweet. These Mediterranean flavours go very well with the olive croûtes.

750 g (1¹/₂ lb) red peppers
500 g (1 lb) plum tomatoes
2 onions, halved, roots trimmed, unpeeled
6 garlic cloves, crushed with the flat of
  a knife
1 chicken stock-cube
300 ml (¹/₂ pint) boiling water
salt, if necessary
For the croûtes:
12 wafer-thin slices of stale baguette
1 tablespoon olive paste
For the garnish:
150 ml (5 fl oz) crème fraîche (optional)
12 basil leaves

Preheat the oven to Gas Mark 6/ 200°C /400°F. Put the peppers on a heavy roasting pan. Stand the tomatoes on their core ends and place the onion halves cut-side down. Tuck the garlic cloves between the vegetables. Roast the vegetables for 30 minutes.

Remove the tray from the oven and turn over the onions and the peppers – their skins will be starting to blister and blacken, and juices will be starting to run from the tomatoes. Roast for a further 30 minutes.

Leave the vegetables to cool for 10 minutes before removing the stalks, seeds and as much of the skins as possible from the peppers. Peel away the skin from the tomatoes and onions; scrape the soft garlic flesh out of its skin. Tip all the flesh, juices and all, into the bowl of a food processor. Dissolve the stock-cube in the boiling water and pour the stock into the processor. Liquidise the soup. Pour the soup through a fine sieve into a saucepan. Bring it up to a simmer, taste it and add salt if necessary.

To make the olive croûtes, first toast the baguette slices. Spread them thinly with olive paste.

Serve the soup with a dollop of crème fraîche topped with basil leaves, shredded if you like, and hand the olive croûtes separately.

Roasted Red Pepper and Tomato Soup
with Basil Cream and Olive Croûtes

Chilled White Soup

Preparation time: 5 minutes + 4 hours chilling
Serves 6

This unusual cold soup combines white bread, almonds, water, salt and garlic to produce a subtly flavoured, thick white soup that's served with white grapes. It's known as ajo blanco con uvas in Spain, where it originated a thousand years ago, when the Moors ruled much of the country. Depending on the proportions of the key ingredients, it's also known as almond soup, grape soup, bread soup and garlic soup. Others call it white gazpacho.

It certainly appeals to garlic lovers, because the garlic packs quite a punch; the garnish of sweet grapes adds a vital and interesting balance of flavour.

250 g (8 oz) stale white bread, crusts removed

900 ml (1¹/₂ pints) iced water

125 g (4 oz) blanched almonds

3 fat garlic cloves, crushed with the flat of a knife

2 teaspoons salt

6 tablespoons olive oil

3 tablespoons white-wine vinegar or sherry vinegar

250 g (8 oz) seedless white grapes, halved

Tear the bread into pieces and leave it to soak in the iced water.

Meanwhile, place the almonds, garlic and salt in the bowl of a food processor. Process until the almonds are very finely ground. Squeeze most of the liquid from the bread (reserving the water) and, with the motor running, add the bread to the almond mixture. Keep the motor running and pour in the oil in a thin stream. Then add the vinegar, followed by the reserved soaking water. Transfer the soup to a large china or glass bowl and add the grapes. Cover the soup with cling film and refrigerate it for 4 hours before serving.

Autumn Soups

Autumn is a rich and abundant season for soup-makers. This is the time to make thick vegetable purées, choosing between artichoke, celery, onion, potato and carrot, amongst others. These are soups that don't need stock to give them body: if you use plenty of vegetables they can be made with water and will still be packed with flavour.

Leeks are also plentiful now and are useful in soups that need a subtle onion flavour; remember, too, that leeks give a glossy, smooth texture to puréed soups.

Now is the time for pumpkin and other squashes. They are delicious added to robust vegetable stew-soups; and when cooked with spices they will be transformed into exotic, golden purées.

And as the leaves drop from the trees and the evenings turn more wintry, this is also the time to serve comforting split-pea soups, or a steaming bowl of mussel soup made butter-yellow and aromatic with saffron.

Middle-Eastern Spinach and Lentil Soup with Meatballs

Preparation and cooking time: 1 hour 10 minutes
Serves 6–8

This soup is a complete meal but is still very good and quite filling even without meatballs. It's even better if you cook the lentils the day before you plan to eat the soup.

For the soup:

250 g (8 oz) brown lentils (preferably Puy lentils)

1 chicken or vegetable stock-cube

1 small onion, peeled and stuck with a clove securing a bay leaf

1.5 litres (2¹/₂ pints) water

1 tablespoon olive oil

1 large onion, chopped

2 garlic cloves, crushed with 1 teaspoon of salt

1 teaspoon ground cumin

750 g (1¹/₂ lb) spinach leaves, stalks removed, shredded finely

2 tablespoons finely chopped fresh coriander

1 tablespoon finely chopped fresh mint

5 cm (2-inch) strip of lemon zest, chopped

pepper

For the meatballs:

250 g (8 oz) minced lamb

1 small onion, grated, or 4 spring onions, chopped

1 tablespoon finely chopped fresh coriander

a generous pinch of ground cinnamon

3 tablespoons white breadcrumbs

1 egg, beaten

salt and pepper

Rinse the lentils, and put them in a large pan, with the stock-cube, onion stuck with clove and bay leaf and water. Bring the water to the boil and then let it simmer, uncovered, for 40

Autumn Soupe au Pistou

Middle Eastern Spinach and Lentil Soup with Meatballs

Artichoke Soup with Bacon Soufflé Toasts

minutes or until the lentils are tender.

Meanwhile, make the meatballs by placing all the ingredients in a bowl. Mix thoroughly and squeeze all the ingredients together with your fingers. With wet hands, break off nuggets of the meat mixture and form them into marble-sized balls. Cover them with cling film and set them aside.

Heat the olive oil in a medium-size pan, and, when it's hot, stir in the onion and garlic. Cook over a medium heat for 8 minutes or until the onions are soft and golden. Add the cumin and season generously with pepper.

When the lentils are ready, drain them in a colander and reserve the cooking liquid in a large pan. Discard the whole onion and tip the lentils into the onion-garlic mixture. Add the spinach, 1 tablespoon of the coriander, the mint and the lemon zest. Stir thoroughly and cook for 5 minutes. Turn off the heat.

Re-heat the lentil cooking water, and, when it's boiling, add the meatballs. Simmer gently for 6–8 minutes. Carefully spoon the lentil mixture back into the pan, and stir in the remaining coriander. Re-heat the soup, remove the strip of lemon zest and serve at once.

Artichoke Soup with Bacon Soufflé Toasts

Preparation and cooking time: 1¼ hours
Serves 6–8

This soup is made with the small knobbly tubers called jerusalem artichokes. They're devils to peel – young, small ones only need to be scrubbed – and there's often a lot of wastage. When boiled, they flop and collapse, and generally look very unappetising.

However, when they're liquidised, as they are in this soup, they transform into a thick, fluffy purée. This texture and their subtle and haunting flavour lends itself perfectly to soup. Served with a few scraps of crisp bacon or with parmesan croûtons, this is one of the best soups I know; with bacon soufflé toasts it's a meal in itself.

For the soup:

75 g (3 oz) butter

1 large onion, chopped

1 large garlic clove, bruised but unpeeled

1 kg (2 lb) jerusalem artichokes, chopped
    coarsely

1 celery stick, chopped, leaves reserved
    and chopped

1.2 litres (2 pints) light chicken or
    vegetable stock (page 10 or 11)

300 ml (½ pint) milk, or half milk and half
    double cream

salt and pepper

For the soufflé toasts:

6 streaky bacon rashers, chopped

2 eggs, separated

2 teaspoons Dijon mustard

a pinch of Cayenne pepper

16 thin slices of stale baguette, toasted

1 tablespoon of fresh grated parmesan
    cheese

salt and pepper

Preheat the oven to Gas Mark 6/200°C /400°F.

Melt 50 g (2 oz) of the butter in a large saucepan and fry the onion, without browning, for 5 minutes. Add the garlic, artichokes and celery, stirring thoroughly so that everything is coated with butter. Cover the pan and let the vegetables sweat for 10 minutes.

Pour on the stock, bring it up to the boil and simmer briskly for about 15 minutes, or until the artichokes are tender.

Meanwhile, make the bacon soufflé toasts. Fry the bacon until it is crisp. Drain it on kitchen paper. Mix together the egg yolk, mustard and Cayenne pepper. Stir in the bacon and season with salt and pepper. Whisk the egg white until it's stiff and then fold it into the yolk mixture. Top the toasted baguette slices with a little of the soufflé mixture, sprinkle them with parmesan cheese and transfer the toasts to a baking tray. Bake them for 5–7 minutes or until the toasts are golden and slightly risen.

When the artichokes are cooked, liquidise the soup in batches. Pour it through a sieve into a clean pan and add the milk or milk and cream mixture. Re-heat the soup and taste and correct the seasoning. Whisk in the last of the butter, garnish with the reserved, chopped celery leaves and serve very hot, accompanied by the soufflé toasts.

Autumn Soupe au Pistou

Preparation and cooking time: 1 hour
Serves 6–8

I've adapted this substantial summer soup from Provence by using autumn vegetables. You can vary the quantities and mixture of vegetables according to what's available: the important point is to cook everything in a sensible order, so that you don't end up with a bowl of mush.

Traditionally the pistou, which is interchangeable with pesto, is stirred into the soup just before serving. I like to serve it separately, for people to help themselves. Any leftovers can be puréed – you may need to add more water and half a chicken or vegetable stock-cube – and served with a garnish of cream, chopped chives and garlic croûtons (page 84).

I've included a recipe for pistou, but bottled red or green pesto is a good substitute if you're short of time.

For the soup:

250 g (8 oz) broccoli or cauliflower

50 g (2 oz) butter

2 large garlic cloves, chopped finely

1/2 fennel bulb, chopped finely

250 g (8 oz) white part of leek, chopped
    finely

1.5 litres (2 1/2 pints) boiling water

175 g (6 oz) potato, cubed

375 g (12 oz) carrot, chopped

50 g (2 oz) soup pasta, e.g. stellette, pepe
    bucato or conchigliette piccole

400 g can of flageolet or haricot beans,
    drained and rinsed

375 g (12 oz) courgettes, cubed

3 tomatoes, peeled, de-seeded and
    chopped

1 tablespoon chopped fresh flat-leaf parsley

salt and pepper

For the pistou:

3 garlic cloves

3 tablespoons pine kernels

leaves from a large bunch of basil

leaves from a small bunch of fresh flat-leaf
    parsley

4 tablespoons olive oil

3 tablespoons grated parmesan cheese

salt and pepper

Begin by making the pistou. Place the garlic, pine kernels, basil, parsley and a little salt and pepper in a food processor. Whizz the mixture to a paste, and, with the motor running, add the olive oil in a thin stream to produce a loose-textured purée. Pour into a bowl and stir in the parmesan cheese.

To make the soup, first remove bite-sized individual florets from the broccoli or cauliflower and cube the stalks.

Melt the butter in a large pan, and, when it begins to foam, stir in the garlic, fennel and leek. Season generously with salt and pepper and cook for 6 minutes. Add the boiling water, and, when it's bubbling away, add the potato and carrot. Let it simmer for 5 minutes. Add the broccoli or cauliflower stalks and pasta and cook them for 5 minutes more. Add the beans and, when the soup has come back to the boil, add the broccoli or cauliflower florets. Cook for 1 minute, add the courgettes and tomatoes and turn off the heat. Taste and adjust the seasoning.

Sprinkle with the chopped parsley and serve immediately, offering the pistou separately for people to spoon some over their soup.

Cream of Celery Soup with Fried Breadcrumbs and Parmesan

Preparation time: 20 minutes + 1 hour 5 minutes cooking time

Serves 6

This is a lovely, thick soup that's rich and full of flavour and utterly redolent of autumn. It's also very good eaten with toasted bacon sandwiches, in which case it's a meal in itself.

For the soup:

75 g (3 oz) butter

2 heads of celery, leaves reserved,
    chopped roughly

1 onion, chopped finely

1 leek, chopped

2 potatoes, chopped

1.2 litres (2 pints) light chicken or
    vegetable stock (page 10 or 11)

1 teaspoon celery seeds

celery salt and pepper

Cream of Celery Soup with Fried
Breadcrumbs and Parmesan
Saffron Potato Soup with Mussels

For the breadcrumbs:

4 slices of brown bread, toasted lightly

1 tablespoon vegetable oil

25 g (1 oz) butter

To serve:

about 2 tablespoons single cream

4–6 tablespoons grated parmesan cheese

Melt the butter in a heavy-based pan and sweat the celery and onion together, covered, on a very low heat, for 30 minutes, stirring occasionally. Add the leek and potatoes and cook for a further 15 minutes. Add the stock, celery seeds, a pinch of celery salt and a generous grinding of pepper. Bring the soup to the boil and simmer for 20 minutes.

Meanwhile use a food processor to turn the toast into coarse breadcrumbs.

Heat the vegetable oil and butter in a small frying-pan. When very hot, stir in the breadcrumbs and stir-fry them until they are golden and crisp, but don't let them burn. Tip the bread-crumbs on to kitchen paper to drain.

When all the vegetables are soft, liquidise the soup very thoroughly to break down the fibrous flesh. Push and pour the purée through a sieve into a clean pan. Taste and adjust the seasoning. Serve very hot, with a swirl of cream and the reserved, chopped celery leaves; hand the fried bread-crumbs and parmesan cheese in separate bowls for people to help themselves.

Saffron Potato Soup with Mussels

Preparation time: 30 minutes + 35 minutes cooking

Serves 6

*This is a Rolls-Royce version of moules marinières that's simple to make. The mussels
are cooked with wine, taken out of their shells and served in a velvety purée made with
potatoes, leeks and onions. The soup's beautiful buttercup-yellow colour comes from
saffron, and the flavour is enriched with fish stock. Serve it with crusty bread and butter.
To make this soup into a complete meal, double the quantity of mussels.*

1 kg (2 lb) live mussels

150 ml ($^1/_4$ pint) dry white wine

50 g (2 oz) butter

1 small onion, chopped

250 g (8 oz) white of leek, chopped

500 g (1 lb) potatoes, peeled, cubed and
   rinsed

1 bay leaf

900 ml (1$^1/_2$ pints) fish stock (page 12)

$^1/_2$ teaspoon saffron threads or powder

salt and white pepper

snipped fresh chives, to garnish

Scrub the mussels and remove the
beards. Discard any with damaged
shells or that do not close when given
a sharp tap. Put the cleaned mussels in
a large pan with the wine. Cover and
cook over a fierce heat, shaking the
pan a few times, until the mussels
open. This takes about 5 minutes.

Discard any unopened mussels.
Place a colander over a bowl and tip in
the mussels, taking care not to spill any
of the liquid. Leave the mussels to cool
while you attend to the vegetables.

Melt the butter in a medium-size
pan and stir in the onion, leek and
potatoes. Cook gently for 5 minutes,
stirring a couple of times.

Meanwhile, strain the mussel liquid
through clean muslin or a J-cloth – this
is essential to catch sand and bits of
shell – into the pan with the vegetables.
Add the bay leaf and fish stock and
bring the liquid up to the boil. Turn
down the heat, stir in the saffron and
leave to simmer for 25 minutes.

While the soup simmers, take most
of the mussels from their shells. The
soup looks prettier if you leave some
of the shells on – a good compromise
is to remove one shell from half the
mussels.

When the soup is ready, remove
the bay leaf and liquidise the soup in a
food processor or blender. Pass it
through a sieve into a clean pan. Stir
in the mussels, reheat and check and
correct the seasoning. Serve with a
sprinkling of chives.

Red-onion and Red-wine Soup with Ciabatta Thyme Croûtes

Preparation and cooking time: 1 hour 40 minutes

Serves 6

In this departure from the classic French onion soup, a large quantity of red onions is slowly cooked with tomatoes, red wine and garlic, seasoned with thyme and orange zest. The result is a rich, mellow and satisfying soup that's even better heated up the next day.

For the soup:

4 tablespoons olive oil

1 large onion, chopped

1 kg (2 lb) red onions, quartered and
    sliced finely

two 400 g cans of tomatoes

4 large garlic cloves, crushed with
    ¹/₂ teaspoon sea salt

a bouquet garni made with 1 bay leaf,
    6 thyme sprigs and a 5 cm (2-inch)
    strip of orange zest

300 ml (¹/₂ pint) red wine

1.2 litres (2 pints) stock, made with garlic
    and herb or vegetable stock-cubes

salt and pepper

For the ciabatta croûtes:

12 thin ciabatta slices

3 tablespoons olive oil

1 tablespoon fresh thyme leaves

extra-virgin olive oil, to garnish

Using a large heavy-based pan with a good-fitting lid, heat the olive oil. Sauté the chopped onion for about 10 minutes, until soft and beginning to colour. Add the sliced red onions, stirring to coat them thoroughly with the oil. Cook slowly, stirring occasionally, for 30 minutes or until the onions soften and wilt.

While the onions are cooking, drain the canned tomatoes, reserving the juice. Squeeze the pips out of the tomatoes and roughly chop the flesh. Measure 300 ml (¹/₂ pint) of strained tomato juice.

When the onions are ready, stir in the salty garlic paste, the chopped tomatoes, bouquet garni and tomato juice. Cover the pan and leave to stew over a gentle heat for 15 minutes. Add the wine and boil vigorously until the liquid is reduced by half. Pour on the stock and simmer, partially covered, for 25 minutes.

Meanwhile, to make the croûtes, first preheat the oven to Gas Mark 6/200°C/400°F. Paint both sides of the slices of bread with olive oil. Sprinkle each slice with thyme leaves. Place them on a wire rack that is resting on a baking sheet and bake them for 4–5 minutes, until crisp and golden.

When the soup is ready, remove the bouquet garni and check and correct the seasoning.

To serve, place two croûtes in each bowl, pour over the soup and garnish with a drizzle of olive oil.

**Red-onion and Red-wine Soup with
Ciabatta Thyme Croûtes**

Pumpkin Soup with Coriander and Chilli Gnocchi

Preparation and cooking time: 1¹/₂ hours

Serves 6–8

The slightly sweet, mild flavour of pumpkin goes very well with celery, and when pumpkin is puréed with leeks it takes on a silky texture. For this soup I've pepped up the flavour with lots of garlic, sage and thyme. The coriander and chilli potato gnocchi (dumplings) are a surprising but very successful optional addition.

For the soup:

1 kg (2 lb) slice of pumpkin

2 tablespoons olive oil

4 garlic cloves, crushed with 1 teaspoon salt

1 tablespoon chopped fresh sage

1 tablespoon chopped fresh thyme

1 large onion, chopped

1 leek, chopped

1 carrot, chopped

2 celery sticks, chopped

1.75 litres (3 pints) water

Tabasco sauce

vegetable oil

1 tablespoon finely chopped fresh parsley

salt

For the gnocchi:

herb potato gnocchi (page 80), made with 2 tablespoons finely chopped fresh coriander and 2 small red chillies, chopped very finely

Cut the pumpkin into manageable pieces, scoop out the seeds and reserve them. Peel the pumpkin and cut it into 2.5 cm (1-inch) cubes.

Heat the olive oil in a large pan and stir-fry the garlic with the sage and thyme, but don't let it burn. Add the onion, leek, carrot, celery and pumpkin flesh, and increase the heat slightly, stirring the vegetables around for about 5 minutes until they begin to soften. Cover with the water and bring to the boil, and then simmer gently, half-covered, for about 15 minutes or until all the vegetables are soft.

While the soup is cooking, prepare the gnocchi following the recipe on page 80 and mix in the chopped chillies and the coriander.

When the vegetables are tender, liquidise the soup in a food processor or blender and pour it through a fine sieve into a clean pan. Adjust the consistency and taste by adding more water and salt as necessary. Re-heat and add Tabasco sauce to taste; 6–8 drops should be sufficient.

Preheat the oven to Gas Mark 4/180°C/350°F. Meanwhile, cook the gnocchi as described on page 80 and set them aside, covered, on a warm plate. Wash the pumpkin seeds under cold running water to remove the strings of flesh. Lay the cleaned seeds on a baking tray, drizzle them with a little vegetable oil and sprinkle them generously with salt. Bake for 10 minutes, turning with a spoon occasionally, until they are golden brown and nicely crisp.

A couple of minutes before you are ready to serve the soup, slip four or more gnocchi into hot soup bowls, pour on the soup, sprinkle with some of the pumpkin seeds and garnish with the parsley.

Yellow Split-pea Soup

Preparation time: 40 minutes + 45 minutes cooking
Serves 6–8

Yellow and green split-peas make excellent soups, particularly when simmered with a ham-bone. They also work very well with spicy flavours, to give a soup with an unexpected depth of flavour that's comforting and exotic at the same time. Here I've seasoned yellow split-peas with cumin, and garnished the soup with coriander and yogurt.

375 g (12 oz) yellow split-peas
1 tablespoon groundnut or olive oil
1 large onion, chopped
3 garlic cloves, chopped
1 bay leaf
2 cloves, balls only
2 teaspoons ground cumin, plus a little
    extra to garnish
2 carrots, chopped
2 tomatoes, chopped
2 litres (3¹/₂ pints) water
2 tablespoons chopped fresh coriander
salt, pepper and lemon juice
150 g carton of Greek-style yogurt, to serve

Rinse the split-peas under cold running water. Heat the oil in a large pan, and, when it's hot, add the onion. Stir-fry for five minutes until the onion is golden and then add the garlic, bay leaf, balls from the two cloves and cumin. Stir everything together and cook over a medium heat for 3 minutes, until the garlic has started to colour. Add the carrots, tomatoes, split-peas and water. Bring to the boil, and then let the soup simmer for about 45 minutes, until the split-peas have collapsed.

Liquidise the soup in a food processor or blender and pour it through a sieve into a clean pan. Add salt, pepper and lemon juice to taste – you will find you need to be generous with the salt. Simmer for 5 minutes, stir in the coriander and serve each bowlful with a spoonful of yogurt and a pinch of ground cumin.

Note: The 'balls' of cloves hold all the flavour, so it's easiest to discard the stalks for this liquidised soup.

Avocado Soup with Red-pepper Salsa and Spicy Tortilla Chips

Preparation time: 25 minutes + 20 minutes chilling
Serves 4

Cold soup for autumn? I love avocados, which are in their prime at that time of the year, but I've never found a successful recipe for cooked avocado soup. Hence this idea for a liquid guacamole, which heats up the system without being hot. It's a good dinner party soup to serve before a hearty casserole, and is packed with vitamin C.

For the soup:

2¹/₂ ripe avocados, peeled and chopped

juice of 1 lime or a small lemon

4 spring onions, sliced

4 tomatoes, chopped roughly

³/₄ small red pepper, de-seeded and
    chopped roughly

1 small garlic clove, crushed with
    ¹/₂ teaspoon of salt

300 ml (¹/₂ pint) own chicken stock (page
    10) or strained canned consommé

150 g (5 oz) carton of Greek-style yogurt

a generous pinch of paprika

pepper

For the garnishes:

¹/₂ ripe avocado, cubed

1 teaspoon lemon juice

1 firm tomato, peeled, de-seeded and
    chopped finely

¹/₄ red pepper, chopped finely

a few fresh coriander leaves, (optional)

spicy tortilla chips, to serve

Mix the avocado thoroughly with the lime or lemon juice in a chilled glass or china bowl. Add all the other ingredients and mix well. Cover with cling film and refrigerate for 20 minutes.

Pour the mixture into a liquidiser or food processor and whizz it to a smooth purée. Check the seasoning. Pass it through a sieve into individual bowls. Divide the garnishes between the bowls and accompany the soup with spicy tortilla chips.

Winter Soups

On a bitter winter evening, nothing restores the spirits faster than a thick rib-sticker of a soup. Cabbage soup with dumplings, a purée of parsnips flavoured with curry, a hearty stew of black beans seasoned with cumin and coriander and beef soup with horseradish dumplings, are the sort of soups I'm talking about. Easy to prepare and cook, and simple to serve and eat, these soups have the double advantage of being easy on the budget too. Serve them with plenty of bread and follow with fruit and cheese or an old-fashioned pudding with custard, and they make the perfect winter supper.

Curried Parsnip Soup with Croûtons

Preparation time: 30 minutes + 40 minutes cooking

Serves 6

This is my all-time favourite soup – my slightly altered version of Jane Grigson's recipe, devised for an Observer *article in 1969.*

Its colour is a deep saffron, the texture is thick, fluffy and creamy and its flavour is subtle and intriguing. The perfect winter warmer.

50 g (2 oz) butter

1 large onion, chopped

1 large garlic clove, crushed with the flat of a knife

1 kg (2 lb) parsnips, cut in even-sized chunks

175 g (6 oz) potato, chopped roughly

1 tablespoon medium-hot curry powder

1 litre (1³/₄ pints) hot chicken stock (page 10)

142 ml (5 fl oz) carton of single cream

salt and pepper

snipped fresh chives, to garnish

For the croûtons

50–75 g (2–3 oz) clarified butter (page 84)

4 slices of country-style white bread, crusts removed, cut in 1 cm (¹/₂ inch) cubes

Melt the butter in a large pan and when it's hot, stir in the onion, garlic, parsnips and potato. Cover and cook over a medium heat, stirring occasionally, for 10 minutes.

Stir in the curry powder, and, after a couple of minutes, gradually add the hot stock. Season with salt and pepper. Simmer for 30–40 minutes, until the parsnips are tender.

To make the croûtons, melt the butter in a small frying-pan and fry the bread-cubes for a few minutes on all sides, until golden and crisp.

Liquidise the soup in a food processor or blender and pour it through a sieve into a clean pan. Correct the seasoning, pour in the cream and re-heat without boiling. Garnish with chives and croûtons.

Green Soup with Bacon and Parmesan Croûtons

Preparation and cooking time: 30 minutes
Serves 4

Many people don't like brussels sprouts. This soup, perked up with sherry and a double garnish, has been unknowingly devoured by brussels-haters, and is a good way of using up leftovers. It can also be made successfully with frozen sprouts. The contrast of crisp bacon pieces and parmesan croûtons with the silky-smooth soup is particularly good, with the double advantage of disguising the sprouts' pervasive smell.

For the soup:

25 g (1 oz) butter

1 small onion, chopped

about 500 g (1 lb) brussels sprouts,
    cooked and chopped

1 small potato, cooked and chopped

600 ml (1 pint) hot light chicken stock
    (page 10)

150 ml (¹/₄ pint) dry sherry

salt, pepper and freshly grated nutmeg

For the garnish:

3 rashers of streaky bacon

2 tablespoons crème fraîche

parmesan croûtons (page 84)

snipped fresh chives

Using a large pan, heat the butter and soften the onion in it. Stir in the sprouts and potato. Sauté for 5 minutes.

Add the stock and simmer for 5 minutes. Add the hot stock and simmer for 5 minutes, or until the potato is tender.

Add the sherry and season with salt and pepper. Liquidise the soup in a blender or food processor and pass it through a sieve into a clean pan. Reheat, taste and adjust the seasoning with salt, pepper and nutmeg.

Fry the bacon in its own fat in a small frying-pan until it is crisp. Drain it on kitchen paper and then crumble it.

Serve the soup very hot, giving each portion a spoonful of crème fraîche and an equal share of the bacon and the parmesan croûtons. Sprinkle with chives and more grated nutmeg.

Borscht

Preparation time: 35 minutes + 35 minutes cooking
Serves 8–10

Borscht, the famous beetroot soup from the Ukraine, is ideal for a party, hence the large quantity given in this recipe. It's easy to make half the quantity if you prefer. It can be served hot or cold, but always with a dollop of soured cream and a sprinkling of chives. Traditionally it's served with buttered black bread or little pasties called piroshkis, *which are filled with scraps of meat or minced mushrooms bound in a cream sauce.*

50 g (2 oz) butter

1 large onion, chopped

3 garlic cloves, crushed with 1 teaspoon salt

1 large carrot, cubed

1 kg (2 lb) raw beetroot, peeled and grated

250 g (8 oz) tomatoes, skinned, de-seeded and chopped

4 tablespoons red-wine vinegar

1 teaspoon sugar

2 litres (3½ pints) rich chicken stock (page 10)

2 potatoes, peeled and cubed

1 kg (2 lb) white cabbage, cored and shredded

1 large cooked beetroot

juice of ½ a lemon

salt, pepper and sugar

To serve:

142 ml (5 fl oz) carton of soured cream

snipped fresh chives

Melt the butter in a large pan and cook the onion and garlic for 5 minutes. Stir in the carrot and raw beetroot and cook for another 5 minutes. Add the tomatoes, vinegar, sugar, a generous seasoning of pepper and 300 ml (½ pint) of the stock. Simmer for 15 minutes.

Add the potatoes, cabbage and the rest of the stock. Bring the soup back to the boil and simmer, half-covered, for 20 minutes.

Ten minutes before the end of cooking, peel and grate the cooked beetroot. Mix it and its juices into the soup – this will freshen up the colour and flavour. Cover the soup and leave it to stand for 10 minutes. Check the seasoning, adjust it with salt, pepper, sugar and lemon juice. Serve in deep soup bowls, with a spoonful of soured cream and a sprinkling of chives.

Cod Chowder with Puy Lentils and Salsa Verde

Borscht

Cabbage Soup with Dumplings

Cabbage Soup with Dumplings

Preparation and cooking time: 1 hour + 20 minutes resting

Serves 6

This is good plain cooking, the sort of food I was reared on, and loved by everyone.

For the soup:

50 g (2 oz) butter

6 smoked streaky bacon rashers, cut in
    thin strips

1 large onion, halved and sliced finely

1 potato, cubed

1.2 litres (2 pints) chicken, ham or
    vegetable stock (page 10 or 11)

1 Savoy cabbage, shredded finely

salt and pepper

For the dumplings:

125 g (4 oz) self-raising flour

50 g (2 oz) dried shredded suet

1 heaped teaspoon chopped fresh thyme

1 tablespoon chopped fresh parsley

about 100 ml (3$^{1}/_{2}$ fl oz) cold water

$^{1}/_{2}$ vegetable or chicken stock-cube

450 ml ($^{3}/_{4}$ pint) boiling water

salt and pepper

Begin by making the dumplings. Sift the flour into a mixing bowl with the suet and herbs and season generously with pepper and a pinch of salt. Add just enough of the cold water to make a pliable, firm but not-too-sticky dough. Leave to rest for 20 minutes.

With floury fingers, break off small nuggets of dough and roll them between your palms into cherry-sized balls. Dissolve the stock-cube in the boiling water and gently heat the resulting stock in a large frying-pan or similar shallow dish. When it's hot, add the dumplings and let them simmer gently for 15 minutes.

To make the soup, heat the butter in a large pan, and, when it starts to froth, add the bacon and cook until the fat begins to run out. Add the onion and cook for 10 minutes. Add the potato and stock, bring the soup to the boil and cook for 10 minutes.

Add the cabbage to the soup and let it simmer vigorously for 5 minutes. Add the dumplings (reserving the cooking liquid for another use if you like) and serve.

Cod Chowder with Puy Lentils and Salsa Verde

Preparation and cooking time: 40 minutes

Serves 4–6

Chowder is the American name for a quickly made rough-and-ready soupy stew, usually containing seafood and potatoes. In New England it tends to be made with milk; New-York-style it is made with tomatoes and water. My version uses a light chicken stock to give the soup more body, and I've included previously seasoned Puy lentils, to add interest and make it more substantial. The salsa verde, made here with basil and parsley, is served separately and brings the whole thing to life.

For the lentils:

75 g (3 oz) Puy lentils

1/2 chicken stock-cube

1 small onion, peeled and stuck with a clove securing a bay leaf

300 ml (1/2 pint) water

For the soup:

40 g (11/2 oz) butter

4 slices unsmoked streaky bacon, sliced in thin strips

1 large onion, chopped

500 g (1 lb) potatoes, cut in 1 cm (1/2-inch) cubes

25 g (1 oz) plain white flour

150 ml (1/4 pint) dry white wine

900 ml (11/2 pints) light chicken stock (page 10)

750 g (11/2 lb) cod fillet, skinned and cut in 5 cm (2-inch) chunks

salt and pepper

2 tablespoons finely chopped fresh parsley, to garnish

For the salsa verde:

2 fat garlic cloves, crushed

1 large bunch of fresh flat-leaf parsley

1 large bunch of fresh basil

6 tablespoons olive oil

50 g (2 oz) pine kernels

salt and pepper

Begin by preparing the lentils. Put the lentils, half stock-cube and onion with bay leaf and clove in a small saucepan. Add the water and bring to the boil. Simmer gently for 30 minutes until the lentils are tender and the water absorbed. Taste and season with salt and pepper. Discard the onion. Keep warm.

Next make the salsa verde. Place the garlic, parsley and basil and a little oil in the bowl of a food processor and process for 1 minute. With the motor running, add the pine kernels and the rest of the olive oil in a thin trickle. Season with salt and pepper.

Now make the soup. Heat the butter in a spacious pan and cook the bacon over a medium heat until the fat runs out and the bacon begins to crisp. Add the onion and potato and sauté without browning for 5 minutes. Sprinkle on the flour and stir quickly to make a thick mixture. Pour in the wine, stirring all the time, and, after a couple of minutes, add the stock. Keep stirring while you bring the liquid up to the boil, and then turn down the heat and simmer gently for 10 minutes, or until the potato is almost cooked.

Add the chunks of fish. Push them under the liquid, and cook until the fish turns milky-white; this will only take 2–3 minutes. Check and correct the seasoning. Serve sprinkled with parsley and give each serving a spoonful of lentils and a dollop of salsa verde.

Lentil Soup

Preparation time: 45 minutes + 45 minutes cooking

Serves 6

This is a wonderfully comforting soup that is markedly improved if left for 24 hours before it's eaten. I tend to make it with the liquid left after I've cooked a piece of ham, but I sometimes buy a ham-bone specially.

1 tablespoon groundnut oil

25 g (1 oz) butter

125 g (4 oz) streaky bacon, chopped

1 large onion, chopped

2 large garlic cloves, chopped

250 (8 oz) green, brown or red lentils

150 ml (¼ pint) dry white wine

1 large potato, cubed

2 carrots, chopped

2 celery sticks, chopped

1 leek, chopped

1 small onion, spiked with 2 cloves
   securing a bay leaf

2 litres (3½ pints) ham stock or 1 ham-bone
   and 2 litres (3½ pints) water

juice of ½ a lemon

salt and pepper

To garnish:

2 tablespoons finely chopped fresh parsley

extra-virgin olive oil

Heat the oil and butter in a large, heavy pan. When they are hot, cook the bacon until the fat begins to run. Stir in the onion and garlic and cook for 5 minutes, without browning. Add the lentils, cook for 10 minutes and then pour on the wine. Let it bubble up and then add the potato, carrots, celery, leek, onion spiked with cloves and bay leaf and the ham stock or ham-bone and water.

Bring the soup to the boil, season generously with pepper and leave the soup to simmer for 45 minutes, or until everything is cooked.

Remove the onion and bay leaf, and the ham-bone, if using. Liquidise 300 ml (½ pint) of the soup in a food processor or blender, return it to the pan and give the soup a thorough stir – this stage may be omitted; it merely helps stop all the ingredients sinking to the bottom of the pan.

Check the seasoning, adjusting it with salt, pepper and lemon juice and stir in the parsley. Serve with a swirl of your best olive oil and some crusty bread.

Lentil Soup

Beef Soup with Horseradish Dumplings

Beef Soup with Horseradish Dumplings

Preparation and cooking time: 1¹/₄ hours

Serves 6

This is a variation on boiled beef and carrots and makes an excellent winter soup-supper. It's worth shelling the broad beans – under their grey, rubbery skins the beans look like bright green jewels. Don't be tempted to over-cook them.

For the soup:

2 tablespoons groundnut oil

50 g (2 oz) butter

500 g (1 lb) stewing beef, sliced finely

1.75 litres (3 pints) beef stock

500 g (1 lb) carrots, sliced thickly

500 g (1 lb) leeks, sliced thickly

250 g (8 oz) frozen broad beans, blanched
    and shelled

salt and pepper

For the horseradish dumplings:

250 g (8 oz) potatoes

1 small onion, chopped

25 g (1 oz) butter

15 g (¹/₂ oz) semolina

1 tablespoon finely chopped fresh parsley

1 tablespoon creamed horseradish

1 egg yolk

about 25 g (1 oz) plain white flour, sifted

salt and pepper

To serve:

English mustard

Worcestershire sauce

Heat the oil and butter in a frying-pan and quickly sauté the beef until all sides have changed colour. Using a slotted spoon, transfer the beef to a large, heavy pan. Add the beef stock and simmer very gently for 40 minutes.

Meanwhile, make the dumplings. Cook the potatoes until soft and then mash them until smooth. Cook the onion in the butter until soft. Sift the semolina into the potato and stir in the cooked onion. Add the parsley, horseradish and seasoning. Incorporate the egg yolk and add enough flour to make a soft, cohesive dough.

With floury fingers, form small pieces of the dough into cherry-sized dumplings. Drop them into lightly salted water and cook for 2 minutes. Remove with a slotted spoon.

When the 40 minutes is up, add the carrots and leeks to the beef stock and cook for a further 15 minutes until everything is tender. Adjust the seasoning with salt and pepper and add the blanched broad beans and the dumplings. Cook for 5 minutes and serve with a pot of English mustard and a bottle of Worcestershire sauce for people to help themselves.

Thai Hot and Sour Prawn Soup

Preparation and cooking time: 45 minutes
Serves 6

Tom yum koong *is the Thai name of this wonderfully lemon-sour and chilli-hot soup, which combines the characteristic balance of sweet, sour, salty, bitter and hot that features in so much Thai food. Part of its intriguing flavour comes from Thai fish sauce, called* nam pla, *which is made with fermented salted anchovies.*

Traditionally, this soup is made with large, uncooked, deep-water prawns, but the smaller Mediterranean prawns will do. I've also made tom yum *with chunks of white fish (allow 125 g/4 oz per person) and with slivers of chicken (allow one leg or thigh per person).*

Incidentally, the juices in raw chilli peppers will burn delicate parts of the body, so take care not to touch your eyes or lips while handling them and be sure to wash your hands in soapy water immediately afterwards.

500 g (1 lb) raw, unpeeled large prawns
1.5 litres (2¹/₂ pints) fish stock (page 12)
4 lemon grass stalks
2 garlic cloves, peeled and chopped finely
6 kaffir lime leaves
2 tablespoons Thai fish sauce
125 g (4 oz) button mushrooms, sliced
6 spring onions, sliced finely
2–4 small green chillies, de-seeded and
    sliced finely
1 tablespoon fresh lime juice
2 tablespoons chopped fresh coriander
salt

Peel the prawns and place their shells, and heads if they have them, in a pan with the fish stock and bring to the boil. Simmer for 10 minutes and then strain the stock into a pan large enough to hold the entire soup.

Remove the dry, outer leaves of the lemon grass and cut the stalks into 2.5 cm (1-inch) pieces. Bash them with a rolling pin to release their flavour. Add the lemon grass, garlic, kaffir lime leaves, Thai fish sauce and a generous pinch of salt to the strained stock and let it simmer for 15 minutes. Add the mushrooms, spring onions and chilli rings and simmer for 3 minutes.

Meanwhile, using a small, sharp knife make a shallow cut along the back of each prawn and remove the dark visceral vein.

Add the prawns and lime juice to the pan, bring the soup back to the boil and simmer for a couple of minutes until the prawns turn pink. Adjust the flavour with salt and more lime juice if necessary. Stir in the chopped fresh coriander and serve (the kaffir lime leaves and lemon grass aren't edible: remove them if possible).

Smoked-haddock Cream with Poached Eggs and Parmesan Croûtons

Preparation and cooking time: 45 minutes
Serves 4

Smoked haddock and soft-poached eggs are one of those culinary marriages made in heaven. In this soup, which is based on Scotland's 'cullen skink', the fish is puréed with potato and the poached egg provides a rich 'sauce'. Cheesy croûtons give a lovely crunch to this satisfying and filling soup.

1 large onion, chopped

2 potatoes, peeled and cubed

1 bay leaf

25 g (1 oz) butter

600 ml (1 pint) milk

600 ml (1 pint) fish stock (page 12)

500 g (1 lb) Finnan haddock with skin, cut in two

pepper

To serve:

4 eggs

4 tablespoons single cream

snipped fresh chives

parmesan croûtons (page 84)

Place the onion, potatoes, bay leaf, butter, milk and fish stock in a pan and simmer for 15 minutes. Lay the pieces of haddock in the pan and simmer gently for 6 minutes. Use a slotted spoon to remove the fish to a plate. Remove the bay leaf.

When the fish is cool enough to handle, go over it for bones before flaking the flesh off the skin. Return half the fish to the pan and season with pepper. Liquidise the soup in a food processor or blender. Pour it through a sieve into a clean pan, using a wooden spoon to push through as much of the fibrous fish as possible. Add the rest of the fish to the pan and re-heat.

Poach the eggs for a few minutes until they are only just set.

Serve each bowl of soup with a soft-poached egg, a swirl of cream and a sprinkling of chives. Offer the parmesan croûtons separately.

Black-bean Soup with Tomato and Avocado Relish

Preparation time: 4 hours soaking + 45 minutes + 3 hours cooking
Serves 6–8

Black beans, not to be confused with black-eyed beans, are small, shiny and kidney-shaped. Their slightly sweet flavour is complemented by onions and garlic, goes well with coriander, cumin and tomatoes, and needs to be pepped up with chilli. This soup combines all those flavours and the result is an intriguingly aromatic, thick and chunky soup, freshened up with a 'salad' of raw tomato and avocado seasoned with lemon juice.

Serve it with coriander garlic bread (page 86) and it's a meal in itself – perfect if there's a vegetarian in the family. I like it accompanied by a shot of dry sherry.

For the soup:

3 tablespoons vegetable oil

2 large onions, chopped

4 fat garlic cloves, crushed with the flat of a knife

1 teaspoon ground cumin

1 teaspoon ground coriander

1 teaspoon dried oregano

1 bay leaf

250 g (8 oz) dried black beans, soaked for at least 4 hours and drained

two 400 g cans of tomatoes, chopped, or two cans of chopped tomatoes

1 tablespoon tomato purée

about 75 g (3 oz) fresh coriander, chopped

1 scant teaspoon Tabasco sauce

1.75 litres (3 pints) hot water or vegetable stock (page 11)

$^1/_2$ teaspoon salt

$^1/_2$ teaspoon ground black pepper

For the relish:

1 avocado

1 tablespoon lemon juice

2 plum tomatoes, peeled, de-seeded and chopped

142 ml (5 fl oz) carton of fresh soured cream, to serve

a few fresh coriander leaves, to garnish

Heat the oil in a large pan and sauté the onions and garlic for 5 minutes, until soft but not brown. Stir in the cumin, coriander, oregano and bay leaf, before adding the beans. Stir-fry for 5 minutes and add the tomatoes and their liquid, tomato purée, chopped fresh coriander, Tabasco sauce and hot water or stock. Bring to the boil and boil rapidly for 10 minutes. Turn down the heat and simmer very gently for 3 hours.

Discard the bay leaf. Purée half of the soup in a blender or food processor. Pass the puréed soup through a sieve into a clean pan and add the unpuréed soup. Re-heat the soup and adjust the seasoning as necessary.

For the relish, peel and chop the avocado and mix it with the lemon juice. Mix in the tomatoes.

Serve each bowlful with a swirl of soured cream, a spoonful of tomato and avocado relish and a few coriander leaves.

Storecupboard Soups

These are the soups that can be conjured out of the cupboard, vegetable rack and deep-freeze, using cans, packets and everyday staples. They aren't, however, boring soups, but imaginative ways with old favourites. Some rely on frozen stock, others need stock-cubes or just water.

Stracciatelle

Preparation and cooking time: 15 minutes
Serves 6

This is one of those marvellously simple soups that is as quick to make as it is delicious to eat. It must, however, be made with decent stock, and the best flavour comes from freshly grated parmesan cheese. The soup gets its name from the look of the finished soup – stracciatelle means 'little rags'.

3 eggs, beaten

4 tablespoons fine fresh white bread-
    crumbs

4 tablespoons freshly grated parmesan
    cheese, plus extra to serve

a generous pinch of freshly grated nutmeg

finely grated zest of 1 lemon

1.5 litres (2¹/₂ pints) cold chicken stock
    (page 10) or chicken consommé,
    sieved

salt and pepper

Place the eggs, breadcrumbs, parmesan cheese, nutmeg, lemon zest and a pinch of salt and pepper in a bowl. Stir in 250 ml (8 fl oz) of the cold stock or consommé and mix thoroughly.

Bring the remaining stock to the boil. Pour the egg mixture into the stock and stir quickly and thoroughly with a fork. Reduce the heat and cook at a gentle simmer for 2 minutes, breaking up the eggs with a fork until they resemble little rags. Serve immediately, with more parmesan cheese.

Risi e Bisi

Stracciatelle

Spanish Chick-pea
Soup with Mint
and Garlic

Spanish Chick-pea Soup with Mint and Garlic

Preparation and cooking time: 15 minutes
Serves 4

Canned chick-peas are an under-rated storecupboard standby. Drained and puréed with lemon juice and garlic, they become hummus; dressed with vinaigrette they make a filling salad, and they are a tasty addition to curries, casseroles and stir-fries.

In Spain and Portugal, chick-peas are the key ingredient in a number of hearty soups. In this version, which is really a liquid hummus, I think it's worth passing the soup through a sieve to give a silky-smooth finish before adding the fresh herbs. This soup is also very good with a poached egg slipped into individual bowls just before serving.

two 432 g cans of chick-peas

2 fat garlic cloves, chopped

6 tablespoons olive oil

2 tablespoons lemon juice

a generous pinch of Cayenne pepper

2 tablespoons chopped fresh mint leaves

**2 tablespoons finely chopped fresh
   coriander or flat-leaf parsley**

salt and pepper

olive oil, to garnish (optional)

Drain the liquid from the chick-pea cans into a measuring jug. Add water to make up the liquid to 900 ml (1½ pints). In a food processor or blender, purée this liquid with the chick-peas, garlic, olive oil and lemon juice.

Pass the soup through a sieve into a saucepan. Season it with salt, pepper and Cayenne and stir in most of the mint and coriander or parsley. Boil the soup hard for two minutes. Remove from the heat and adjust the seasoning with salt, pepper and lemon juice. Stir in the rest of the herbs and serve, if liked, with a swirl of olive oil.

Risi e Bisi

Preparation and cooking time: 40 minutes
Serves 4

This is a storecupboard version of the famous pea and rice soup-risotto of Venice. There it's made with tiny, young peas, pancetta (Italian bacon), and freshly grated parmesan cheese. The essential ingredient is Italian risotto rice, which has a distinctive round shape and cooks to retain a slight bite.

In Venice risi e bisi *is regarded as a cross between a soup and risotto, and is always served as an appetiser; my version is definitely a soup.*

25 g (1 oz) butter

1 teaspoon olive oil

2 bacon rashers, chopped

1 small onion

100 g (3^1/$_2$ oz) Italian risotto rice (Arborio)

1.2 litres (2 pints) boiling chicken stock (page 10)

375 g (12 oz) frozen peas

20 g (^{3}/$_4$ oz) parmesan cheese, grated

1 tablespoon (15 g/^{1}/$_2$ oz) butter

2 tablespoons chopped fresh flat-leaf parsley

salt and pepper

Heat the butter and olive oil in a medium-size saucepan and gently sauté the bacon and onion until the onion is soft but not brown. Stir in the rice and season with salt and plenty of pepper. Start to add boiling stock, a ladleful at a time, stirring constantly. As the liquid is absorbed, continue to add more stock. After 15 minutes, add the remaining boiling stock and simmer for a further 10 minutes.

Stir the frozen peas into the pan. Bring the soup back to the boil, turn down the heat and cook for 5 minutes. Stir in the parmesan cheese, butter and parsley and serve immediately.

Tomato-rice Soup with Orange and Herbs

Preparation and cooking time: 20 minutes

Serves 4

This is a comforting sort of soup that's quick and easy to make and uses a number of ingredients that most people have most of the time. The final addition of a quantity of fresh herbs is a lovely contrast of colour and gives the soup another layer of flavour.

I've taken to keeping a supply of frozen herbs in my deep-freeze, for the occasions when fresh herbs aren't available, and these are perfect in this soup.

50 g (2 oz) quick-cook basmati or long-
    grain rice

grated zest of ¹/₂ and juice of 1 orange

1 carrot, chopped

1 potato, peeled and cubed

400 g can of chopped tomatoes

2 tablespoons tomato purée

1 chicken or vegetable stock-cube

600 ml (1 pint) water

25 g (1 oz) butter

2 tablespoons finely chopped watercress,
    parsley, chives or coriander, or a mixture

salt and pepper

Begin by putting the rice on to cook according to the packet instructions.

Place the orange zest and juice, carrot and potato, chopped tomatoes and their juice, tomato purée, and chicken or vegetable stock-cube in a medium-size pan. Add the water. Bring the liquid to the boil and boil hard for 8 minutes. Liquidise the soup and pass it through a sieve into a clean pan. By now, the rice will be cooked. Drain the rice and add it to the soup. Re-heat thoroughly before adjusting the seasoning with salt and pepper. Stir in the butter and herbs and serve immediately.

Cream of Sweetcorn Soup

Preparation and cooking time: 20 minutes + 4 hours chilling (optional)
Serves 4

This soup is a real star – the perfect storecupboard standby. It uses canned sweetcorn, milk and a little seasoning and can be served hot or cold. It's worth the extra effort of sieving the finished soup.

25 g (1 oz) butter

a bunch of spring onions or 1 onion, chopped finely

326 g can of sweetcorn, rinsed and drained

750 ml (1¼ pints) milk

a generous pinch of freshly grated nutmeg

salt and pepper

To garnish:

a generous pinch of paprika

1 tablespoon snipped fresh chives

Melt the butter in a medium-size saucepan and soften the spring onions or onion. Stir in the sweetcorn and cook gently for a couple of minutes. Add the milk, nutmeg, and a little salt and pepper. Bring the soup to the boil, lower the heat and simmer gently for 5 minutes. Pour it into the bowl of a food processor or blender and liquidise until smooth. Pass the soup through a sieve into a serving bowl. Adjust the seasoning if necessary.

Serve with a dusting of paprika and the snipped chives. If serving cold, chill for at least 4 hours before garnishing.

White-bean Soup

Preparation and cooking time: 25 minutes

Serves 4–6

This is a good cheat's version of a classic Italian soup and it's perfect heart-warming fuel on a cold winter's day.

Although delicious eaten as soon as it's made, the flavours will develop and improve if the soup is left overnight; in which case you may need to add a little more liquid.

1 tablespoon olive oil

1 large onion, chopped finely

2 garlic cloves, chopped finely and then pounded with 1 teaspoon salt

4 streaky bacon rashers, cut in thin strips

a generous pinch of dried thyme or rosemary

two 400 g cans of haricot, cannellini or navy beans, drained and rinsed

900 ml (1½ pints) chicken stock (page 10) or equivalent using stock-cubes

2 tablespoons bottled pesto sauce

1 peperoni sausage, sliced finely (optional)

juice of ½ small lemon

salt and pepper

To garnish:

chopped fresh parsley

extra-virgin olive oil

Heat the olive oil and gently sauté the onion for 5 minutes, without letting it brown. Add the garlic, bacon and thyme or rosemary and cook for 5–10 minutes, until the bacon starts to crisp. Stir in the white beans and add the stock. Bring the soup up to the boil, season generously, and simmer for 5 minutes.

Scoop half the beans and some of the liquid into the bowl of a food processor or liquidiser and process until smooth. Pour it back into the pan and re-heat the soup. Stir in the pesto sauce, the peperoni sausage slices, if using, and the lemon juice. Cook gently for 5 minutes and serve garnished with the chopped parsley and a slick of your best extra-virgin olive oil

This is very good with chilli croûtons (page 84).

Baked-bean Soup

Preparation and cooking time: 10 minutes
Serves 4

A wonderful soup and the best way to stretch a can of beans between four.

4 streaky bacon rashers

1 onion, chopped finely

4 tablespoons fresh breadcrumbs

400 g can of beans in tomato sauce

2 chicken stock-cubes dissolved in 900 ml
   (1 1/2 pints) water

1/2 teaspoon Worcestershire sauce

salt and pepper

To serve:

parmesan croûtons (page 84)

Tabasco sauce

Lay the bacon in a frying-pan and cook it until it is evenly crisp. Lift the bacon out with a slotted spoon and put it aside to cool (before crumbling it). Gently sauté the onion in the bacon fat. When the onion is soft but not browned, transfer it to a medium-sized saucepan. Stir in the breadcrumbs and add the beans and chicken stock. Season with salt and pepper and half a teaspoon of Worcestershire sauce. Bring the soup up to the boil, give it a good stir and leave to simmer for 5 minutes.

Just before serving, mix in the crumbled bacon. I also like to add chunky parmesan croûtons and a few shakes of Tabasco sauce.

Pea and Pear Soup

Preparation and cooking time: 15 minutes + 4 hours chilling (optional)
Serves 4–6

This is an unlikely-sounding combination that's intriguingly delicious; it is as good cold as it is hot.

500 g (1 lb) frozen peas, defrosted

two 411 g cans of pears in natural juice

2 tablespoons finely chopped fresh mint or
   2 tablespoons mint jelly

900 ml (1 1/2 pints) light chicken stock
   (page 10)

salt and freshly ground white pepper

Cook the peas in salted water for a few minutes until tender. Drain. Purée the peas, pears and mint or mint jelly with the chicken stock in a liquidiser or food processor. Pour the soup through a sieve into a medium-size pan, pushing the peas through with the back of a wooden spoon. Heat the soup through and season it to taste with salt and white pepper. Serve it immediately, or chill for at least 4 hours before serving it cold.

Minted Pea Soup

Preparation and cooking time: 20 minutes
Serves 4–6

When I made this for a cookery demonstration at Olympia, no one believed how I could transform frozen peas and concentrated mint sauce into a soup good enough to serve at a dinner party. It's one of the best storecupboard soups I know and everybody loves it. Serve it with a swirl of cream and a sprig of fresh mint, if you have it. It's also very good with scraps of crisp grilled bacon and parmesan croûtons (page 84).

1 chicken stock-cube dissolved in 600 ml (1 pint) water

1 kg (2 lb) frozen peas

1 teaspoon concentrated mint sauce

142 ml (5 fl oz) carton of single cream

150 ml (¼ pint) milk

salt, pepper and sugar

Bring the stock to the boil and add the peas and mint sauce. Bring the liquid back to a steady simmer, cover and cook for 10 minutes.

Pour the contents of the pan into the bowl of a liquidiser or food processor. Whizz at top speed for 2 minutes. Pour the soup through a sieve into a clean pan. Use the back of a wooden spoon to push through as much of the purée as possible – this is quite hard work!

Add the cream and milk, re-heat the soup without boiling and remove the pan from the heat immediately. Taste and adjust the seasoning with salt and a pinch of sugar if necessary.

Spinach Soup

Preparation and cooking time: 30 minutes
Serves 4–6

It's only recently that I've discovered frozen spinach. It cooks to an unattractive slop but it's perfect for sauces and makes wonderful soups. To make a quick, simple cream of spinach soup, liquidise 500 g (1 lb) de-frosted spinach with 600 ml (1 pint) of hot stock and whisk two egg yolks and 2 tablespoons of grated parmesan cheese into the soup after it has boiled. Simmer gently for 2 minutes and serve. This recipe doesn't rely on eggs for its richness – both are perfect storecupboard soups.

50 g (2 oz) butter

1 large onion, chopped

2 garlic cloves, chopped finely

2 potatoes, cubed

500 g (1 lb) frozen spinach

a generous pinch of freshly grated nutmeg

2 chicken or vegetable stock-cubes dissolved in 900 ml (1½ pints) water

salt and pepper

Melt the butter in a medium-size saucepan and stir in the onion. Cook gently and after 10 minutes add the garlic and potatoes. Season generously with salt and pepper, cover and leave to sweat for 5 minutes.

Add the frozen spinach and nutmeg and stir until the spinach is de-frosted.

Pour on the stock, bring the soup to the boil and simmer for 10 minutes or until the potatoes are tender.

Pour the soup into the bowl of a blender or food processor and liquidise it. Pour the purée through a fine sieve into a clean bowl. Taste, adjust the seasoning as necessary, and serve very hot.

To make more of this soup, garnish it with curls of parmesan cheese shaved with a potato peeler from a block of cheese. Alternatively, accompany it with parmesan croûtes, made by topping thin slices of baguette with grated parmesan cheese. Place the croûtes under a hot grill until the cheese melts and colours slightly.

Garnishes and Embellishments

Part of the pleasure of soup-making is the opportunity the finished 'canvas' provides to turn even the most modest soup into a minor work of art. Almost anything goes, but there should always be a point to the garnish. It must relate in some way to the taste and/or the aroma, as well as to the visual appeal of the soup.

For example, a simple broth can be dramatically changed with a garnish of chopped fresh tomato and a scattering of chopped fresh herbs. Similarly, a smooth puréed soup looks stunning when garnished with a swirl of a contrastingly coloured purée. Texture can be introduced with scraps of grilled bacon, crunchy croûtons or with a mound of super-fine, deep-fried pasta, vegetables or crisps, balanced on a spoonful of cream or yogurt. Equally, a selection of complementary garnishes can be served at the table for guests to make up their own compositions.

A small amount of a luxury ingredient, such as a few grains of caviare, an oyster or a slice of pan-fried scallop, can be used to transform humble soups and add interest to clear, intensely flavoured soup.

Garnishes can also be used to make more of a soup. Eggs, for example, can be whisked with cream and stirred in at the last moment to enrich and thicken. They can be poached and slipped into the soup just before serving, or cooked as an omelette or pancake and sliced finely to be sprinkled on to the soup. Dumplings, like gnocchi made with mashed potato, have the two-fold advantage of a garnish that looks attractive and is very filling.

Many of the soups in this book incorporate their own garnish or embellishment, with ingredients that inter-relate to the soups' main ingredients. Use my ideas to inspire your own – there's no limit to the possibilities.

Herb Potato Gnocchi

Preparation and cooking time: 20 minutes

Makes 35 (serves 6–8)

The Italian dumplings called gnocchi are a great way of using up cold, leftover boiled potatoes. I like to add them to a bowl of well flavoured stock or canned consommé, with a garnish of fresh herbs and parmesan cheese for grating into individual servings.

You can use any variety of potato for gnocchi.

250 g (8 oz) peeled potatoes, cooked

65 g (2¹/₂ oz) plain flour, sifted

2 heaped tablespoons finely chopped
 fresh herbs, e.g., parsley, basil or
 coriander

1 egg yolk

1 teaspoon olive oil

salt, pepper and freshly grated nutmeg

Mash the potatoes until quite smooth. Season them with salt, pepper and a pinch of nutmeg. Tip the mashed potatoes on to a floured surface. Make a well in the middle and add a quarter of the sifted flour, and then the herbs and egg yolk. Sprinkle on the olive oil. Using your fingertips, quickly work the mixture to incorporate the flour, adding more as you do so. You will end up with a soft and light but surprisingly durable dough.

Divide the dough in half and roll each half into a long, 2.5 cm (1-inch) thick sausage. Chop it into 1 cm (¹/₂-inch) lengths. The gnocchi can be cooked like this but if you want the authentic look, press the ball of dough into the concave curl of a fork with the index finger so that the tines of the fork leave a pronounced indentation. Gently roll the gnocchi off the fork with your index finger. This should give it a slight curl.

Drop the gnocchi into a large pan of boiling, salted water, cooking them in batches of 10 or 12. They will pop up to the surface after about 20 seconds – any longer and they'll be tough – scoop them out with a slotted spoon. Drain the gnocchi and slip them into the soup tureen or into individual bowls.

Herb Potato Gnocchi
Puff-pastry Lids
Rocket Pesto

Puff-pastry Lids

Preparation time: 10 minutes + 20 minutes cooking
Makes 6 lids

This impressive 'garnish' can be used for any soup but is particularly good with Mushroom Soup with Mushroom Gremolata (page 18) and other aromatic soups. You will need to use bulbous rather than flat-style soup bowls, which will also need to be ovenproof.

500 g (1 lb) ready-made puff or shortcrust pastry

1 egg yolk, whisked with 1 teaspoon milk or water

1 egg white, whisked to a froth

Preheat the oven to Gas Mark 7/220°C/425°F. Roll out the pastry 5 mm (¼ inch) thick and cut it into circles about 4 cm (1½ inches) wider than the soup bowls. Working quickly on one bowl at a time, paint a 4 cm (1½ inch) band of egg white round the outer rim of the bowl. Pour in the hot soup level with the base of the egg-white rim. Take a circle of pastry and place it across the bowl without stretching it. Seal down the sides, nipping and tucking to make it neat and using more of the egg-white 'glue' if necessary. Paint the entire pastry lid with the egg-yolk solution.

Place the bowls on a baking tray and bake for 15–20 minutes until slightly risen, crisp and golden. Serve immediately.

For an alternative approach, use the bowl as a template to draw round, and float the circle of puff pastry on the soup. Bake in the same way.

Rocket Pesto

Preparation time: 10 minutes
Makes about 150 ml (¼ pint) (serves 4–6)

The distinctive, bitter, lemony tang of rocket goes well with bland foods like potato, beans and pasta, and creamy seafood like squid and scallops. This pesto is bitter and creamy at the same time; it is delicious stirred into soups made with these ingredients just before serving. Serve it in its own bowl for people to help themselves.

two 30 g bags of rocket, rinsed and dried
1 garlic clove
3 tablespoons of pine kernels, toasted
**   lightly**
4 tablespoons olive oil
3 tablespoons grated parmesan cheese
salt and pepper

Put the rocket, garlic, pine kernels and a little salt and pepper in the bowl of a food processor. Work to a paste and, with the motor running, add the olive oil in a thin stream to produce a loose-textured purée. Pour into a bowl and stir in the parmesan cheese.

Tomato and Mint Salsa

Preparation time: 5–10 minutes
Serves 6

Salsa means 'sauce' in South America and usually refers to a spicy mound of finely diced raw vegetables, heavily laced with chilli. Its texture is somewhere between a sauce and a salad; and it's served as a relish with cooked fish and meat, and vegetarian patties. Salsas are also an interesting way of freshening up soups, and go particularly well with vegetable and bean purées. Serve them as a garnish: stir them into soups just before serving, or serve them separately for people to help themselves. This version goes well with pea or courgette soups.

1 extra-large tomato or 3 plum tomatoes
1 dessertspoon finely chopped fresh mint
1 teaspoon finely chopped fresh parsley
salt and pepper

Completely cover the tomatoes with boiling water. Leave for 30 seconds – they are ready when the skin curls back when you pierce the tomato with the point of a sharp knife. Drain and immerse the tomatoes in cold water to stop them softening. Pull away the skin and cut the tomatoes into quarters. Pull out their seeds and cores, and slice the tomatoes into 5 mm (¼-inch) dice. Season and mix with the mint and parsley.

Garlic Croûtons

Preparation time: 20 minutes

Serves 4–6

Croûtons can be cooked in butter or oil and made in a frying-pan or in the oven. If you're using butter, which I prefer for plain croûtons and these delicately flavoured garlic croûtons, unsalted is best. It needs to be clarified first to stop it burning.

I make croûtons in batches and store them in an old ice cream container in the fridge.

1 large garlic clove, crushed with the flat of a knife

50-125 g (2–4 oz) clarified butter (see note)

1 small stale baguette, cut in 1 cm (¹/₂-inch) cubes

Rub a frying-pan with the garlic, leave it in the pan and then pour in the butter. Over a low heat, stir-fry the garlic for 30 seconds until it begins to colour. Remove the garlic. Add the bread-cubes to the pan and sauté them, shaking the pan occasionally, and stirring the bread around to cook it uniformly. Drain on absorbent kitchen paper.

Note: to clarify butter, melt the butter in a small pan over a low heat. When the liquid bubbles, remove the pan from the heat and skim off the froth that will have formed. Allow the liquid to cool slightly and pour through muslin, cheesecloth or a coffee filter-paper into a clean storage jar, leaving the milky solids behind. Store in the fridge for up to a month and use as required.

Parmesan Croûtons

Preparation and cooking time: 20 minutes

Serves 4–6

3 slices from a Farmhouse white loaf, crusts removed, cut into 1 cm (¹/₂-inch) cubes

3 tablespoons of olive oil

2 heaped tablespoons of grated parmesan cheese

Preheat the oven to Gas Mark 6/200°C/400°F. Pour the oil on to a plate and sprinkle the parmesan cheese on to a second plate. Roll the bread first in the olive oil and then in the parmesan cheese. Place the croûtons on a wire rack that is resting on a baking sheet and bake for 10 minutes, until crisp and golden. Drain on kitchen paper.

Variation: To make chilli croûtons, omit the parmesan and stir 6 drops of Tabasco sauce into the olive oil before rolling the bread cubes in the oil.

Parsley and Chive Pancake Strips

Preparation and cooking time: 10 minutes

Serves 6–8

Serving finely sliced, savoury rolled pancakes as a soup garnish is an oriental idea. They work particularly well with clear soups that rely on a good quality stock, but they are also good with thick vegetable purées, and contribute extra protein.

I like to flavour the pancakes with fresh herbs, and you can ring the changes to complement your soups; basil, for example, goes very well with tomato soup, and watercress goes with cucumber or lettuce.

50 g (2 oz) self-raising flour, sifted

a pinch of salt

1 egg, beaten

150 ml (¹/₄ pint) milk

1 teaspoon finely chopped fresh parsley

1 teaspoon finely snipped fresh chives

oil for frying

Sift the flour and a pinch of salt into the egg and gradually add the milk to form a smooth batter. Stir in the parsley and chives. Heat a scant tablespoon of oil in a frying-pan until it smokes and then turn down the heat slightly.

Have ready in a cup 2 tablespoons of the batter. Pour and quickly swirl the batter around the pan and cook for 20 seconds. Flip the pancake over with the help of an egg slice and remove it after 10 seconds. Place the pancakes to drain on kitchen paper.

When they are cool enough to handle, roll each pancake into a tight cigar and finely slice it with a sharp knife. Sprinkle the ribbons on to the soup just before serving, or serve them separately for people to help themselves.

Accompaniments for Soup

Bread is the obvious choice to serve with soup. Dunking a piece of crusty bread into a bowl of steaming-hot soup is one of life's great pleasures. I like to complement my soups with bread. Dainty Melba toast goes with elegant soups and consommés; herb scones are a treat with delicate vegetable soups; whereas rustic garlic breads go well with robust, country-style soups.

The style of bread served as an accompaniment alters the perception of the soup it accompanies. For example, ciabatta or foccacia make more of an event of an Italian soup such as stracciatelle and pappa al pomodoro; garlic bread with fresh herbs turns a simple vegetable soup into a treat. Home-made breads, rolls and scones, like the herb scones on page 91, can be tailored to suit particular soups by adding grated parmesan cheese, fresh herbs and other seasonings.

Some soups, such as borscht, the Ukrainian beetroot soup, and French-onion soup come with their own idiosyncratic accompaniment. This is an idea I like to borrow. I enjoy dreaming up things to serve with particular soups and regard it as a good way of adding interest to yesterday's soup. This needn't involve a lot of work or time and can often be done with scraps of leftovers. Filo pastry, which defrosts quickly and gives foolproof results, is my favourite standby for making miniature pasties to serve with soup.

Many of the soups in the main body of recipes have their own accompaniments: use them as an inspiration to make up your own.

Coriander Garlic Bread

Preparation and cooking time: 20 minutes
Serves 4–6

This version of garlic bread oozes with butter and is for dedicated garlic lovers – if you prefer a subtler flavour, use less garlic. Parsley, celery leaves, mixed herbs or chives can be used in place of coriander.

1 stale baguette
125 g (4 oz) butter
4 garlic cloves, chopped finely
1 tablespoon chopped fresh coriander

Preheat the oven to Gas Mark 6/200°C/400°F.

Melt the butter with the garlic in a small pan. Stir in the coriander.

Make diagonal slashes in the loaf – as if you were slicing the loaf but without cutting right through – at 5 cm (2-inch) intervals. Place the loaf in the middle of a large sheet of foil. Spoon the coriander butter on to each side of the slices, pouring any leftovers on the top. Seal the parcel and bake in a hot oven for 10 minutes.

Potato Sticks

Preparation time: 10 minutes + 15 minutes cooking
Makes 20 sticks

This is another good recipe for using up leftover cooked potatoes and one that is endlessly versatile. I sometimes add finely chopped fresh herbs, grated cheese, a few drops of Tabasco sauce or pounded anchovy fillets to the mixture, and serve the potato sticks as an alternative to bread. You can vary the shapes too.

I particularly like them hot from the oven dunked into piping-hot Baked-bean Soup (page 76), but, if stored in an airtight tin, they will remain moist for several days.

1 egg
125 g (4 oz) soft butter or margarine
125 g (4 oz) self-raising flour
a pinch of salt
175 g (6 oz) mashed potato
milk
1 dessertspoon of oat flakes, or caraway,
dill, sesame, poppy or celery seeds

Preheat the oven to Gas Mark 5/190°C/375°F. Cream the egg with the butter until smooth and glossy. Sift in the flour, a pinch of salt and, using your fingertips, work in the mashed potato. The dough will be soft and pliable – if it seems too floppy, sift over a little more flour.

On a floured surface roll the dough about 1 cm (1/2 inch) thick and cut it into 5 × 1 cm (2 × 1/2-inch) sticks. Brush the top with milk and sprinkle with salt, and oatflakes or seeds. Transfer to a well greased baking-sheet, leaving a space between each stick, and bake for 15 minutes.

Coriander Garlic Bread

Potato Sticks

Basil and Chive Böreks

Basil and Chive Böreks

Preparation time: 15 minutes + 20 minutes baking
Makes 16 böreks

Böreks are cork-shaped filo pastry parcels. The basic stuffing is mashed potato, laced with finely sliced spring onions and plenty of fresh herbs. The filling can be varied to suit the soup they will accompany.

For the pastry:

16 filo pastry sheets, measuring about
    18 x 25 cm (7 x 10 inches)

50 g (2 oz) butter, melted

For the filling:

50 g (2 oz) butter

90 ml (3 fl oz) milk, scalded

500 g (1 lb) mashed potato

2 spring onions, sliced finely

2 tablespoons chopped fresh basil

1 tablespoon snipped fresh chives

salt and pepper

Preheat the oven to Gas Mark 4/180°C/350°F. If you are using cold mashed potato, first melt the butter in the hot milk and stir it into the mash before you mix in the spring onions, herbs and seasoning.

Lay out the sheets of filo pastry and cover with a damp tea towel. Working with one sheet at a time, paint it with butter and place a dessertspoon of the filling in the centre. Roll and tuck the pastry to make a cork-shaped parcel and use melted butter to seal it.

Lay the böreks on oiled baking-sheets and bake for about 20 minutes, until they are crisp and golden. Serve hot, warm or cold.

Brown Herb Scones

Preparation time: 10 minutes + 20 minutes cooking

Makes 9 scones

250 g (8 oz) self-raising wholemeal flour

1/2 teaspoon salt

125 g (4 oz) butter or hard margarine

2 tablespoons finely chopped mixed
    fresh herbs

150 ml (5 fl oz) milk

egg-wash (optional)

Preheat the oven to Gas Mark 5/190°C/375°F.

Tip the flour into a mixing bowl with the salt. Cut the butter or margarine into small pieces and rub it into the flour, until the mixture resembles rough breadcrumbs. Stir in the herbs and gradually add the milk to form a soft, pliable dough. Turn it on to a floured surface and gently pat and mould the dough to form a slab 18 × 25 cm (7 × 10 inches). Cut across its width into three equal pieces and divide each band into three triangles. Transfer to a flat, well greased baking tray and brush the tops with the egg-wash, or dust them with flour.

Bake for 10 minutes, lower the oven temperature to Gas Mark 2/150°C/300°F and cook for a further 10 minutes until puffed and golden.

Melba Toast with Pimiento Butter

Preparation and cooking time: 15 minutes
Serves 4

Melba toast, those wafer-thin crisp triangles of toasted bread, go well with any delicate soup. I like to serve it with a flavoured butter that has some connection with the soup. This particular butter is delicious with Roasted Tomato Soup with Green Dumplings (page 20).

For the Melba toast:
8 slices of stale white medium-sliced
    bread

For the pimiento butter:
125 g (4 oz) canned red peppers, drained
125 g (4 oz) soft butter

To make the Melba toast, toast the bread, remove the crusts and slice the toast horizontally through the middle to make two thin slices. Cut these into triangles and toast the uncooked side briefly under a hot grill, allowing the toast room to curl. Cool on a rack.

To make the butter, liquidise the red pepper. Cream the butter until it's soft and fluffy. Beat the red pepper purée into the butter. Turn into individual pots. The purée will keep for three days if refrigerated.

Crisp Parmesan Biscuits

Preparation time: 10 minutes + 8 minutes baking
Makes 15–20 biscuits

These very thin, elegant biscuits are delicious served with beef consommé. They can be turned into tuiles by curling them round a clean broom-handle or shaped round a cup while they are still warm.

50 g (2 oz) plain white flour
75 g (3 oz) flaked almonds
75 g (3 oz) parmesan cheese, grated, plus
    a little extra
40 g (1½ oz) butter, melted
1 egg white, beaten with a pinch of salt

Preheat the oven to Gas Mark 6/200°C/400°F. Sift the flour into a bowl and mix in the almond flakes, parmesan cheese and melted butter. When thoroughly mixed, fold in the egg white and form into a dough. Flour a suitable surface and roll the dough into a very thin sheet. With an 8 cm (3-inch) pastry cutter or an upturned glass, cut the pastry into circles and lay them, well spaced apart, on a well oiled baking-sheet. Bake for 6–8 minutes until pale golden. Remove with a palette knife and place on a wire rack to cool. Dust with extra parmesan cheese before serving.

Melba Toast with Pimiento Butter
Crisp Parmesan Biscuits

Soda Bread

Preparation time: 10 minutes + 45 minutes baking
Makes 1 large round loaf

Bread and soup were made for each other, particularly when the bread is crusty and freshly made. Soda bread doesn't need yeast or lengthy proving, and it's child's-play to make. Eat it hot from the oven, cut into chunks with plenty of butter.

500 g (1 lb) wholemeal flour

175 g (6 oz) plain white flour

1 rounded teaspoon bicarbonate of soda

1 teaspoon salt

25 g (1 oz) butter or margarine, chilled and
cubed

about 450 ml (3/4 pint) buttermilk

Preheat the oven to Gas Mark 6/200°C /400°F. Mix the flours, salt and bicarbonate together in a mixing bowl. Rub in the butter with your fingertips, lifting the mixture high above the bowl to get air into the dough. Continue until it resembles fine breadcrumbs. Using a wooden spoon, stir in the buttermilk (depending on the flour you may need less or more) to make a soft dough. Turn on to a floured surface and knead lightly until the dough is smooth. Form into a circle about 4 cm (1½ inches) thick and place on a well floured baking-sheet. Slash the top with a deep cross, dust with flour and bake for about 45 minutes, until the loaf is crusty and browned.

If the loaf is not to be eaten immediately, cool it on a wire rack. If you want to keep the crust soft, wrap the hot loaf in a tea towel.

Index

THE AMERICAN LOVER:
AND OTHER STORIES

ROSE TREMAIN

Chatto & Windus

LONDON

Published by Chatto & Windus 2014

4 6 8 10 9 7 5

First published in Great Britain in 2014 by
Chatto & Windus
Random House, 20 Vauxhall Bridge Road,
London SW1V 2SA

www.randomhouse.co.uk

Addresses for companies within The Random House Group Limited can be
found at: www.randomhouse.co.uk/offices.htm

The Random House Group Limited Reg. No. 954009

A CIP catalogue record for this book is available from the British Library

Hardback ISBN 9780701185220
Trade paperback ISBN 9780701189273

The Random House Group Limited supports the Forest
Stewardship Council® (FSC®), the leading international forest-certification
organisation. Our books carrying the FSC label are printed on
FSC®-certified paper. FSC is the only forest-certification scheme supported
by the leading environmental organisations, including Greenpeace.
Our paper procurement policy can be found at
www.randomhouse.co.uk/environment

Typeset in Sabon MT by Palimpsest Book Production Limited,
Falkirk, Stirlingshire

Printed and bound in Great Britain by
Clays Ltd, St Ives plc

THE AMERICAN LOVER

For Vivien Green, with love

CONTENTS

The American Lover

1.

All day long, lying on the sofa in the sitting room of her parents' London mansion flat, Beth hears the clunk of the elevator doors opening and closing.

Sometimes, she hears voices on the landing – people arriving or departing – and then the long sigh of the elevator descending. She wishes there were no people, no elevator, no pain. She stares at the old-fashioned room. She stares at her crutches, propped up against a wing chair. In a few months' time she is going to be thirty.

There is a Portuguese maid, Rosalita, who comes in at two o'clock every day.

She is never late. Rosalita has a gentle face and plump, downy arms. As she sprays the furniture with beeswax polish, she will often talk about her old life, and this is the only thing that Beth enjoys – hearing about Rosalita's old life in a garment factory in Setúbal, making costumes for matadors. The places Rosalita describes are hot and bright and filled with the sound of sewing machines or brass musical instruments. She describes how the matadors used to flirt with the seamstresses. They were young, she says, and full of ardour and their sweat was scented with incense, from the number of visits they made to the bullring chapels. These things remind Beth that there were days long ago when she was innocent enough to worship the ordinary beauty of the world.

In 1964, the lover came.

He was American. His name was Thaddeus. He came in and looked at Beth, who was nineteen years old. He was forty-eight, the same age as Beth's father. He was a commercial photographer, but when he saw Beth, with her serious, exquisite face, he said: 'I have to photograph you.'

Beth knew that she shouldn't go near him, that his skin would burn her, that his kiss would silence her. But she went.

Her mother said to her: 'I know what you're doing. I haven't told your father. I really think you should end this. He's much too old for you. It's shameful.'

But all Beth could think was, I love this shame. I'm on fire with shame. My shame is an electric pulse so strong, it could bring the dead to life.

Thaddeus had an estranged wife named Tricia, an ex-model who lived in California. Something he liked to do with Beth was to describe the many ways he used to make love to Tricia. Sometimes, at moments of wild intensity, he called Beth 'Tricia'. But Beth didn't mind. She could be anyone he chose: Beth, Tricia, Julie Christie, Jean Shrimpton, Jeanne Moreau, Brigitte Bardot . . . it didn't matter. Whatever self she'd had before she met him was invisible to her now. At certain moments in a life, this is what a person can feel. She was her lover's lover, that was all.

* * *

While Rosalita is dusting Beth's crutches, which she does very tenderly, from time to time, Beth shows her pictures from her press file.

The picture Rosalita likes best is of the car. It's in colour. There's nobody in the photograph, just the car, parked on the gravel of the house Beth once owned in the South of France: a pillar-box-red E-Type Jaguar soft-top with wire wheels. Rosalita shakes her head and whispers, 'Beautiful car.'

And Beth says, 'You know, Rosalita, there was a time when it was very easy for me to buy a car like that. In fact, it was given to me, but I could have bought it. I had all the money in the world.'

Thaddeus had no money. Only what he earned from his photography for the ad agencies of domestic appliances and food and hotel exteriors and yachts and London bobbies on bicycles, wearing what he called 'those droll Germanic helmets'.

'Jealousy of David Bailey,' joked Thaddeus, 'is my only flaw.'

Beth looked at him. He was thin and dark. There were dusty patches of grey in his chest hair. He let his toenails grow too long. He was beginning to go bald. There were times when Beth thought, He's just a very ordinary man. He doesn't have the grand, sinewy neck of Charlton Heston or the swooning brown eyes of Laurence Olivier. He's not even tall. But she knew that none of this made the least difference to her feelings.

In the car crash, Beth's legs had been broken in five places. They had been the legs of a dancer, strong and limber, shapely and thin. Now, her bones were bolted together with metal and coffined in plaster of Paris. What they would look like when the plaster of Paris was one day cut away,

Beth couldn't imagine. She thought they might resemble the legs of a home-made rag doll, or those floppy limbs the women seem to have in paintings by Chagall, and that forever more, she would have to be carried through life in the arms of people who were whole.

Sometimes, while Rosalita is trying to clean the flat, the power goes off. This is now 1974 and the Three Day Week is going on. 'All caused,' says Beth's father, 'by the bloody NUM. Trade unions hold this country to ransom.'

Though Rosalita shakes her head in frustration when the Hoover falls suddenly silent, she has sympathy for the coal miners, towards whom Beth is indifferent, just as she is indifferent to everything else. Rosalita and Beth smoke Peter Stuyvesant cigarettes in front of the gas fire – Beth on the sofa, Rosalita on the floor – and try to imagine what the life of a coal miner might be like.

'The thing I wouldn't mind,' says Beth, 'is the darkness.'

'Darkness may be OK,' says Rosalita, 'but there is also the heat and the dirt and the risk of the fire.'

'Fire?'

'Fire from methane gas. Fire coming out of the tunnel wall.'

Beth is silent, thinking about this fire coming out of the wall. She says to Rosalita: 'I was burned.'

'In the crash?'

'No. Not in the crash. The car never caught fire. I was burned by a man.'

Rosalita looks up at Beth. It is getting dark in the flat, but there is no electricity to turn on, so Rosalita lights a candle and sets it between them. By the light of this candle, whispering as if in church, Rosalita says: 'Your mum tell me this one day. Your American man. Your mum is crying. She says to me, "Beth was going to have a beautiful life . . ."'

'I did have a beautiful life. It ended early, that's all.'

Thaddeus lived in Kensington, when Kensington rents were cheap back then.

He'd furnished his studio flat entirely from Habitat, down to the last teaspoon. The carpet was rough cord. The bed was hard. On the hard bed, he took intimate photographs of Beth, which he threatened to sell to *Penthouse* magazine. He said Bob Guccione was a friend of his and Guccione would gag for these. He said, 'Why waste your beauty, Beth? It'll be gone soon enough.'

Beth replied: 'I'm not wasting it. I'm giving it to you.'

And so he took it. He kept taking, taking, taking.

One night, as he was falling asleep, Beth said: 'I want to be with you for ever. Buy me a ring and marry me. Divorce Tricia. You don't love Tricia any more.'

'I don't love anyone any more,' he said.

These words sent a shock wave through Beth's heart. It began to beat very fast and she found it difficult to breathe.

'Why don't you?' she managed to say.

He got up and went to the window, staring out at the London night. 'You will see,' he said, 'when you're my age, when your life hasn't gone as you imagined . . .'

'See what?'

'I mean that you'll understand.'

She didn't understand, but she was always careful, with Thaddeus, not to show ignorance or stupidity. He'd often said he thought American girls were smarter than

English girls 'in important ways'. She tried to visualise
the ring he would buy her: a diamond set high in a
platinum claw.

Now, she thinks again about what he'd said – that his life
hadn't *gone as he'd imagined*. And this leads her to wonder
about the lives of her parents.

She knows she doesn't think of them as *having lives*, as
such; they're just performing the duty of existence. They
have dull, well-paid jobs, working for a Life Assurance
company called Verity Life, with offices in Victoria Street,
not far from the flat.

They pay for things. They watch television. The mother
is half in love with Jack Lord, star of *Hawaii Five-O*, who
drives a police motor launch at breathless speed. She loves
it when a suspect is apprehended by Jack and he barks,
'Book him, Danno!' to his second-in-command. To the
NUM hot-head, Arthur Scargill, defending the strike that
has taken Britain into darkness, the mother often shouts,
'Book him, Danno!' And this always makes the father smile.
The father's smile is like a weak gleam of sunlight falling
upon the room.

The parents have survived all that Beth has done to them,
all that has been done to her. Beth tells Rosalita that they
will outlive their own daughter and this makes Rosalita
bustle with agitation and reach for the crutches and tell her
to get off the sofa and walk round the room. Beth tells her
it's too painful to walk, but Rosalita has cradled in her arms
matadors with lethal wounds; she's impatient with people
complaining about pain. She gives the crutches to Beth and
says, 'If you walk to the fireplace and back again, I will

make hot chocolate with rum.' So Beth does as she is told and the pain makes her sweat.

The taste of the rum reminds her of being in Paris with Thaddeus.

She let herself get sacked from her job in the Gift Wrap counter in Harrods before they left, because part of her had decided they would never come back. They would live like Sartre and de Beauvoir on the Left Bank. Thaddeus would make a name for himself photographing French actors and models and objets d'art. They would drink black coffee at the Flore. She, Beth, would begin her career as a writer.

Thaddeus told her he'd been loaned an apartment 'with a great view' by an American friend. The view turned out to be of the Cimetière de Montparnasse, but Thaddeus continued to call it 'great' and liked to walk there, taking pictures of gravestones and mausoleums and artificial flowers, early in the morning. He said nothing about how long they would be staying in the City of Light.

The apartment had almost no furniture, as though the American friend hadn't yet decided to move in. The floors were wooden and dusty. The hot-water boiler screamed when it was turned on. Thaddeus and Beth slept on a mattress under a crocheted blanket of many colours.

Thaddeus said he had no money to buy sheets, but he had money, it seemed, to take them to an expensive gay and lesbian nightclub called *Elle et Lui*, where the personnel greeted him like a long-lost star and where a tall, beautiful woman called Fred became their friend and lover.

Fred lived in a hot little garret not far from their own empty, echoing apartment. Here, they drank rum and coke and made what Fred called *l'amour exceptionnel*. She said love between three people was *radioactive*; once you'd experienced it, it stayed in your blood for ever. She called Thaddeus 'Thad'. She whispered to Beth: 'Thad brought you here for this. It's the only kind of love he values because it's a democratic love. *Tu comprends?*'

She wanted to ask, does that mean what we had in London wasn't precious to him? But she didn't want to hear the answer. And she liked the way being touched by Fred excited Thaddeus. He called them 'the two most beautiful women in the world'.

'How long did you stay in Paris?' asks Rosalita.

Beth can't remember. Sometimes, she thinks it was a whole year and the seasons turned in the cemetery and the snow remoulded the tombs. Sometimes, she guesses that it was about a month or six weeks – until Thaddeus ran out of money.

She says to Rosalita: 'It was a kind of dream.'

She can't remember a summer season to the dream; only a cold spring arriving and the great grey *allées* of horse chestnut trees clothing themselves with green. There used to be a sequence of photographs of her, leaning out over the churning river in that same springtime, with her hair cut short like Jean Seberg, but these have been put away somewhere and their hiding place forgotten.

She can remember being ill for a while with *la gripe*. Fred came round, bringing an old fur coat, and covered her with this. Then Thad and Fred stood at the window, silhouetted against the wan light of day, and Beth could see them thinking, What is to be done now? – as though all human activity had come to a sudden end. And she knew that they would soon arouse each other by deft, secretive means and ask her to watch whatever they decided to do next. But she closed her eyes and breathed in the scent of mothballs on the fur and knew that she was drifting far away on a tide of naphthalene. She tells Rosalita: 'I can remember that feeling of floating out of my life, while fellatio was taking place.' And Rosalita crosses herself and whispers: 'Such things you have seen. Try to forget them now.'

She wants to forget them, but she can't. She says to Rosalita, 'Tell me something else about Setúbal and the matadors.'

Rosalita replies that she should really get on and clean the bathroom, but then she goes to her bag and takes out a photograph of a young man in a matador costume. It's a faded picture, but the weight of gold sequins on the shoulder pads still cast a spangled luminescence onto the soft skin of the young man's face.

'My brother,' says Rosalita quietly. Then she lights a cigarette and sighs and inhales and explains: 'In Portugal we don't kill the bulls. We say there is no need for this blood. The *cavaleiros* on horseback stab them with *bandarilhas* and the *forcados* tease them until they are still.'

'And then what happens?'

'Then the matadors must come and risk their lives against them. Instead of killing with a sword, they stab with one last *bandarilha*. But a bull does not know it is not going to be killed. It will try to wound the matador with its horns. And this is what happened.'

'To your brother? He was wounded.'

'Yes. Antonio. You see how beautiful he was. More beautiful than me. He died of his wounds. And I see my parents thinking, It should have been Rosalita who was taken from us, not Antonio. So this is when I left Portugal and came to England.'

Beth is silent. She reaches out and holds Rosalita's hand.

Thaddeus and Beth came back from Paris. Perhaps it was summer by then, or autumn. Seasons are of no account in the way Beth remembers what happened next. It just happened in time, somewhere, and altered everything.

She became pregnant. She knew she would have to move out of her parents' flat; her father wouldn't tolerate her presence any more, once he knew her story.

While he and her mother were at work, she packed two suitcases with everything she owned, which came down to very little, just a few nice clothes, including a grey sleeveless dress from Mary Quant and four pairs of high-heeled boots. Pressed in among these things was the notebook she'd taken to Paris, which was meant to be full of notes towards a novel, but which contained no notes at all, only ink drawings of Thaddeus and Fred and of the dilapidated bedroom window, beyond which strange creatures floated in the Parisian sky: winged lambs, feathered serpents.

There were a few other things. A copy of *Le Petit Prince* by Saint-Exupéry and Tolstoy's *Anna Karenina*. There was a wooden tennis racket and two silver cups she'd won at school – one for being tennis champion, the other for 'good citizenship'. She would have left these behind but for the sentimental idea that she might one day show them to her child and the child might laugh and be proud.

She got into a taxi and arrived at Thaddeus's apartment towards the end of morning. She'd long ago asked to have her own key, but Thaddeus had said, 'Oh no. I never do this.' He had a way of making his utterances absolute and incontrovertible, like the authority of the CIA was behind them.

She got out of the taxi and rang the bell. Arriving at this door always made her heart lift, as though she was coming home to the only place that sheltered her. She set the suitcases down beside her, like two arthritic dogs who found movement difficult.

A stranger answered the door. Or rather somebody who was not quite a stranger, a French architect whom they had met once for lunch in Paris at the Dôme in Montparnasse. His name was Pierre.

Pierre said in his accented English: 'Thad said you would come. The flat belongs to me now.'

'What?' said Beth.

'Yes. I 'ave taken it on. Thad has gone back to California. I am sorry. May I offer you some tea?'

Beth says to Rosalita, 'I died there. Right there, between the two suitcases. That's when the real Beth died.'

Rosalita is sympathetic and yet sceptical. She says, 'I have seen many deaths, including Antonio's, and you have seen none. Death is not like that.'

'You don't understand, Rosalita,' says Beth. 'There was the girl who was loved by Thaddeus and when he left for California, that girl ceased to be.'

'But you are here. You are alive.'

'This "I" is not that "I". It's the person who took over

from her. It's the person who wrote the bestselling book called *The American Lover.*'

2.

The book was begun the day after the abortion.

The first scene was set in the abortionist's house (or 'clinic', as the surgeon called it) in Stanmore. It had a panelled hall and a view of a semi-rural recreation area.

Beth (or 'Jean', as she named her protagonist) was given an injection that she was told would make her forget everything that was going to happen. But the one thing she could remember was her inability to stop crying, and a nurse came and slapped her face, to make her stop, and afterwards there was a mark on her cheek where the slap had landed. The mark became a bruise and the bruise took a long time to fade.

Then, Beth's unborn baby was gone. She was a new self, who had no baby and no lover. Her bones felt as brittle and empty as cuttlefish shells and her head as heavy as a heap of wet earth and stones. It was difficult to make this wet earth function as a brain. It needed some skilled potter's hand to do it, but no such person was nearby.

Beth had a friend called Edwina, whom she'd known since schooldays, and thanks to Edwina – a girl with very clear skin, untouched by life – who drove her to Stanmore and collected her again, she was able to hide the abortion from the parents. They thought she and Edwina had gone on a boating picnic that day with some friends in Henley. She told them she'd got the bruise on her face by being accidentally hit by an oar.

On the way back from Stanmore, Edwina asked Beth what she was going to do now. Beth felt sleepy and sick and didn't want to have to answer questions. She stared out at the night folding in on the long and terrible day. She said: 'I'm going to become Jean.'

'Who's Jean?' asked Edwina.

'A kind of heroine, except there's nothing heroic about her. I'm going to write her story and then try to sell it to a publisher.'

'Do you know anybody in the publishing world?' asked Edwina.

'No,' said Beth.

The abortion 'scene' began the story, but wasn't its beginning. It wasn't even its ending, because Beth had no idea what the ending would be, or even if there would *be* a proper ending, or whether the narrative wouldn't just collapse in upon itself without resolution.

What mattered was writing it: the act of words.

Beth began it in her Paris notebook. She let the words travel over the faces and bodies of Thad and Fred and over the window frame and the winged lambs beyond. To write about the abortion, about Thaddeus's desertion, wasn't difficult; what was difficult was writing about the happiness that had come before. But she knew she had to do it somehow. You couldn't ask readers to care about the loss of something unless you showed them what that something had been.

The story began in London, then moved to Rome instead of Paris. Jean and her American lover, Bradley, were loaned an apartment just outside the Vatican City. Their transgressive love with a third person, Michaela, took place within two blocks of one of the holiest places on earth. The ringing of St Peter's bells tolled upon their ecstasy. In the apartment below them lived a lowly priest, whose life became a torment. Beth worked hard upon the sexual agonies he suffered. She wanted everything about the book to be shocking and new.

Beth wrote every day. She thought her parents would nag her to find a job to replace her old one at the Harrods Gift Wrap counter, but they didn't. It seemed that if you were a writer, you could get away with doing nothing else. Other people would go out to work and come back and you would still be there, unmoving in your chair, and they would make your supper and wash it up and you would collapse onto the sofa to watch *Juke Box Jury*. They would place forgiving goodnight kisses on your agitated head.

The father sometimes asked questions about the book, but all Beth would say was, 'You're probably going to hate it. It's about a girl going crazy. It's about things you don't talk about at Verity Life.'

But this didn't seem to make him anxious. It made him smile a tolerant smile, as though he thought Beth had underestimated him. And one Saturday morning, he took Beth to a second-hand shop off Tottenham Court Road and helped her choose a typewriter, and paid for it in cash. It was an old industrial Adler with a body made of iron and a pleasing Pica typeface and a delicate bell that tinkled when the carriage reached the end of a line. After Beth set the Adler on her desk, she felt less alone.

A letter came from California.

Thaddeus had that childish, loopy writing many Americans seemed to think was adequate to a grown-up life and his powers of self-expression were weak.

When Beth saw that the letter began *Dear Beth*, she laid it aside for a while, knowing it was going to smite her with its indifference.

Later, she took it up again and read: *I tried to tell you several times that I couldn't promise to stick around in London but I think you weren't listening. When you are my age, you will see. Money is important. I have to be a man of the world as well as a lover. Tricia has inherited her mother's house in Santa Monica. It's a nice beach-house, which I could never on my own afford. You would like it. And I can bathe in the ocean most days and forget about the cold of Europe. You will be OK. If you go to Paris, see Fred and tell her the Old American has gone back to the sun. Love, Thad.*

Beth folded the letter into her notebook and went and lay down on her bed. She thought about the crocheted blanket that had covered them in Paris: the rich smell of it, which was both beautiful and tainted. She thought about the lens of Thaddeus's camera pointed at her body and the shutter opening and closing, opening and closing, gathering her further and further into a prison from which there was no exit.

There was only the book.

It was written in eleven weeks. Everything that Beth had experienced with Thaddeus was relived through Jean and Bradley. The slow, exquisite way a single orgasm was achieved sometimes took a page to describe. Fred/Michaela became a male-to-female transsexual with handsome white breasts. Bradley became a painter. His own genitals, both aroused and dormant, featured repetitively in his art. Jean was a beauty, with a mouth men tried to kiss in the street and tumbled blonde hair. She was Desire Absolute. Bradley and Michaela screamed and wept over her and sometimes lost all control and beat the floor, while the poor priest lay in his narrow bed beneath them and jabbered his Hail Marys as a penance for his own sexual incontinence.

It was typed out on the Adler, with a blotchy blue carbon copy underneath. Beth stared at this carbon copy. She thought, Jean is the smart top-copy of a person now, and I'm the carbon, messed up and fragile and half invisible. But she also understood that no book quite like this had ever been written by a twenty-year-old girl. The pages crackled with radioactive heat. Readers could be contaminated in their thousands – or in their millions.

Beth now remembered that she knew nobody in the publishing world. She'd had no idea it was a 'world', exactly. She'd imagined there were just writers and printers and the people who paid them doing some slow gavotte together, which nobody else ever saw. All she could do was buy the *Writers' and Artists' Year Book* from Smith's, choose an agent from its pages who promised 'international representation' and send off the book.

Rosalita sometimes says how sad it is that most of what she and Beth talk about in the winter afternoons is concerned with endings of one kind or another. But she likes the next bit of Beth's story. What happened next seemed to promise new happiness: Beth was taken on by an agent.

'The agent was called Beatrice,' Beth tells her. 'After she'd read the book, she invited me round to her office in Canonbury Square. There was a bottle of champagne waiting. She said, "I can sell this novel in forty countries."'

'Forty countries!' gasps Rosalita. 'In Portugal, we probably couldn't name more than half of those.'

'Well,' says Beth, 'I probably couldn't either. I never knew Panama was a country, I thought it was a canal. And I've forgotten the list of all the places where the book was sold. All I know is that money started to come to me – so much money I thought I would drown in it.'

'And then you buy the red car?' asks Rosalita.

'No. Not that car. That was a gift, which came later. I bought another car, a Maserati. But a car didn't seem much to own, so I bought a house in Kensington and then I drove to France with Beatrice and I bought a second house in St-Tropez.'

'Were you happy?' asks Rosalita.

'No. I was famous. I made the cover of *Paris Match* and *Time* magazine. I perfected the way I looked. Not like I look now, Rosalita. It was my moment of being beautiful. I got letters from all over the world from people wanting to go to bed with me. I probably could have slept with Jean-Paul Belmondo and Marcello Mastroianni, if I'd tried.'

'Ah, Mastroianni. What a god!'

'Yes, he was, I suppose,' says Beth. 'But I never met him.'

As if to affirm the disappointment of not meeting Mastroianni, the lights in the flat go out suddenly and the afternoon dark presses in. Rosalita goes hunting for candles, but can't find any, so she lights the gas fire and by its scented blue light changes the subject to ask Beth what her mother and father thought about the book.

'Oh,' says Beth. 'Well, I remember the way they looked at me. Sorrow and pity. No pride. They told me I'd sold my soul.'

'And what did you say?'

'I said no, I gave my soul away for nothing. Thaddeus still has it. He keeps it somewhere, in a drawer, with old restaurant bills and crumbs of stale tobacco and discarded Polaroids that have faded to the palest eau-de-Nil green.'

Rosalita doesn't know what to say to this. Perhaps she doesn't understand it? Her comprehension of English is known to falter now and then. The gas fire flickers and pops. Rosalita gets up and puts on her coat and before leaving places a kiss on Beth's unwashed hair.

After *The American Lover*, there would need to be another book, a follow-up, so Beatrice said. Did Beth want the world to think she was a one-book wonder?

Beth replied that she didn't care what the world thought. She was rich and she was going to live. She was going to live so fast, there would be no moment in any part of the day or night to remember Thaddeus. She would crush him under the weight of her new existence.

She went to St-Tropez, to redesign the garden of her house. She drank most nights until she passed out and slept sometimes with a beach lifeguard called Jo-Jo, who liked to stare at pornographic magazines in the small hours.

The garden progressed. In a shaded area of Corsican pines, Beth built a temple, which she filled with an enormous daybed, hung with soft white linen. She spent a long time lying on this daybed alone, drinking, smoking, watching the sea breezes take the pines unaware.

News came from Beatrice that *The American Lover* had been sold in five more countries. A Swedish director wanted to turn it into a film. An Icelandic composer was writing

The 'American Lover' Symphony. Pirated copies had reached The Soviet Union and a young Russian writer called Vassily wrote to say he was writing a sequel to the novel, in which Bradley would be executed by a KGB agent in Volgograd. *This*, he wrote, *will be a very violent death, very terrible, very fitting to this bad man, and I, Vassily will smuggle this decadent book out of Russia to the USA and it will become as famous as your book and I will be rich and live in Las Vegas.*

In this cold, dark winter of 1974, Beth spends more and more time looking at her press file. There is not one picture of Thaddeus in it. He is the missing third dimension in a two-dimensional world. Beth's vacant face, caught in the white glare of photographers' flashbulbs, looks more and more exhausted with the search for something that is always out of sight.

She can remember this: how she looked for Thaddeus in Iceland, in shabby, raucous nightclubs, in hotel dining rooms, in the crowd of tourists congregating at a hot spring. Later, she searched for him in Canada, on the cold foreshore of Lake Ontario, in a brand-new shopping mall, in the publisher's smart offices, on the precipice of Niagara Falls.

And then in New York, where, finally she went and was fêted like a movie star, she kept finding him. He was at a corner table in Sardi's. He was standing alone in the lobby of the Waldorf Astoria. He was in Greenwich Village, walking a poodle. He was buying a silk scarf in Bloomingdale's. He was lying on a bench in Central Park. He was among the pack of photographers at her book launch.

She thinks that he came back to her so strongly there, in America, because of all the voices that sounded like his.

And one evening, as she was crossing Lexington Avenue, she heard yet another of these voices and she stumbled and fell down, slayed by her yearning for him. The man she was with, a handsome gallery owner of Persian origin, assumed she was drunk (she *was* often drunk) and hurled her into the first cab he could flag down and never saw her again.

She sat in the back of the cab like a dead person, unable to move. The sound of the cab's engine reminded her of the motor launch Thaddeus had once hired on the Seine. The day had been so fine that Thaddeus had taken off his shirt and she had put her arms round his thin torso and stroked his chest hair. And the ordinariness of him, the way he tried so hard and did so much with this fragile, unremarkable frame of his, had choked her with a feeling that was not quite admiration and not quite pity, but which bound her to him more strongly than she had ever been bound, as though her arms were bandages.

In the screeching New York night, Beth wondered whether, after all, after living so hard to forget him, she wouldn't fly to California and stand on the beach in front of his house at dawn, waiting until he got up and came to her.

She imagined that when he came to her, they would stand very still, holding on to one another and the sighing of the ocean would soothe them into believing that time had captured them in some strange, forgiving embrace.

When Beth came back from America, she got married. Her husband was an English aristocrat called Christopher. He was a semi-invalid with encroaching emphysema, but he was kind. He told her she needed someone to care for her, and she felt this to be true: she was being suffocated by the surfeits of her existence. Christopher said that, on his part, Beth would 'decorate' his life in ways he had often thought would be appropriate to it, but he reassured her that he preferred sex with men and would let her sleep alone. His house in Northamptonshire had a beautiful apple orchard, where he built her a wooden cabin. He suggested she might write her books in this cabin, and he furnished it with care.

She spent some time there, playing Bob Dylan songs, watching the apple blossom falling in the wind, but she knew she would never write another book. She had no life to put into it, only the half-life that she'd been leading, since writing *The American Lover*. And the years were beginning to pass. She was being forgotten. People knew that she was the author of what had come to be known as a 'great classic about transgressive first love' but times were changing, and they couldn't quite remember what all the fuss had been about.

Beth liked Christopher because he sheltered her. When her house in St-Tropez burned down, Christopher began on her behalf a long wrangle with a French insurance firm. But he couldn't win it. The house had been struck by lightning, so the insurers said, and nobody could be insured against 'acts of God'.

Christopher lamented all the money Beth had poured into this house, but she found that she didn't really care about it – either about the house or about the money. The person who got mad was Beatrice. She screamed at Beth that she was letting everything slip through her fingers. 'You will soon see,' she said, 'that the money will dry up, and then what are you going to do?'

She didn't know or care. With Christopher, she had suddenly entered upon a period of quiet. It was as if her heart had slowed. She liked to work in the greenhouses with Christopher's gardeners (one of whom, a handsome youth called Matty, was his most favoured lover), potting up seedlings, tending strawberries, nurturing herbs. Only now and again did some resistance to this quiet life rise up within her. Then she would get into the new red E-Type Jaguar that Christopher had given her and drive at terrible speed down the Northamptonshire lanes, screaming at the sky.

'Were you trying to die?' Rosalita asks her.

'Not trying,' Beth replies. 'Just laying a bet.'

'And you didn't think, maybe you hurt or kill someone else?'

'No. I didn't think.'

'This is not good,' says Rosalita. 'You were like the bull which wounded my brother. You had a small brain.'

One time, she just went on driving until she got to London. She called Christopher to say that she was safe and then stayed in her Kensington house, doing nothing but drink. Her wine cellar was emptying but there were still a few cases of champagne left, so she drank champagne.

She'd intended to drive back to Northamptonshire the following day, but she didn't. She was glad to find herself in a city. She found that if she went to bed drunk, Thaddeus would often visit her in her dreams. He would come into her room very quietly and say, 'Hey, kid.' He would remove the hat that he sometimes wore and sit on the bed and stroke her hand. This was as far as the dreams ever got, and Beth began to work out that this affectionate, silent figure was waiting for something. He would never say what. He sat very still. Beth could smell his aftershave and hear his quiet breathing.

Then, one morning, she believed she understood. Thaddeus was asking for her forgiveness.

She typed out a letter on the old Adler. She felt very calm, almost happy.

She told Thaddeus that she'd been crazy with grief and this grief and its craziness just wouldn't let her alone. She said: *I guess the book said it all, if you read the book. Jean loves Bradley way too much and when he leaves her, she's destroyed. I let Jean die, but I'm alive (in certain ways, anyway) and I have a husband with a very English sort of kind heart.*

But when it came to typing the word 'forgive' Beth faltered. Though in her dream, Thaddeus had been affectionate and quiet, Beth now thought that he would find the whole idea of 'forgiveness' sentimental. She could hear him say: 'You're way off, *ma pute*, way off! We had a few turns on the merry-go-round, or whatever the British call that little musical box thing that takes you round in a circle. And then one of us got off. That's all that happened. There was no crime.'

Beth tore the letter out of the Adler and threw it away. She opened another bottle of champagne, but found the taste of it bitter. She asked herself what was left to her by way of any consolation, if forgiveness was going to be refused.

'After that,' she tells Rosalita, 'I gave up on things. I drove back to Christopher. His emphysema was beginning to get very bad. I stayed with him through his last illness until he died. I ran out of money. Christopher left his whole estate to Matty, his gardener friend, so I had to leave Northamptonshire. I missed the apple orchard and my little cabin there. The Kensington house was valuable, but it was all mortgaged by then. And after that there was the crash.'

'Tell me . . .' says Rosalita.

It's a winter afternoon, but the lights are still on. Rosalita is coiling up the Hoover cable.

'Well, I'd hung on to that car. It seemed like the only thing that anyone had given to me and not taken away again. But I hadn't taken care of it. It was a heap of rust. People were right not to give me things, I guess. My brain wasn't big enough to take care of them.

'I wasn't trying to kill myself, or anything. I was driving to see my friend, Edwina, the one with the lovely skin, who'd helped me through the abortion.

'I was on some B-road in Suffolk. I braked on a bend and the brakes locked and that's all I can remember. The car went halfway up a tree. That long snout the E-Type has, that was concertina'd and the concertina of metal smashed up my legs.'

'Right,' says Rosalita, putting the Hoover away. 'Now you are going to do some walking, then we will have rum and hot chocolate.'

The Three Day Week has ended with the miners' defeat. Britain tries to get 'back to normal'.

'There is no normal,' says Beth to Rosalita. 'The only "normal" has been talking to you in the afternoons.'

But that is ending, just as everything else seems, always,

to end. Rosalita is leaving London to return to Setúbal, to nurse her dying mother.

'She doesn't deserve me,' Rosalita comments. 'She only loved Antonio, never me. But in my blood I feel I owe her this.'

'Don't go,' pleads Beth.

'Alas,' says Rosalita, 'it has to be like this. Some things just have to be.'

On Rosalita's last day both she and Beth feel unbearably sad. As Rosalita walks out of the flat for the last time, she says: 'All the secrets you told me I shall keep inside me, very safe.'

'And your brother, Antonio, the matador,' says Beth. 'I will keep his memory safe. I will think about the light on his face.'

Beth waits for the clunk of the elevator's arrival. Then she hears Rosalita get into the elevator and close the door and she remains very still, listening to the long sigh of the lift going down.

A year after Rosalita leaves, Beth is able to walk once more, with the aid of a stick.

One day she takes the bus to Harrods, suddenly interested to visit the place where she'd worked long ago, cutting wrapping paper with mathematical care, fashioning bows and rosettes out of ribbon, making the most insignificant of gifts look expensive and substantial. It had seemed to her a futile thing to be doing, but now it doesn't strike her as futile. She can see that a person's sanity might sometimes reside in the appreciation of small but aesthetically pleasing things.

Holding fast to her stick, she gets on to the familiar

escalators. The feeling of being moved around so effortlessly, whether up or down, has always given her pleasure. As a child, she used to beg to be brought here, to the escalators. She loved to watch the people moving in the opposite direction, like dolls on a factory conveyor belt.

She's watching them now, these human dolls: a multitude of faces, ascending to Soft Furnishings, descending to Perfumerie and Banking, all locked away in their own stories.

Then she see Thaddeus.

He's descending. She's going up. She stares at him as he passes, then cranes her head round to keep watching him as he goes on down. And she sees that he, too, has turned. Changed as she is, he has recognised her. His face is locked on hers.

She gets off the escalator at the first floor (Lingerie, Ladies' Shoes, Children's Clothes). Her heart cries out for her to run to the descending escalator, to follow Thaddeus, to rush into his arms. But her body is too slow. Her legs won't let her run. She stands on the first-floor landing, looking down.

She sees Thaddeus stop and look up. Then he joins the people surging towards the exit doors and follows them out.

Captive

Owen Gibb grew up on a hundred-acre farm in south Norfolk, with apple orchards and a pond for geese and ducks, and fields of lush grazing for a fine herd of Herefords. Wooden chicken houses, set out across a muddy rise, were shaded by ancient oaks. In the cool dairy, butter was churned.

When Owen's parents died, he had to sell the farm. What remained to him, when all the tax and all the debts had been paid, was a small bungalow, once occupied by his grandmother, and a piece of land, half an acre long, leading down to a quiet road. The new owners of the farm rooted out the apple trees and turned the dairy into a holiday cottage.

Owen knew that it was important, with a legacy as meagre as this, to make an immediate plan for it. Delay would get him nowhere. He was fifty and alone. His only companions were his black Labrador dogs, Murphy and Tyrant, and it was they who inspired his plan.

He designed a set of boarding kennels. He'd heard you could make a good living out of people's longing to be rid of their pets, in order to holiday in Spain or Florida – or just to be rid of them, full stop. For that was part of human nature: a longing to be rid of the things you'd thought you might be able to love, and found you couldn't.

All Owen had to do was build the kennels with care, make them solid and comfortable, so that he could designate them 'superior'. Long before the building work was complete, he'd chosen the wording for his sign: 'Gibb's Superior Dog-Homing Facility'.

He set the kennels in two rows, running down towards the road, with a green exercise space to the west of them. In each pen, he installed a shelter, made of wood planking and bedded with straw, which reminded him of the old henhouses. The open areas in front, where the dogs could walk round and round – as prisoners do in a yard – were fenced with sturdy chain-link. The flooring was concrete (the only practical solution) but underneath the concrete, Owen laid in a network of heating pipes that would run off the bungalow's oil-fired boiler. 'Your pet,' Owen heard himself announce to his future clients, 'will never suffer from cold in this facility.'

He decided, too, that his kennels would be available to all-comers.

After failing to halt his plans at the local council office, the owners of the farm had tried to get him to promise that he wouldn't take in dangerous dogs, but he'd refused. He knew that housing Staffordshire bull terriers, Dobermanns or Rottweilers would put up his Public Liability Insurance premiums. But Owen Gibb was a man who felt some affection for all animals. It didn't trouble him that some of them possessed a harsh kind of nature. He thought he could have grown accustomed to wolves, or even jackals – provided that there wasn't a whole pack of them: too many to love.

* * *

Word circulated quickly around the local area: 'Gibb's Superior' was the best and most economical place to board your dog. The food and shelter were good, with the heated floors providing reassurance in winter. The animals got proper exercise every day – in rotation according to their breed, size and sex. And, most important of all, if you stayed away longer than you'd agreed, Owen would always 'sort something out'.

Soon, Owen's booking ledger was so crammed that he began to consider nibbling some land from the exercise space, in order to extend the kennels beyond the thirty places provided at present. It troubled him to turn an animal away, as though this act of his would condemn it to unacceptable suffering, or even death. Because people were hard-hearted: this he knew. If a pet stood between them and their restless desires, they weren't ashamed to have it put down, or turn it out into some wasteland, far from home, to 'fend for itself' – whatever they thought that might mean.

Owen drew up plans for ten more units. He hired a plumber to find a way of running a spur off the underfloor heating grid and ordered a second oil tank.

Work was almost ready to begin when, on the first day of a new year – the kennels full to capacity with assorted boarders – a front of arctic weather drove south from Scandinavia and settled over East Anglia.

Snow fell and rested on the frozen earth and piled up on the wooden roofs of the shelters. Owen stood at his front window, watching.

The dogs came out of the shelters and smelled the frosty air and raised their heads into the whirl of snowflakes, trying to bite them as they fell. Though the blizzard was obliterating the path to the road, Owen was exhilarated to see that where it fell onto the concrete pens, it quickly melted. The heating pipes were doing their job.

Owen knew the dogs would still be cold in these conditions – especially the two Staffordshire bull terriers he'd boarded since Christmas, whose smooth skin appeared almost as vulnerable to Owen as the skin of a man's body – but they'd survive. He'd increase their food ration, shred newspapers to add to the straw, put coats on the Staffies and on the overweight little Dachshund bitch called Cherry.

It snowed all day, pausing at night to uncover stars and a deep frost, and began snowing again the following morning. It felt, to Owen, as he worked on the paper-shredding, as though the fat snow would never stop, but keep falling and falling into the heart of the year's beginning, blocking any artery that led to spring. But he and the dogs would endure it together, as the Herefords had endured it through his childhood, as the old apple trees had endured it, motionless in the wind, under their white burden.

Two days later, Owen was woken at seven, in darkness, by the sound of the dogs howling.

His bedroom was icy. He drew back the curtains and saw snow piled a foot high on the outer sill. He fumbled for the warmth of the radiator under the window, but it was cold.

Owen tugged on a fisherman's sweater, cords and worn slippers and padded to the kitchen, where he knew what he would find: the boiler was out.

The boiler was old, difficult to light. Owen kneeled down

and took the housing off the ignition box, smelling oil, surprised at how quickly the appliance, which had been burning strongly at midnight, had cooled.

His hands were shaking. The sound of the dogs' howling choked him. Murphy and Tyrant, their tails optimistically wagging, crowded round Owen's crouching figure, and he didn't push them away, but kept them near to him for comfort.

He tried to think clearly. He spoke aloud to the Labradors: 'Useless to try to relight the boiler if snow's piled up on the chimney stack, eh, lads?' he said. Murphy licked Owen's face. Tyrant's tail beat against the boiler-housing. 'Boiler'll cut out straight off if there's anything blocking the outflow. So, what's to do next, Murph? Tyrant? Get a ladder, I guess, and clear the stack. Right? Then come back in and try the old relighting procedure. Pray it works.'

Owen tugged on heavy socks and boots and his warmest farm coat and opened the back door and Murphy and Tyrant went out to do their business, jumping through the snow to reach a favourite spot.

But Owen stood motionless on the threshold of the door. Hoisting a ladder, clearing snow from the stack: these tasks didn't trouble him. What he dreaded was the sight that awaited him at the kennels. He sniffed the outside air and could guess at a temperature of minus 5 or 6 degrees. Animals without fur succumbed quickly to hypothermia in cold of this intensity. They were howling now, but unless he got the boiler going, they would soon enough fall silent.

He's out in it now. He keeps looking back at his footprints in the snow, leading away from the oil tank, finding it hard to believe what he's just seen.

He carries a bucket of high-protein food. He stands by the pens. Some of the dogs come out from the shelters and try to push through the deep snow towards him. He throws bits of food through the wire. There is no sign of the Staffies.

He longs for someone to help him. He thinks wistfully of the days when his parents were alive, companionable voices to console and advise. Because he's trapped. In the night – the coldest night of this winter – somebody came and committed a crime against him. He keeps vainly hoping that he's imagined it, but he knows he hasn't. Silently in the snow, these criminal people unlocked his oil tank and siphoned out every last drop of oil. Every drop.

He believes these criminals are his neighbours, the family who walk the loved land where he grew up, but who detest him and his dogs and want to bring all his endeavours to nothing. He can't be sure it was them, of course, and he believes that he will probably never get to the bottom of a thing so steeped in hate, but suspicion will linger. The very people who own what should have been his are intent upon his ruin.

He must defy them.

He's called all the oil-delivery merchants he can find in the phone book. Most – because it's the week of the New Year – aren't answering; those that answer say demand for heating oil is so heavy they won't be able to get to him for another nine or ten days.

Owen walks on slowly down the line of kennels. One of the pit-bulls lies dead with his jaw clamped round the chain-link gate, as though trying to bite his way out. The

Dachshund, Cherry, is a lifeless, snow-covered mound. Owen shivers as he stares at the fat little corpse. From the bungalow comes the sound of his landline ringing: dog-owners calling from ice-bound stations or airports, asking him to keep the dogs until the thaw comes.

There will be no thaw. This is how it feels to Owen. He and the animals are imprisoned for all time in a frozen world.

He tries to master his shivering and to think clearly. He knows that he has no choice. He will have to bring the dogs inside the bungalow. Twenty-eight dogs.

He'll try to separate them, as he does for their exercise routine, so that they don't constantly mate and fight with each other. But still, their animal natures, confined, confused, will create turmoil around him. Their barking and howling and rampaging will fill his every waking hour and make sleep impossible. Murphy and Tyrant will cower in corners, hide in cupboards, their familiar territory usurped by strangers. And everything that Owen possesses will be torn and stained and brought to desolation.

But there's no other way to save the dogs. No other way. He feels paralysed, as though he's suddenly become ill or old.

He turns away from the kennels and walks towards the house. The howling and whimpering of the dogs resume as they watch him leave.

But he needs a moment of respite. He remembers that he still has electricity. He's going to make himself a cup of tea, something to warm him, at least, before he faces all that he has to face in the coming day.

He fills the electric kettle. He stands waiting for the homely sound of its boiling to mask the noises outside, which now come to him as though from a faraway country, a barbaric place, where there is no order or kindness, the sort of place he'd hoped never to inhabit.

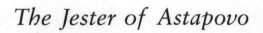

The Jester of Astapovo

A few weeks before the main events of this story disturbed forever the life of its protagonist, Ivan Andreyevich Ozolin, he had believed himself to be in love with an older woman, Tanya Trepova.

The year was 1910. Ivan Andreyevich Ozolin was the stationmaster of Astapovo, an insignificant little stop some 120 miles south-east of Moscow, on the Smolensk–Dankovo section of the Ural railroad line. He was forty-six and had been married to his wife, Anna Borisovna Ozolina, for twenty years. Tanya Trepova was a widow of fifty-three with excellent deportment, but whose pale face wore an expression of perpetual and affecting melancholy. It had been this melancholy of hers that Ivan Ozolin had longed to alleviate. On one of his days off (which were few) he arranged to go on a bicycling trip to the forest with Tanya Trepova, pretending to Anna Borisovna that he was going mushroom-picking.

Ivan Ozolin and Tanya Trepova sat down on the mossy earth, where there were indeed a few pale mushrooms nestling among the tree roots. Ivan wanted to lean over and kiss Tanya, but he felt that to touch with his lips features still set in such a sorrowful arrangement was tantamount to an insult. So what he decided to do was to lean back on his elbows and cross one leg over the other and point out to his would-be mistress the ridiculous appearance of his white cycling socks.

'Look at these!' he said with a guffaw. 'And look at the little bit of my leg showing between the top of the sock and the bottom of my trousers. How can we take anything seriously – anything in the world – when we catch sight of things like this? Life's a joke, don't you think so, Tanya? Every single thing in life is a joke – except love.'

A smile did now appear on Tanya Trepova's face. It remained there long enough for Ivan to get up the courage to say: 'I'd like to make you happy. I'm serious about that. My wife thinks I'm a fool who jokes about everything, but to jest is better than to despair, don't you think?'

The September sun, coming and going between clouds, flickering through the trees, now suddenly laid on Tanya Trepova's pale skin a steady and warming light. But as soon as this light arrived there, her smile vanished and she said: 'Sometimes despair is unavoidable.'

Then she got to her feet and brushed down her skirt and said: 'I shouldn't have come to the forest with you, Ivan Andreyevich. I can't think what I was doing. I only agreed because I was flattered by the kind attention you've shown me since my husband died, and because I enjoy cycling. But please let's go back now.'

Ivan was a courteous man. Despite his strong feelings for Tanya Trepova, he wasn't the type to take advantage of any woman – even here, in the eternal silence of the woods.

So he got up obediently, tugging down his trouser leg over his rucked white sock, and he and Tanya Trepova walked to where their bicycles were parked, then rode back to Astapovo, side by side, talking only of inconsequential things.

When Ivan Ozolin got home to his red-painted stationmaster's cottage, Anna Borisovna asked: 'Where are the mushrooms, then?'

'Oh,' said Ivan, swearing silently at his forgetfulness. 'I couldn't find any. I searched and searched. I didn't find a single one.'

Anna Borisovna stared accusingly at her husband. After twenty years of childless living with him, he wearied her. Was this just another of his stupid jokes?

'It's September and the sun's out after the long rains we've endured and there are no mushrooms in the forest?'

'No. Or rather, I'm absolutely certain there *had been* mushrooms, but other people gathered them before I got there. You know there is now a local group calling itself The Mushroom League?'

'What?' said Anna Borisovna.

'Yes, yes. The League believes that eating mushrooms makes a man – how can I put it so as not to shock you? – more *virile*.'

Anna Borisovna sniffed and turned away. 'I would have thought Russian men were quite "virile" enough,' she said.

In October, winter began to close in on Astapovo, as it did at this time each year.

Ivan Ozolin supervised the cleaning and oiling of the

ancient snowplough kept in a dilapidated shed on a siding on the Smolensk side of the tracks. He chopped wood for the pot-bellied stoves that heated his own cottage, the two waiting rooms (ladies' and gentlemen's) and the station buffet on the Dankovo side. His mind, as he went about these familiar tasks, was preoccupied by his failed attempt to have a love affair with Tanya Trepova. Most men that he knew had love affairs and even boasted about them. But he, Ivan Ozolin, hadn't been able to manage even this! It was laughable!

Ivan thought, My life's at a standstill. Trains come and go, come and go past my door day and night, but I live without moving at a way-station where nothing stops for long or endures – except the monotony of all that's already here.

The idea that this state of affairs would just go on and on and nothing important would happen to him ever again began to terrify him. One evening, he deliberately got drunk with his old friend Dmitri Panin, who worked in the one-man Telegraph office at Astapovo station and began to pour out his heart to him.

'Dmitri,' he said, 'how on earth are we meant to escape from the meaninglessness of life? Tell me your method.'

'My method?' said Dmitri. 'What method? I'm just a Telegraph operator. I send out other people's messages and get messages back.'

'At least you're in touch with the wider world.'

'I may be in touch with the wider world, but I don't have any message of my own. Life has not . . . Life has not . . . equipped me with one.'

'Equipped you? Have another drink, my friend. I think

we're both talking drivel, but it seems to me there are three ways and only three of escaping it.'

'Escaping what?'

'Meaninglessness. The first is ignorance. I mean the ignorance of youth, when you haven't seen it yet.'

'Seen what?'

'Death waiting for you. Inevitably waiting. You know?'

Dmitri said that he knew that perfectly well and that meanwhile he'd order them another bottle of vodka and a piece of special Smolenski sausage to keep them from falling under the table. Then he asked Ivan Ozolin to hurry through the other 'two ways of escape' because he had a feeling that they were going to bore him or depress him, or both.

Ivan gulped more vodka.

'Well,' he said, 'the second is through religion, when you believe, as my wife does, that this life is a temporary hell, entirely without meaning, but that a condition of marvellousness attends you when you die.'

'A condition of marvellousness? What's that? D'you mean the kind of feeling one gets after five or six vodkas?'

'I don't know. Perhaps it's even better than that? If it were no better, why would you wait out a whole life for it? You might as well just keep drinking the vodka.'

Dmitri nodded and sighed. Ivan went on to express his profoundly held opinion that, in his view, human beings were merely 'randomly united lumps of matter', but that some gullible people, such as his wife, Anna Borisovna, refuted this and believed that human life had been created by God. 'She thinks,' said Ivan Ozolin, 'that, contrary to all evidence, God is benign . . . but to me that is illogical. I ask myself why a benign being would have decided to create the Russian winter.'

'Well,' said Dmitri, 'I'm pretty sure we already know that twaddle and counter-twaddle. What's the third way of escape?'

Ivan Ozolin scratched his head, balding on the crown, growing sensitive to winter cold. 'I can't remember what it was,' he said. 'I'm sure I knew it yesterday, but now I've forgotten it again.'

'Oh well,' said Dimitri. 'Let's talk about Tanya Trepova.'

Ivan didn't really want to talk about Tanya Trepova, even to Dmitri. He began cutting up the hunk of sausage into manageable pieces.

'That was a farce,' he said.

'A farce?'

'Yes. I didn't even kiss her.' And then he let out one of his famous guffaws.

Dmitri began to cram his face with sausage. 'I can't see what's so funny about that,' he said with his mouth full. 'If it had been me, I would have kissed her, at least.'

On the afternoon of 31ˢᵗ October, a cold day marked by an icy wind and flurries of snow, a southbound train from Tula arrived at Astapovo station.

Ivan Ozolin, wearing his stationmaster's uniform, was standing alone on the platform, holding his flags, waiting to see if anybody was going to disembark before waving his green flag to send the train onwards towards Dankovo. He saw the door of one of the Second Class carriages open and a young woman step down and come towards him. She was plump, with a wide, homely face and wearing a peasant scarf over her brown hair.

'Stationmaster!' she called. 'We need your help. Please. You must help us . . .'

Ivan Ozolin hurried towards her. Her voice, he noticed at once, was not the voice of a peasant.

'What can I do?' said Ivan.

'My father is on the train. We were trying to get to Dankovo, but he's been taken ill, very ill. A doctor is with us. The doctor says we must get off here and find a bed for my father. Or he could die. Please can you help us?'

Ivan Ozolin now saw that the young woman was trembling violently, whether with cold or agitation, or both, and he knew that he would have to do whatever he could to help her and her sick father; it was his duty as a station-master and as a human being. He followed her to the open door of the Second Class carriage. Steam billowed all around them in the freezing air. He climbed aboard the train and was led along the crowded carriage to one of the hard leather benches where an elderly man was lying, covered by a thin blanket. By his side, kneeled a man wearing a black coat, who was presumably the doctor. From all the other benches passengers were staring and whispering.

'Dushan,' the young woman said to the doctor. 'Here's the stationmaster. Between the two of you, you can carry Papa to the waiting room and then this good man is going to find us a bed for him, aren't you, sir?'

'A bed? Yes, of course . . .'

'There's an inn here, I suppose? What's this place called?'

'Astapovo.'

'Astapovo. I've never heard of it, have you, Dushan? But everywhere has some little inn or hotel. Hasn't it?'

Her agitation was growing all the time. He saw that she could hardly bear to look down at her father, so greatly did the sight of him lying there in his blanket upset her. Very calmly, Ivan Ozolin said: 'There is no inn in Astapovo. But the fact that there is no inn here doesn't mean that there are no beds. We can arrange a bed for your father in my cottage . . . just over there on the Smolensk side of the track . . . that red house you can glimpse . . .'

'Dushan,' said the young woman, now breaking down into tears, 'he says there's no inn. What are we going to do?'

The doctor stood up. He put a comforting arm round the young woman's shoulders and held out his other hand to Ivan Ozolin. 'I am Dr Dushan Makovitsky,' he said. 'Please tell me your name, Stationmaster.'

Ivan Ozolin took Makovitsky's hand and shook it. He bowed. 'I am Ivan Andreyevich Ozolin, Doctor,' he said.

'Very well,' said Makovitsky. 'Now let me explain the situation. My patient here is Count Tolstoy: Leo Nikolayevich Tolstoy, the world-famous writer. He was attempting to get as far as Novocherkassk, to stay with his sister, but he has been taken ill. I'm desperately afraid he may have pneumonia. Will you help us to save his life?'

Leo Tolstoy . . .

Ivan Ozolin felt his mouth drop foolishly open. He looked down at the old man, who was clutching in his frail hands a small embroidered cushion, much as a child clutches to itself a beloved toy. For a moment, he found himself unable to speak, but could only repeat to himself, *Leo*

Tolstoy has come to Astapovo . . . Then he managed to pull himself together sufficiently to say: 'I'll do everything I can, Doctor. Everything in my power. Luckily the waiting rooms are on this side of the track, so we haven't got far to carry him.'

Dushan Makovitsky bent down and gently lifted Tolstoy's shoulders. The old man's eyes opened suddenly and he began murmuring the words: 'Escape . . . I have to escape . . .'

His daughter stroked his head. 'We're moving you, Papa,' she said. 'We're going to find you a warm bed.'

Ivan Ozolin took hold of the writer's legs, noting that underneath the blanket he was wearing peasant clothes: a tunic tied at the waist, moleskin trousers tucked into worn boots. When the two men lifted him up, Ivan was surprised at how light his body felt. He was a tall man, but with very little flesh on his bones. They carried him gently from the train and out into the snow. Feeling the snowflakes touch his face, Leo Tolstoy said: 'Ah, it comes round me now. The cold of the earth . . .'

But the distance to the waiting room wasn't great and soon enough Dr Makovitsky and Ivan Ozolin had lain the elderly writer down on a wooden bench near the wood-burning stove. Instructing the doctor to go back to the train for their bags, Tolstoy's daughter did her best to make her father comfortable on the bench, tucking the blanket round him, taking the little pillow from his hands and placing it gently under his head, smoothing his springy white beard.

Ivan hovered there a moment. His heart was beating wildly. He explained that he had an immediate duty to supervise the train's onward departure towards Dankovo, but as soon as this was done, he would run to his cottage and prepare a bed for Count Tolstoy. 'My wife will help me,' he said. 'It will be an honour.'

The cottage had only four rooms: a living room, a kitchen, a bedroom and a small office where Ivan Ozolin kept his railway timetables and his stationmaster's log. Outside the cottage was a vegetable garden and a privy.

When Ivan Ozolin came rushing in to tell Anna Borisovna that Leo Tolstoy, gravely ill, had arrived at Astapovo and needed a bed in their house, she was boiling laundry on the kitchen range. She turned and stared at her husband. 'Is this another of your jokes?' she asked.

'No,' said Ivan. 'On the soul of my mother, this is not one of my jokes. We must give up our bed, Anna. To the poor and needy of this land, Tolstoy is a saint. In the name of all those who suffer today in Russia, we must make our own small sacrifice!'

Anna Borisovna, though tempted to mock the sudden floweriness of Ivan's language (brought on, no doubt, by the unexpected arrival of a famous writer), refrained from doing so, and together she and Ivan went to their room and began dismantling their iron bed. It was heavy and old and the bolts rusty, and this work took them the best part of half an hour.

They carried the bed into their sitting room and reassembled it, dragged their mattress on to it and then laid on clean sheets and pillow cases and woollen blankets from their blanket chest. While Ivan banked up the stove, Anna set a night table by the bed and a chamber pot underneath it. On the table she placed a jug of water and a bowl and some linen towels. She said to Ivan: 'I wish I had some violets to put in a little vase for him.'

'Never mind that,' said Ivan Ozolin. 'Now you must come with me and we'll carry him across the tracks. Only twenty-nine minutes before the Dankovo train.'

When they got back to the waiting room, Tolstoy was sleeping. His daughter, too, had gone to sleep kneeling on the hard floor, with her head lying on the bench, near her father's muddy boots. Dushan Makovitsky kept a lonely vigil at their side and seemed relieved to see Ivan return with Anna Borisovna.

'Good people,' he said in a whisper. 'You can't know how grateful I am. You must understand that this is a terrible business. Terrible beyond imagining. Count Tolstoy left his home in secret two nights ago. He left because his wife had made his life unbearable. He left to try to find peace, far away from the Countess. But he lives in mortal fear of being followed, of his whereabouts being discovered by her, so secrecy is vital. You understand? Nobody but you must know that he's here.'

Ivan nodded. He stared fiercely at Anna until she nodded, too. Nevertheless, Ivan felt himself go cold with sudden terror. He looked down at the old man. Surely he – who must by now be in his eighties – would have preferred to live out his last years peacefully on his estates, and yet he'd run away in the middle of an October night! What marital persecutions had pushed him to make this extraordinary decision? If this was what marriage had done to someone as wise as Leo Tolstoy – to the author of *War and Peace* and *Anna Karenina* – what might it eventually do to him, the humble stationmaster of Astapovo? He glanced up at the waiting-room clock. Seventeen minutes remained before the arrival of the Dankovo train.

'We should hurry,' he said. 'Everything is prepared.'

Now, as darkness came down, the great writer was undressed tenderly by his daughter, who put a clean nightshirt on him and combed his hair and beard and helped him to lie down in the iron bed. He was very tired and weak, but he knew that he was in a strange place. Anna and Ivan, working next door in the small kitchen, heard him say to his daughter: 'Sasha, I know I'm ill. I suppose I could be dying. So I want you to send a telegram to Vladimir Chertkov and ask him to come here. Send it tonight.'

'Yes, all right, Papa. But if Mama finds out that you sent for Chertkov and not for her—'

'I can't help it. To see her face would kill me! I can't set eyes on her ever again. I can't. But I must see Chertkov. There's all the wretched business of my will and my copyrights to settle . . .'

'All of that was sorted out, Father. Vladimir and I know your wishes; that all the copyrights are willed to me and I authorise that your works are to be made available to the Russian people, free of any charge . . .'

'Yes. But Vladimir is to be the Executor. Only him. Not you, not Tanya, not any of my good-for-nothing sons. Vladimir Chertkov alone will decide what's to be published and by whom and when . . . both the novels and all the other work . . . and the diaries your mother tried to steal . . .'

'He knows. You've been through it a hundred times.'

'No, we haven't been through it a hundred times. And

I want him here, Sasha! Don't argue with me! Arguments give me a pain in my heart. Where's Dushan?'

'Dushan's sleeping, Papa. In the waiting room. He hasn't slept for thirty hours . . .'

Then, as Ivan and Anna tugged out their few pieces of good china and Anna began to wash these, they heard the sound of wailing and it reminded Ivan of the noise that a wolf can make when it finds its leg caught in a trap. He stared helplessly at his wife. He tried to summon up a joke to crack, as a weapon against the noise coming from next door, and said: 'I suppose that's the din that all writers make. Their heads are so full of crazy thoughts.'

'Don't be stupid,' said Anna.

'Try to stop crying, Papa,' they heard Sasha say. 'It really does no good. I'm going to send the telegram to Vladimir now. Then I'll be back and we'll see whether you can eat something.'

The front door of their cottage opened and closed. The Ozolins knew they were alone in their house with Leo Tolstoy. Anna Borisovna thought of the long night ahead, with no bed to sleep on. But it was almost time for the 5.18 train from Tula, so Ivan tugged on his overcoat and gloves and took down his red and green flags and went out by the back door. Anna dried the china slowly. After a few minutes, she heard the weeping diminish, breath by breath, as though the weeper had become exhausted with it.

The following morning under a blank grey sky, Vladimir Chertkov arrived on the 9.12 train from Moscow. He was a good-looking man in his fifties with a well-trimmed brown beard. When Sasha greeted the traveller on the Dankovo platform, Ivan Ozolin heard him say: 'Where in heaven's name have I come to? There's nothing here.'

They had to wait for the Dankovo-bound train to leave before they could cross the tracks to the cottage. Ivan Ozolin had hoped to accompany them. He felt that, at last, his own life was bound up with something important and he didn't want to miss a moment of it. But when the steam from the departed train cleared, he saw that Sasha and Chertkov were already walking away over the rails, so he stood there and let them go, while he slowly folded up his green flag.

Then he caught sight of Dmitri Panin running in an agitated way along the Smolensk platform, waving a telegram in his hand. As Chertkov and Sasha passed him, Dmitri stopped and hesitated, then hurried on to the end of the platform and began beckoning frantically to Ivan Ozolin. In the sunless morning, Dmitri's face appeared as red as a beet.

'Look at this!' he gasped, when Ivan reached him. 'It's from Countess Tolstoy – to her husband! What in the world is going on?'

Ivan seized the telegram and read: *We know where you are. Arriving with Andrei, Ilya, Tanya and Mikhail tonight. Special Pullman train from Tula. Signed: Your loyal wife, Countess Sonya Andreyevna Tolstoya.*

'Ivan,' said Dmitri, 'tell me what the hell is happening . . .'

'All right, all right,' said Ivan. 'It's too late for secrecy now, if she knows where he is. But how did she find out? You didn't send a message, did you?'

'Me? Message to who?'

'Somebody must have sent a message. How could it have got out except via your Telegraph office?'

Dmitri wiped a hand across his sweating brow. 'Ivan,' he said, 'I haven't the faintest idea what you're talking about!'

'Oh, the poor man . . .' murmured Ivan. 'He said he'll die, if he catches sight of her!'

'What? Who will die?'

'Count Tolstoy. He's here, Dmitri.'

'Here? What d'you mean? Here, where?'

'In my bed. No, keep your hair on, it isn't one of my jests. I swear. Leo Tolstoy is here, in the bed of the station-master of Astapovo! Now, give me back the telegram. I'd better give somebody this news.'

When Ivan Ozolin went into the dark living room of the cottage, he saw by the soft candlelight a scene that reminded him of a religious picture. Leo Tolstoy was lying, propped up on the white pillows, with his white hair and beard fanning out from his face like a frosty halo. Leaning towards him, one on either side of him, were his daughter Sasha and his friend and faithful secretary, Vladimir Chertkov. Their heads rested tenderly against Tolstoy's shoulders. They stroked his hands, clasping the embroidered cushion. Sasha's dark hair was loose and spread over her blue blouse. The Madonna, thought Ivan. The Madonna (just a little plump) with St John, at the foot of the cross . . .

Though he hesitated to interrupt this scene of adoration – particularly with news he imagined would be so unwelcome – he knew that he had to warn someone about the arrival of the Countess. Fortunately, when Tolstoy saw him come in, he said: 'Oh, my friends, here is the good man, Ivan Andreyevich Ozolin, who has been so very kind to us. Come here, Stationmaster, and let me introduce you to my most beloved friend, Vladimir Chertkov.'

Chertkov stood up and Ivan Ozolin shook his hand. 'Thank you for all you've done,' Chertkov said. 'We fervently hope the Count will soon be well enough to travel onwards, but in the meantime . . .'

'Sir,' said Ivan, 'anything we've been able to do for Count Tolstoy . . . it's done from deep in our hearts. But I wonder whether I might have a word with you in private?'

Chertkov followed Ivan out into the cold, closing the door behind them, and they walked a little way from the window of the living room and stood by the fence that bordered the vegetable garden. Looking distractedly down at the carrots, onions and leeks in their futile rows, Ivan passed the telegram to Chertkov and heard his gasp of horror as he took in the news.

'Disaster!' said Chertkov. 'God in heaven, how could she have known?'

Ivan shook his head. 'I asked my Telegraph man, Dmitri Panin, if anything had gone from here and he swore—'

'No, no. I'm not suggesting you were in any way . . . Oh, but you can't know, Stationmaster, what a fiend that woman is! Mad with jealousy. Prying among the Count's papers and diaries day and night. Threatening suicide. Never giving him any peace . . . And now . . . This is going to kill him!'

At this moment Dr Dushan Makovitsky came over the tracks, from where he'd been taking breakfast in the small buffet which served dry little meals to the few travellers who boarded or left trains at Astapovo. When news of the arrival of the Countess was conveyed to Makovitsky, he remained calm. 'The solution is simple,' he said. 'We'll say nothing to Leo Nikolayevich. We'll just close the doors to the cottage – front and back – we'll close them and lock them and neither Countess Tolstoy nor any of her other children will be allowed to enter.'

'So we're going to be locked in?' said Anna Borisovna to Ivan that afternoon, as she toiled over her bread baking. 'This is getting stupid. We've given up our bed. Now, we're going to be prisoners, are we?'

Ivan looked at his wife. He noticed, as if for the first time, how grey and straggly her hair appeared. He wondered how it would look – and how he would cope with the way it looked – when she was old.

'Well, or you could get on a train and leave, Anna Borisovna,' he said. 'Perhaps Countess Tolstoy would let you take her private Pullman back to Tula?'

'That's not funny,' said Anna Borisovna. 'Nothing you say is funny any more.'

Ivan Ozolin smiled. 'Jokes need the right audiences,' he said. 'A joke is a contract with another human being.'

As Anna turned away from him, they both heard a new sound coming from next door, the sound of hiccups. They heard Tolstoy cry out for Chertkov and then for Makovitsky. They waited. The hiccups continued, very loud. Tolstoy now called out for Sasha, but no consoling voice was heard.

'They must be asleep,' said Ivan. 'Somewhere.'

'Well, and that's another thing,' hissed Anna. 'Just where in the world are all these new arrivals going to be housed? Are you expecting them to sleep under the Telegraph counter with Dmitri?'

'Yes,' said Ivan. 'I was thinking that would be convenient. That way they're on hand to send telegrams to the Press bureaus of the world.'

Anna Borisovna seized a dishcloth covering a bowl of yeast and snapped it in her husband's face, stinging his cheek. He put his hand to his face. He wanted to retaliate by pulling her dishevelled hair, pulling it until it hurt, but he stopped himself. He didn't want to become the kind of pig who beat his wife. He didn't want to become a pig at all. He was enjoying his role as the 'saviour' of Leo Tolstoy's life.

He was on the platform, with Sasha and Dr Makovitsky, when the gleaming Pullman arrived. Once Countess Tolstoy and her four eldest children had descended and had been led into the ladies' waiting room by Sasha, Ivan Ozolin, as instructed by Chertkov, told the driver of the Pullman to shunt the two carriages into the siding running parallel with the Dankovo track and leave them there.

He then went into the waiting room. He found the Countess weeping in Sasha's arms and the other grown-up children standing around with faces set in expressions of grumpy disdain. When the Countess raised her head to acknowledge his presence, he saw a fleshy face, every part of which appeared swollen, whether by grief or malady or an excess of cream cakes, he was unable to say.

'So it's you!' she said, flinging out an accusing gloved finger. 'It's you who are hiding him!'

'Hush, Mama,' said Sasha.

'You should know,' said the Countess to Ivan, 'that

wherever my husband goes, I go too. If he's in your bed, then that is where I am going to sleep!'

She broke again into a storm of weeping, which calmed only a little when Anna Borisovna came into the waiting room with a tray of hot tea and some slices of cinnamon cake, which everybody fell upon. It was now near to midnight. Dr Makovitsky drew Ivan aside.

'Are the Pullman cars staying here?' he asked.

'Yes,' Ivan was able to say. 'But I think the train company is going to levy a charge.'

'Friend,' said Makovitsky, 'in any crisis, there are always roubles to pay.'

All night, Leo Tolstoy coughed and hiccupped. At around three o'clock, Sasha woke Anna and Ivan and asked if some infusion could be made to relieve these sufferings.

They staggered, exhausted, to the kitchen and put water on to boil and took down jars of dried sage and comfrey and cloves.

'How much longer is this going to go on?' asked Anna. 'Sleeping on the floor makes my bones ache.'

'Ah,' said Ivan, 'but think how good it is for the posture!'

'That's another thing about your jokes that I can't stand,' said Anna Borisovna. 'They're always founded upon lies.'

Ivan smiled. He began asking himself whether this were true or not, but was too tired to be able to decide.

He carried the infusion to the living room, which was very dark, the candles having burned low. He laid the jug down on the cluttered night table. Vladimir Chertkov, in his nightshirt, was lying across the end of Tolstoy's bed. Dr Makovitsky was taking the old man's pulse. The great writer was curled up in the bed, seeming small like a child. Ivan glimpsed blood on his pillow.

'Escape . . .' he was heard to murmur once again. 'I must escape . . .'

Ivan Ozolin rose early to see in the 7.12 from Moscow via Tula to Dankovo.

In the normal way, perhaps two or three passengers got off, or the train crew changed here. But this morning, every single door all the way down the train opened and fifty or sixty people disembarked.

Ivan Ozolin stared at this crowd. Perhaps he'd known they'd come, eventually, that the life of Leo Tolstoy was as precious to the people of his country as the earth itself and that, if he was going to die, they would want some part in his dying. He could see straight away that many of the arrivals were newsmen with cameras and as they milled around on the platform – looking in vain for some grand Station Hotel or the presence of a commodious Telegraph office – he felt himself surrender to them, to the grand circus that was accumulating at Astapovo. He wanted to embrace them, to say, 'You were right to come! Life is uneventful, my friends! Don't I know it! But here's an event: the dying Tolstoy trying to keep his wife at bay! So come and get your bit of it and remember for ever whatever you think it teaches you.'

Now, the two waiting rooms, the station buffet, the Pullman cars and the freezing anteroom that adjoined Dmitri Panin's Telegraph office were crammed with reporters, all trying to buy food, send messages, write copy and above all to catch a glimpse of the writer, as he lay gasping and hiccupping in Ivan Ozolin's iron bed. Dmitri, made faint by cigarette smoke, noise and rudeness, struggled on at his post.

To ease his friend's lot, Ivan Ozolin laboriously wrote out a notice, which he pinned above Dmitri's small counter. It read: *Your Telegraph Operator has not read the works of L. N. Tolstoy, so please do not waste time by asking him any questions about them. Signed: I. A. Ozolin, Stationmaster.*

More journalists arrived by every train. And then from across the surrounding countryside, as the news spread, peasant farmers, blacksmiths, carpenters, laundresses, wheelwrights, slaughterers, seamstresses, milkmaids and bricklayers began to converge on Astapovo. These last slept out in the open, or in hay barns, made fires in the fields, seeming not to mind cold or hunger. A cohort of sausage-makers did a brisk trade. Potatoes were dug up by hand and roasted in the fires. Snatches of the patriotic song 'Eternal Memory' floated out across the dark earth. Normal existence was put to one side. Astapovo was where life had paused.

Ivan felt immoderately proud of this, as though he himself had been responsible for organising it. He hoped – foolishly, he knew – that Tanya Trepova might arrive here and, when she saw him at the centre of this altered world, discover that she had feelings for him far stronger than those she had expressed on their cycling outing.

Chertkov ordered that the windows of Ivan's cottage be boarded up from inside. Though, with every hour, Leo Tolstoy was growing weaker, his determination not to let his wife come near him never faltered. While reporters came and went from the Pullman cars, where the Countess was giving interviews, Sasha, Makovitsky and Chertkov kept round-the-clock guard at the door of the cottage. Anna Borisovna worked tirelessly in the kitchen, making soups and vegetable stews bulked out with barley, to feed the exhausted household.

Then, on the morning of 4th November, after Ivan Ozolin had dispatched the early train to Smolensk, he turned to go back to his cottage and saw the unmistakable figure of Countess Tolstoy making her way towards his door. Behind her came several press reporters, some of them carrying cameras. Ivan Ozolin followed.

Countess Tolstoy beat on the front door of the cottage with her fists. 'Sasha!' she cried. 'Let me in!'

Ivan couldn't hear whether any reply came from inside. He watched the Countess lay her head against the door. 'Open up!' she wailed. 'Have pity, Sasha! Let people at least believe I've been with him!'

Still the door didn't move. The photographers jostled to get pictures of Countess Tolstoy begging to see her dying husband and being refused. But then Ivan saw his wife, who had been pegging out washing in the vegetable garden, approach the distraught woman and take her arm and lead her gently round towards the back of the house.

Anna Borisovna had a back-door key. The posse of journalists followed the two women, clumping along the little path beside the privy. And it was at this moment that Ivan Ozolin discovered the role that destiny had kept up its sleeve: he was going to be Leo Tolstoy's bodyguard!

He ran to the front door. His hands were shaking as he

let himself in. He called out to Chertkov and Makovitsky: 'She's coming in the back door! My wife has a key!'

The two men rushed out into the hallway, but Ivan was the first at the door. He caught a momentary glimpse of his wife, with the Countess at her shoulder. He just had time to execute a formal bow before he slammed his weight against the door to close it in their faces. Chertkov and Makovitsky now joined him to hold the door shut. Ivan reached up and slid an iron bolt into its housing. He heard his wife crying out: 'This isn't fair! You men! We slave for you and you keep us out of your hearts!' He could hear the growl of the pressmen, pushing and questioning outside in the cold day.

'Well done, Ozolin,' said Chertkov.

'Yes, well done,' said Makovitsky. 'You may have saved his life.'

That night, as they lay on their hard floor, trying to sleep, Anna said: 'Countess Tolstoy says he's only doing this to draw attention to himself.'

'What?' said Ivan. 'Dying, d'you mean? I must try that sometime when I want to get your attention.'

She turned away from him. She tugged a cushion under her shoulder.

He was up early the following day for the Tula train. A priest with an impressive beard alighted from the train and came towards him. 'I'm here to save Tolstoy's soul,' he said. 'Am I in the right place?'

'I don't know,' said Ivan. 'I thought Leo Tolstoy had been excommunicated many years ago.'

The priest was old but had lively, glittering eyes. 'The Church can punish,' he said, 'but it can also forgive.'

'Follow me,' said Ivan Ozolin. Then he added: 'My wife is a church-goer, but I am . . . well, I think I'm nothing. I'm just a stationmaster.'

The priest didn't smile. As they crossed the tracks, he said: 'To be a stationmaster is not enough for a man's soul.'

'Well, I don't know,' said Ivan Ozolin. 'I've thought a lot about that. You see, I think I bring quite a fair bit of gladness to *other men's souls* – just by existing. When people on the trains catch sight of me in my uniform, on the freezing platforms, they say to themselves, "Look at that poor idiot, with his red and green flags. At least we're not stuck in this nowhere of Astapovo! We're fortunate compared to him. We have destinations!"'

'But you have none,' said the priest.

'On the contrary,' said Ozolin. 'I have one. I understand it now. My destination is here. I am the guardian of Count Tolstoy's dying wish.'

'Is that not a rather pretentious thing to say?'

'It may be,' said Ivan. 'But for once I am not joking.'

The priest – despite his beard and headdress, which gave him such gravitas and authority – fared no better than Countess Tolstoy. Nobody inside the cottage would open the door to him and he had to be housed in the Pullman with, by now, so many people aboard the two carriages that the luggage racks were being used as hammocks and the on-board commode was full to overflowing.

This last inconvenience occasioned so many complaints that Ivan took upon himself the unsavoury task of emptying it. He lugged the great stinking drum as far as the outskirts of the woods and tipped the excrement into a ditch, where the benign earth would, in time, absorb it and weeds and grass come to cover it. He found himself smiling as he wondered whether, next season, mushrooms would spring up here. And the thought amused him. This feeling of amusement was so intense that he felt joyful to be alive.

When he returned to the cottage, Tolstoy's daughter whispered to him that the last hours of Tolstoy's life were now slipping by. She told him that his temperature wavered between 102.5 and 104. He was unconscious most of the time, yet bouts of hiccupping still tormented him.

It had grown very dark in the room, owing to a shortage of candles. In this foetid darkness, Sasha asked Ivan to prop up the bed. It seemed that one of the bolts had sheared off under the weight of the 'holy family' constantly sitting or leaning on the mattress. All Ivan could find to use was a pile of snow-covered bricks, stacked near the privy, so he brought some of these inside and inserted them laboriously one by one, as the patient cried out in his sleep. Ice from the bricks melted and formed a pool on the floor, not far from where the chamber pot had been placed. Ivan snapped out a handkerchief and hastily mopped up the ice-water. There were, he thought, confusions enough in everybody's hearts without adding others of a domestic nature.

'When will it be over?' Anna Borisovna asked for the third or fourth time. 'When will we be free?'

'When he decides,' replied Ivan breezily. 'Writers make up their own endings.'

It came at last. On the early morning of Sunday 7th November, Countess Sonya Andreyevna Tolstoya was permitted to come into the sickroom – but not to approach the bed. She sat in a rocking chair, vigorously rocking and praying, with her older children clustered round her, scowling in the half-light. Sasha begged her to rock and pray more quietly, in case the patient suddenly awoke to find her there. But the patient heard nothing. And at 6.05 Dushan Makovitsky noted the final cessation of Tolstoy's breath.

The children wept – not only Sasha, but the grumpy ones as well. Vladimir Chertkov tried not to weep, but was unable to hold back his tears. Dr Makovitsky closed the dead man's eyes and folded his arms across his chest. The Countess lay her head on the bloodstained pillow and howled.

And then the great cavalcade began slowly to depart from Astapovo. As the reporters queued up at Dmitri's office to send their last messages, an engine was once again joined to the Pullman cars and the locomotive took away the body of Leo Nikolayevich Tolstoy. To wave off the Pullman with his green flag, Ivan had to push through a pungent throng of peasants, present to the last, singing 'Eternal Memory', with their arms raised in a passionate farewell and their faces blank with sorrow.

When the train had finally gone, Ivan Ozolin felt very tired and yet strangely triumphant, as though he himself had achieved victory over something that had always eluded him. He wanted to savour this victory for a little while, so he went into the now deserted station buffet and ordered a tot of vodka and a slice of cinnamon cake and sat at one of the tables with his eyes closed and his heart beating with a steady and beautiful rhythm. He knew there were many tasks still to be done; he shouldn't remain sitting like this for long, but he felt so elated and happy that it was tempting to order a second vodka and a second slice of cake . . .

He was on his third vodka and his third slice when Dmitri came into the buffet with a telegram. 'I just took this down,' said Dmitri, whose habitually red face, Ivan noticed, looked suddenly pale. 'It's from your wife.'

Ivan Ozolin reached up and took the telegram and read: *Women, too, have the right to escape. I am leaving you, Ivan Andreyevich. I hope to start a flower shop in Tula. Please do not follow me. Signed: Your unhappy wife, Anna Borisovna Ozolina.*

Ivan reread this message several times, while Dmitri stood by him, with his arms hanging limply by his sides.

'What do you make of it?' said Dmitri at last.

'Well,' said Ivan, 'she's left me.'

'I can see that,' said Dmitri, 'but why?'

'She was always fond of flowers, especially violets.'

'That doesn't explain it. You're a good man, Ivan. Why would she leave you?'

'I have ridiculous legs. When I look at that bit of my legs between the end of my trousers and the beginning of my sock, I see how absurd they are.'

'That's no reason, either. Most men's legs look ludicrous.'

'Oh well, I expect Anna's left because she's tired of my jokes. I don't blame her at all.'

Dmitri sat down. He yawned. He said in a melancholy voice that Anna's absence wasn't the only one they were going to have to suffer. History itself, he said, had come to them and taken up residence with them for a while and was now abandoning them. He asked Ivan what he planned to do once they found themselves quite alone once more.

Ivan thought about this question for a long time and then he said: 'The time has come.'

'What d'you mean "the time has come"?' asked Dmitri.

'Oh,' said Ivan, 'it just feels as though it has. The time for mushroom-picking. I believe the time for this has come.'

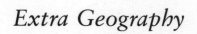

Extra Geography

For two sublime years, we were the wingers. We could outrun the field.

For those two years, at Upton Hall School, all lacrosse matches depended upon us.

'Pass to the wing!' the captain would screech to the fumbling, tangled slow-coaches in midfield. 'Pass to Minna! Pass to Flic!'

With the ball caught, cradled, we'd fly over the muddy grass. And the goal would tremble into sight and the opponents' keeper would lumber out in her creaky shin-pads and our own forwards would prance up, neighing for the ball. But most times, our momentum just carried us on, we couldn't resist it, and one of us would score a goal and then the whole team would come crowding round and clash their lacrosse sticks with ours in a victory salute.

But in summer, there were no lacrosse games. We weren't heroines any more, just ordinary girls, and this felt worrying, as though we might soon die.

One hot day, as we sat in the Upton Hall rose garden, bored with everything, inattentively reading *A Midsummer Night's*

Dream, Minna said to me: 'Flic, I've got an idea. Let's fall in love with someone.'

My gaze moved up from Shakespeare's text and rested on Minna's features. She was growing into a beauty, with grey eyes and chestnut hair and a chocolate mole on her thigh. We were both fourteen. I said: 'Who've you got in mind?'

Minna said: 'No one. Let's make it random, like Titania falls in love with that idiot disguised as a donkey. Let's choose the next person we see.'

The next person we saw was the geography teacher, Miss Delavigne.

Along she came, with her black hair gleaming in the sunshine, wearing a coral-coloured dress.

'Hello, Miss Delavigne,' said Minna.

'Hello, Minna. Hello, Flic.'

She stopped and made polite conversation. She came from the South Island of New Zealand and her pronunciation of certain vowel sounds was something new to us at Upton Hall School. When she went on her way, we appraised her. Her first name was Rosalind. Her skin was tanned, but her ankles looked chunky in navy canvas shoes. Minna said New Zealand women probably didn't know anything about fashion, but we couldn't let that matter to us; love was meant to be blind. We had noticed, however, that Miss Delavigne's eyes were violet-blue and her teeth white as cuttlefish. We decided her age was thirty-nine.

We thought we'd start by being romantic and courtly. We stole a rose and walked to the bungalow Miss Delavigne occupied beyond the lacrosse field, and scattered the rose petals at the bungalow gate. When we came away, I felt sexy and strange, as though the rose petals had been virgin's blood.

Then we decided we'd better get good at geography, so we stared at maps of New Zealand, trying to memorise place names and rivers and sites of mineral deposits. The place names that appealed to us most were Brightness Gully and Desolation Creek.

We agreed that our prime targets were to get ourselves invited to tea at the bungalow and to persuade Miss Delavigne to let us call her Rosalind.

Later in the term, our class went on an outing to the Science Museum in London. Minna and I held Miss Delavigne's hands – one each – as we gazed at a diorama of a Maori village, and she said: 'What the diorama doesn't show is the sadness of the people.'

I looked at Minna because I had no idea what comment to make. And I saw that Minna had no idea, either. By now, we knew a lot about New Zealand weather and cabbage trees and flightless birds, but nothing about the country's history. Miss Delavigne went on: 'Shall I tell you something not many people know? My grandmother was Maori. She deserted her tribe to marry a white man, a *pākehā*, my grandfather, Josiah Delavigne.'

Minna said: 'Does that make you feel sad, Miss Delavigne?'

'No,' she said. 'I'm proud of my Maori blood. But the Maori haven't been treated well. They've lost far too much of their land.'

'We'd love to see a picture of your grandmother,' I said. 'Have you got one at the bungalow?'

'Yes. I keep one by my bed.'

I didn't dare look at Minna. Pressing my hand against the hot glass of the diorama, I said: 'You could invite us to tea and we could do some extra geography and you could show us the picture.'

In the coach going back to Upton Hall, Minna asked me: 'Are you in love with her yet?'

'I don't know,' I said. 'I liked holding her hand.'

'I like her smell,' said Minna.

I said: 'Let's pretend we're in the Maori village alone with her, wearing skirts made of flax. Let's pretend we're plaiting feathers into her hair.'

So we put our heads close together and closed our eyes and imagined the sunlight depicted in the diorama falling on us and on Rosalind Delavigne and on all the acres of land stolen from her family, rippling away to the horizon. But we were so tired from the long day, we both fell asleep.

Near the end of term, we got our invitation to tea.

Laid out on a teak table was a sponge cake and a plate of Penguin biscuits.

The tea was in a floral china pot. Miss Delavigne had put on crimson lipstick. It was raining outside and Miss Delavigne had turned on the gas fire and lit a cosy little lamp. I tried to imagine that there was nothing beyond the windows, not even the lacrosse pitch or the rain, but only the deep, soft dark of the universe.

We drank the tea and ate the food and passed the picture of Miss Delavigne's grandmother from hand to hand. The grandmother wasn't dressed in a skirt made of flax, but in some starchy old dress, with a white lace collar and button-up boots, and I felt disappointed, except that her face was beautiful, with heavy black hair wrenched into a bun. Looking from her to Miss Delavigne and back again, you could see that some of her beauty had descended down the generations.

After the second cup of tea, Minna said: 'It's fine if we call you Rosalind, isn't it?'

When Minna said this, Miss Delavigne inclined her head, as though she were listening for something, some animal noise out there beyond the windows of the bungalow. Then she said quietly, 'What is it, you two? What is it you want?'

Neither Minna nor I could move or say anything. We just sat there dumb, like stupid lacrosse reserves on the pavilion bench. The fire burned blue. Then Rosalind Delavigne reached out and began stroking Minna's chestnut hair. I saw Minna's head move slowly sideways and I knew what was going to happen next: there was going to be a kiss.

I stared at the kiss, mouth on mouth. When, after a long, silent moment, Minna's face was separate from Rosalind's again, it was smeared with the crimson lipstick and her eyes looked drugged, as though by some weird sleep.

I waited, very still, because I thought that now, my turn for a kiss would come, but it didn't. Rosalind got up suddenly and began pacing about the tiny, lamplit room. 'Gracious!' she said. 'Gracious, how *wrong* of me! I just don't know what happened there. You must go, Minna. Flic, off you go. Goodness me, if the Head knew. Really I dread to think . . .'

We walked back to the dormitories through the rain. I gave Minna my handkerchief so she could wipe Rosalind Delavigne's lipstick off her face.

When she gave the hankie back, I said: 'Minna, was it fantastic?'

But she didn't answer. She strode on, as though what had happened had nothing in the world to do with me.

In the autumn term, there was a new geography teacher, called Miss Smith. When I asked the Head whether Miss Delavigne was coming back, she said: 'No, dear. She's returned to her faraway land.'

The lacrosse games began and we took our wingers' positions on the field. But something was wrong with Minna: she'd lost her speed. The midfielders from the opposing team came charging towards her and tackled her long before she got anywhere near the goal. And soon enough, she was dropped from the team.

I thought she'd be upset about this, but Minna said she didn't care, that lacrosse was for kids and she wasn't a kid any more, hadn't I noticed?

She showed me a photo of a boy called Jeremy she'd met in the summer holidays. She said: 'That Rosalind thing was a laugh, but this is real.'

The winter began seeping in. And as the dark came down on the lacrosse pitch, I'd often stare over at Miss Delavigne's bungalow. It was unoccupied now and I noticed that one window-pane was broken and that the paint was flaking off the door. In my mind, I named it Desolation Creek.

*A View of Lake Superior
in the Fall*

Walter and Lena Parker were in their early seventies when they decided to run away from home.

This was in Millennium year. Friends in their neighbourhood of Greenhills in Nashville, Tennessee, who thought the Parkers had taken leave of their senses, liked to explain the crazy decision by calling it 'Millennium Fever'. But, in fact, it wasn't done feverishly. It was done after long weeks of discussion and planning. Walter and Lena owned a summer cabin on a small island way up on the Canada side of Lake Superior and this is where they ran to. It was in May weather, hot and bright.

When they got to the cabin, Walter said: 'I feel like Henry Fonda.'

'What?' said Lena.

'I feel like tired old Fonda in that film with Katie Hepburn.'

'*On Golden Pond?*'

'That's the one. He thinks about everything that's gotta be done to make the place liveable and then he just sits in his chair and does nothing.'

'It's a stupid film. He does nothing – except get lost in the darned woods – because *she* does it all. She gets in the logs . . . everything. But it's not going to be like that, is it, Walter?'

'I don't know,' said Walter. 'I don't know what it's going to be like.'

But on their first night there, they slept like babies, only waking once to look out at the waning moon above the lake, and to remark on the beautiful silence of the night. And in the morning, eating ham and eggs and drinking strong coffee, they felt something like pure happiness come over them.

'We made a good decision,' Walter said. 'Didn't we?'

Lena got up and came over to Walter and put her arms round him and kissed the top of his grey head. 'I still love your hair,' she said.

They began to make lists of the things they'd need for the winter. Winter was far off, but they knew they'd be staying and not returning to Nashville; they didn't even need to discuss it any more. The priority, they decided, would be to install a wood-burning stove for the living room and some kind of electric heater for their bedroom. Lena, in particular, was susceptible to cold and up here, once the fall was past, you could expect every variety of cold weather you could think of: freezing fog; temperatures so low the water froze at it edges; blizzards, and what the islanders called 'lake-effect snow', which fell in sudden thick waves or streamers, the flakes so densely packed together they seemed to choke up the air.

'It's funny,' remarked Lena, 'I've often imagined the cabin enduring the Canadian winter, on its own. I'd kinda feel *sorry* for it. But now we're going to be in it. I wonder how we'll do.'

'We'll do fine,' said Walter. 'Get a chest freezer, though. We can fill it with moose steaks for when the roads get tough.'

'Maybe buy a TV?'

'If you want. Or we can just play Scrabble and talk about the past.'

'Trouble about the past, it's so full of Shirley.'

'Yup.'

'We might start feeling guilty that we ran away.'

'I refuse to feel guilty. At my age. Don't we have the right to some peace and quiet?'

'I'm not sure what we have a right to, Walter. I'm still confused about this.'

'Don't be. Shirley made our lives hell. That's all you need remember.'

Lena didn't know if 'hell' wasn't too dramatic a word. Some elderly people might have taken things more in their stride. But she and Walter were so gentle and quiet and kind in each other's company, they found it hard to tolerate what Shirley had imposed on them, which felt like a crazy and never-ending carnival of woe.

They tried to let their love for Shirley, their only child, triumph over the chaos that she'd inflicted. She had, after all, suggested her return to her parents' house as an act of kindness, 'so I can take care of you both, now that you're getting on a bit', and it had been too difficult and unkind to tell her not to come. But, as they foresaw, this 'caring' never happened. Shirley was forty-two and at a low point in her life. She'd returned to Nashville to start over. On her first night home, she announced, 'I'm going back to my first love: singing. I should have stuck at music and done that all along.'

Shirley had never stuck at anything. After a college degree in music, which she failed to complete, she got work as a junior assistant in a musician's agency in New York City. At the age of twenty-three, she married a bassoon player called Nate and divorced him within a year. She became the plaything of an older man, a composer of international renown, who had wives in London and Vienna. She left him before he left her, railed against his 'stupid rich life' and dropped out for a while, working in clubs and late-night bars, then joined a women's commune in Brooklyn and fell in love with a woman called Robyn.

She told Walter and Lena that things with Robyn were stable and that they intended to give birth to a child, or adopt one, they didn't know which, but this was what they wanted – to be mothers. Walter and Lena kept mainly quiet on the subject and sent monthly cheques. Shirley told them she was working on a novel and would pay them back 'when I become the new Joyce Carol Oates'. But neither the novel nor the baby ever appeared. Shirley moved on and never spoke any more about Robyn or motherhood. The years kept going by.

She left New York City and worked as a teaching assistant in a small-town school in New Jersey. It was during this time that Walter offered to get her home and employ her in the bookstore that he and Lena had owned and run in Hillsboro Village, Nashville, for thirty years. Shirley told him it was a kind thought, but selling books was 'just too darn monotonous for someone like me'. She'd decided to go back to college now, she announced, to do a degree in management theory. Walter commented to Lena that management theory sounded 'monotonous' to him, and all Lena could find to say was, 'I guess we've got to give her the benefit of the doubt.'

There had been doubt all along, however, that Shirley would ever make a true beginning on her life. When she passed the age of forty and returned to New York to be with yet another married lover, they stopped hoping for any such thing as a 'beginning'. Then, suddenly, a year ago, long after the bookstore was sold and gone and Walter and Lena had bought their cabin on Lake Superior and entered upon a time of quietness and ease, Shirley, alone once more, with her degree course in management theory stretching out from three years to five on a string of low grades and missed assignments, announced her new plan: her return to Nashville to 'care' for them.

At this point, they sat down and asked themselves, 'Do we love Shirley?' or, put less crudely, 'Is the love we feel for Shirley adequate to compensate for all that we're going to give up for her sake?'

Sitting on their porch, watching dusk come on around their favourite red-bud tree, Lena clung to Walter's thin arm. She could feel the sinews and the bone underneath the meagre flesh. 'The thing about marriage,' she said, 'is that some mothers love their children more than they love their husbands, and I guess that's OK. Everybody just gets on with it. But I . . . I've always only really loved you, Walter. I think I'm like Queen Victoria in that respect. She loved Prince Albert, but didn't care much for any of her children. And that's just how it was and how it is.'

Lena laid her head on Walter's chest and he held her

close to him. He didn't say anything. He didn't need to. He knew that what she said was true.

What Walter felt, after he'd got over what he called his 'Fonda moment', was a sudden burgeoning of delight in himself and in his life.

He was still an energetic man. He drove a new Honda CRV with 4x4 drive and heated front seats. Now, it amused him to sing a little rhyme as he drove along:

I'm Henry Fonda,
Riding in a Honda . . .

He'd loved and respected learning all his life and his head was full of poetry. The bookstore had been at the centre of the Hillsboro community for more than thirty years. He was proud of this. Proud of the dedication and the continuity. He hadn't lived in vain. And now he was free. He could walk in the woods, or fish in the lake. He could buy a boat and learn to sail or just get one with an engine and be done with it. He could afford to lay in some nice wine. Sitting on his south-facing porch, he could read Walt Whitman or Emily Dickinson all day, sipping Chablis, if he chose to. Lena wouldn't mind. His happiness was hers. They would eat perch and trout and crayfish for their suppers. They would gorge themselves on fine sunsets. They would have the retirement all Americans dream of and seldom get.

Lena had stuffed the Honda with her favourite orna-ments and china and cushions and lamps from the Greenhills house, so they set about making the cabin 'cosy'. A nice man called Charlie came to install their wood-burner and congratulated them on buying 'top of the range', and said, as he left, 'These little cabin places, I love 'em. Best kind of home you can get.'

The warm May weather carried on into June and Lena and Walter took a daily morning dip in the lake before breakfast. The water was cold. It always had been cold, but Walter felt that this immersion somehow cleansed his blood and prolonged his life. The only thing was, he would have liked a target for his swims – some raft or island to reach each time, so that he could say to himself, 'Here I am!' when he got there. And he thought that if he'd been younger and had woodwork skills he would have been able to construct a raft and tether it by some means to the lake floor, so that it didn't float away.

Then there was the question of a dock. There was no point buying a boat, if there was no dock for getting in and out of it. Even hopeless old Fonda had somehow got himself a dock! So Walter went in search of builders and found one whose name and logo he liked: 'Jim Pride, Superior Builder. Pride of Lake Superior.' And Pride came and stood at the water's edge and made a sketch for Walter of how his dock would look and Walter thought it 'the prettiest darn dock this side of Daisy's dock in *The Great Gatsby*', and he felt his heart swell. He stuffed Jim Pride's fist with down-payment dollars and began going round the boat yards. He knew that he'd name his boat *Lena*.

In their first weeks, Lena wrote letters to old Nashville friends. *Dear Bobbie, Well, here we are, up in Canada, away from it all. Walter's very tickled by what we've done . . . Dear Mandy, Hope nobody's missing us yet. Think we may be gone a while . . .*

But by the time August came and the dock was almost

finished, Lena couldn't be bothered to tell people their news any more. She said to Walter; 'Letter-writing's giving me cramps in my hands, and anyway, what's important is *living* this new life, not bragging about it.' And he said: 'I one-hundred-and-one per cent agree.' So she quit writing letters, quit *thinking* about friends like Bobbie and Mandy, and she found that this liberated a clean space in her head, like her mind was an attic cleared of useless things.

The only person she wrote to, to ask her to 'keep an eye on the comings and goings in the house' was their immediate neighbour, Wilma Thirsk. And Wilma wrote back that Shirley and her friends had 'gotten the habit of playing guitars and banjos in your yard late at night, but I don't like to go round to complain because some of the friends are black and bald and scare me half to death'.

So Lena had to sit Walter down and say, 'What can we do about this, Walter? It just ain't fair on Wilma.' And Walter said, 'There's nothing we can do. Remember how it was when we were there.'

They remembered all right. No sooner did she arrive in Nashville than Shirley got in with a crowd of hangers-on at Opryland. One or two of them were backup singers – which Shirley yearned to be, too. The rest were riggers and costume people and electricians, black and white and Hispanic and Polish. They seemed to move about in one gigantic troupe, invading the house at four in the morning or at two in the afternoon, when Walter was taking his nap, carrying in crates of beer and bottles of whisky, raiding Lena's refrigerator to make sandwiches or cook burgers and playing music day and night. According to Shirley, they were 'the best fun people I've ever known', and she explained that she had to stick with them and show them some hospitality because through them could come some singing work, 'and this is my hope now, my hope for a new life'.

How could they deny their daughter a new life?

They tried to be friendly towards the troupe, but there were so darn many of them, Walter kept forgetting their names. When the gang arrived, he and Lena retreated to Walter's study, where they tried to concentrate on Scrabble through the whine and warble of Country songs and the stink of marijuana, which seemed to be everywhere in the house. 'I guess we could be arrested and sent to jail for possession, or harbouring possessors, or something,' remarked Lena. 'Then what?'

'Then nothing,' said Walter. 'They'd just carry on. Nobody would notice we were gone.'

They patiently restocked and restocked the refrigerator, but the food pillage went on and on. One night, as somebody was frying burgers, an electric plate on the old cooker caught fire and shorted out the main fuse, leaving the house in darkness for two days until the cooker could be ripped out and the wiring renewed. On several mornings, Lena found pools of vomit in the corners of rooms. And then there was the snow of rhinestones each visit left behind on the carpets, as though all the troupe's Opry finery was falling to bits and shedding itself day by day. Lena and her home help, Barbara, kept going round with the vacuum, but rhinestones were like sticky fish scales that seemed to defy suction; they had to get down on their hands and knees and sweep them up with a brush and pan. And one day, as they swept and swept and aired the room to try to get away the vomit stink, Barbara announced, 'I'm sorry, Miz Parker, but I think I gotta be movin' on. I ain't up to this job no more. You need an industrial cleaner here.'

That was when Lena had her first cry about it, in Barbara's arms, and when Walter found her weeping like this, he got so mad at Shirley for causing the distress that he fell backwards over a coffee table and broke it to pieces.

That night, when he heard Shirley come in very late but without the troupe, he got up and put on his dressing gown and tiptoed to her room. He listened a moment, then went in and found his daughter kneeling down and giving head to Womack, one of the black riggers, and she turned and saw him and brought her mouth away from Womack's dick to yell, 'Fuck off, Dad! This is my room!'

Walter fled, his face red and burning. The thing that bothered him most was how pale and fragile and small Shirley appeared beside Womack.

He went down to the kitchen and stuck the kettle on to make tea. He stared at his own reflection in the kitchen window and thought, I guess my life is ruined now. I guess I was a no-good father. I guess I deserve to die.

He sat with the tea till the dawn came up. Overhead, he could hear Shirley's small bed creaking and moving about as she yielded to the convulsive weight of Womack's love. He told himself that perhaps it was someone like this she needed, someone who had no hope of her except as a pretty face, a good fuck, someone she wouldn't disappoint.

It was agreed, up at the lake, that they wouldn't talk about Shirley. For what was there to say? She had their house now. She had her lover and her troupe.

She had the hope of returning to music, even if that hope – like the hope of being a lesbian mother, like the hope of marrying a famous conductor, like the hope of becoming a novelist or a management consultant – appeared frail. Enough time remained in her life for her to surprise them and they prayed that she would. But it was as though their love for her was awaiting this moment to be released and that until then it was smothered by weariness as much as by disappointment.

'We're just going to get on with the summer and forget about it all,' Lena announced.

'Darn right!' Walter concurred.

And what preoccupied them now was finding the right boat. Something sturdy, but not too big, with a reliable engine. Prices seemed high. They had good savings from the sale of the bookstore, but Walter was too careful a man to let them dig too far into them. They knew, too, that once the winter came, boating would be impossible, or if not impossible, then too dangerous to be contemplated. 'We don't want to wind up like old Shackleton,' said Walter. 'I mean crushed by ice.'

In the end, they bought a second-hand wooden boat with an inboard engine in a tiny cabin, called *Maybelle*. The owner was a Dutch sculptor with an Australian wife. They were 'going larger, boat-wise', but had been fond of *Maybelle*, 'especially' they said, 'her dinky little wooden fore-deck'.

'Mind if we change her name?' asked Walter.

'Oh yes,' said the Dutchman, 'this is very bad luck, to change the name of a boat. We should not advise it.'

But Walter thought *Maybelle* was a dumb name. 'If I drive around the lake in the boat called *Maybelle*, people will think I'm a Fonda-style idiot,' he said. So he commissioned a young boat-yard hand to paint it out and rename it *Lena*, and when this was done, he and Lena got into the boat and drove slowly around to the new dock, feeling as pleased with life as they could ever remember. They sat there in the boat at the dock's edge, bouncing just a little on the wavelets.

'I guess we're true islanders now,' said Lena. 'We've taken to the water.'

Most days, after that, they went out in *Lena*. It had a powerful engine, but Walter drove it very slowly. So slowly, in fact, that other boats often came up on their wake and surged past them, waving and screaming with laughter, but Walter didn't care. 'We're in uncharted waters,' he said to Lena. 'And we know nothing about the weather. Let everybody mock.'

They'd never been on the island past the middle of August. Now, to their surprise, as this month went by, they felt some season begin that they'd never experienced. Light left the sky in late afternoon. The shadows of the woods seemed to creep nearer and nearer to the cabin and remain there. Storms growled over the Canada shore. Hail fell out of a blank white sky. In the calendar of their minds, it was still summer – late summer – but there didn't seem to be much trace of summer remaining.

'I guess,' said Lena, as they woke one morning to a hard frost, 'we're just being given a taste of the real winter, to see if we can take it.'

'We can take it,' said Walter. 'Tennessee winters weren't a bundle of fun. Or have you forgotten? Remember the ice

storms? And, Jesus Christ, I nearly broke my back shovelling
snow for Wilma Thirsk. We're here for the duration.'

So they began to think about this word, 'duration', and
what it meant to each of them. Had they thought about it
differently? Did they really believe they were never going to
return to their ordinary lives, built in Greenhills over so
many seasons, so many decades? Lena wasn't sure *what* she
believed. She said to Walter: 'When we get through the
spring, then, I guess we'll know what we really intended.'

Walter was silent a while. Then he said, 'We ran away,
Lena. Remember? We ran away from that carnival. We never
said anything about returning. It just wasn't part of the
picture. Nothing that Nature's planning to dish out could
be worse than what we had to leave.'

'We don't know that yet,' said Lena.

'Yes we do. Think about all the Canadians in the world:
none of 'em go about telling you they died of the *weather*.
They just get on with it.'

'Yes, but we're not Canadians.'

'We are now. By adoption. Don't get faint on me, sweetheart. We're in this together.'

'I'm not getting faint. I'm just pondering things aloud.'

They lit the wood-burner in the mornings and tried to keep
it going twenty-four hours by banking it up before they went
to bed, but by breakfast time there was no heat in it, just
a few embers.

Sometimes, Lena took the quilt off the bed and sat
wrapped up in this while she drank her morning coffee. She
saw how very many man-made things, such as wood-burning
stoves, were somehow less efficient than they should have

been. It was enough, she thought, to make you believe that somewhere in the universe an advanced Alien society existed, where everything was a shining miracle of perfect function, including the Alien brain, which would have considered rhinestones to be trash and a career as a backup singer risible.

'We're so flawed, that's the problem,' she said aloud.

'Who's flawed?' said Walter, as he brought new life to the fire.

'The human race. We're so mediocre.'

Walter stood up, brushing ash off his trousers. 'That could be another thing the long winter's going to be good for,' he said: 'Philosophy.'

It was October now and the leaf fall around the cabin was dense and pungent. Lena made leaf collages on rough cream paper and pinned them to the wooden walls. Varnish on the leaves kept the colours bright. She knew they looked like a child's effort, but she smiled to think that 'children' were the people they'd become. Shirley and her hard-drinking, hard-screwing friends were living complex, grown-up lives; she and Walter were like castaway kids, diverting themselves with making fires and playing simple games, holding on to each other in their new unknown.

The light died earlier and earlier in the day. In the mornings, a dense, cold mist shrouded the water, as though the world ended where the lake began.

Walter walked out onto his dock and stared into the fog. He savoured the idea that it made the territory he now inhabited smaller than ever. 'This is right,' he said to himself. 'When you get old, all you want is a small bit of ground, so you don't have to see too far down any particular road.'

He thought about Shirley and all the roads she'd been

on, stumbling towards this or that endeavour and always quitting, always failing, and wondered why it had been like this. As a kid, he and Lena had tried to get her to persevere with things. She made the school basketball team for a year, then got dropped, but didn't seem to know why or even care. 'Didn't you jump high enough, or what?' Walter remembered asking her.

'I jumped a bit,' she'd replied. 'I guess they just didn't rate it.'

He remembered wanting her to care, wanting her to promise to jump higher, because how could your life have any meaning if you didn't mind about things, one way or the other? Walter realised he nurtured no hope of her becoming a singer, no hope at all. He didn't give her one chance in a hundred. And so he fell to thinking, were he and Lena to blame for it all, too wrapped up in each other to ever get right behind Shirley and push her on? 'We probably were,' he said aloud, 'and it's too late now. We haven't got any *push* left in us.' His voice was small in the freezing mist, but he didn't mind about this, he even *liked* it – his own smallness in the white emptiness.

The winter locked them down. Even the CRV had difficulty getting through the four miles of ice and snow to the stores. They ate the moose steaks and the lake trout they'd put in the freezer, with tins of sweetcorn and beans. They brought their bed into the living room so that they could bank up the burner in the small hours and be warm when they watched TV. When blizzards tormented the cabin, they sometimes mumbled old forgotten prayers. After one fierce storm, Walter put on newly acquired snow shoes and made a circuit of all the summer cabins on their part of the lake, and he saw that they were all shuttered and closed – every single one, except theirs.

'We're nuts, Lena,' he said when he got back. 'Everybody sensible from the summer cabins has gone back south.'

'No, we're not nuts,' she said. 'Because I've been thinking, Walter, it doesn't *matter* how we live our lives, as long as we're not harming anyone. We're all dying, anyway. Being pretend Canadians is perfectly OK.'

'Guess you're right,' he said, 'and let's try not to die yet. I really liked those snow shoes. Get you a pair, sweetheart, and we can go on snow walks.'

'Good idea,' said Lena.

It was a bit like trying to walk on two tennis rackets, but they eventually got the hang of it. They chose days when the sun returned for a few hours and made jewellery out of the trees. And it was after one of these beautiful walks that Lena sat down and decided to write to Shirley. She knew that a letter would tire her. She selected a picture postcard showing 'A View of Lake Superior in the Fall' and wrote in large handwriting:

Shirley dear, Today Dad and I went on one of our walks, wearing our new snow shoes! Guess we look quite droll, but who cares? We saw some black squirrels dancing over the snow and magpies skimming between the branches, and lots of moose prints and the sun was just glorious. Only occasionally can one remember that bits of the world are still grand.

Please tell us how you are, and Womack and your friends. Hope you may have news of some singing work at the Opry. From your loving mother, Lena.

PS. Dad sends his best.

'Best what?' said Walter.

'Oh, don't be difficult, Walter. Best "stuff" . . . you know . . .'

'She won't answer anything that short,' said Walter, as he read it over.

And they looked at each other. 'That's why you chose a card, is it?' he said. 'You don't *want her to answer?*'

'I dunno,' said Lena. 'I absolutely do not know whether I want an answer or not.'

It was on that night that a storm took out the electricity. They'd prepared for this by buying two old-fashioned oil-lamps and these they lit at four in the morning. They banked up the wood-burner and got back into bed and watched the oil-lights flickering as the wind buffeted the cabin walls and screamed all around them in the tall trees.

'Who'd have thought we'd end up here?' said Lena. 'With just *flames* for company.'

'Let's make a resolution,' said Walter.

'Sure,' said Lena. 'What resolution?'

'We won't let the winter beat us. We'll at least hold on till spring.'

Lena snuggled close against Walter. He was as lean and rangy as Clint Eastwood, but his body always seemed to be warm.

'I'm your girl,' she said. 'No giving up. Now, what about some Yeats, or something, to pass the night?'

'OK,' said Walter.

> *I will arise and go now, and go to Innisfree,*
> *And a small cabin build there, of clay and*
> *wattles made;*
> *Nine bean rows will I have there, a hive for the*
> *honey-bee,*

And live alone in the bee-loud glade.'
Walter knew the whole poem by heart. Lena closed her eyes and surrendered to his voice.

Spring came slowly, leaf by slow leaf.

One morning in April, with the sun at last quite high in the sky, Walter went down to the lake and put a toe in the water and decided he'd risk going for a swim.

When he appeared in his faded old Bermudas, carrying a towel, Lena had to smile; the sight of him was such a compound of sweetness and tragedy. 'We should get you some new swim-wear,' she said.

'No,' Walter said. 'I like these fine.'

Lena put on her coat and walked with Walter down to the water's edge. The cry of the gulls was loud. Bright light danced on the surface of the lake.

Walter handed Lena his towel and waded into the water on his thin, white shanks. When he was up to his knees, he stood still and laughed.

'How is it?' Lena called out.

'Just a bit fresh,' he said.

But he dived in then and swam out in his hectic, unco-ordinated crawl to the end of the dock, where he paused and clutched at one of the wooden stanchions.

'Nuts . . .' said Lena to herself. 'He's nuts. It's still far too cold.'

But he swam on, pushing away beyond the dock, bashing and thrashing with his arms until he was just a tiny moving entity in the vastness of the lake. Lena called to him not to go too far. But she knew he couldn't hear a thing. She thought about him saying, last summer, how swimming was cleansing his blood and prolonging his life and she looked forward to seeing his expression when he got back to shore, so pleased with himself and full of euphoria, like he'd come first in a triathlon competition. She laid out his towel, to warm it in the sun.

Walter never returned to shore.

Lena ran to the Honda and drove to the boat yard and a flotilla of small yachts and dinghies set out in search of him. They searched until the light faded and found nothing.

After two days, his pale white body, still partially clothed in the frayed Bermudas, washed up right where he had started, by the wooden stilts on which the dock rested, as though, all the while, he'd been trying to struggle home.

When Lena arrived back in Nashville, she noticed that the house in Greenhills had been steam-cleaned. It smelled of something burned and sweet, like sugar-candy.

There was no sign of Womack or the troupe. Shirley's hair was cut short and dyed pink. Lena observed that her daughter's neck was beginning to pucker.

'Did you get any work as a backup singer?' Lena asked.

'No,' said Shirley. 'It's kind of a closed shop, the Opry. You have to know people.'

'I thought you did know people.'

'Yup. Just not the right people. The whole singing thing sucks in this town. But I've gone back to my novel. This is a good house for writing. I'm using Dad's study.'

This was the first time Lena let herself weep – when she went into Walter's study and saw it strewn with the pages from Shirley's book, most of them torn or scrunched up and hurled onto the carpet. She closed the door and kneeled by Walter's armchair, where he'd liked to sit and read, and put her face against the green velvet cushion where his back had once rested, and howled. She knew the noise she was making was unearthly, like the noises they'd heard up at Lake Superior in the winter nights. But she didn't care.

After Walter's funeral, to which Womack turned up and stood at the back, hunched and sad, like a penitent, Shirley tried to persuade Lena to stay in Greenhills. She said, 'I've been discussing it with Womack. He agrees with me, the cabin was one thing when you had Dad with you, but on your own, it's madness.'

'What's Womack know about it?' said Lena.

'He knows a lot,' said Shirley. 'I told him lots of stuff about you and Dad and the bookstore and my childhood and everything.'

'You did?'

'Yes. Womack and I got married in February.'

'Oh,' said Lena. 'Well, I guess I'm glad.'

'Are you sure you're glad?'

'Yes, I am. Very glad. No one should be alone like you've been.'

Shirley smiled. She touched her mother's grey hair. '*You* shouldn't be alone. Miles from anyone, up in Canada. It's stupid. Stay here with us and we can take care of you. Womack is a very kind man.'

Lena held Shirley close to her and thanked her. They stood this way for some time and both realised that it was the nearest they'd felt to each other in years.

But Lena knew she wouldn't stay in the house. The only

place she wanted to be was on the island. She wanted to stand on the dock, exactly where Walter had often stood, always in the same spot, not quite at the end of it, and stare out at the water and the sky.

She wanted to feel what he had felt in his contemplation of the great and heartless lake.

She wanted to honour him for all that he had been.

Man in the Water

Inspired by the picture *Yarmouth Beach and Jetty* by
Norwich School artist Joseph Stannard (1797–1830)

Fishing was my livelihood and my life.

I'd go out early, on the ebb tide. Put up the ragged sail. Hear my boat, the *Mary Jane*, complaining in the wind. Use my telescope to search the sky for gulls. Watch what the other boats were doing. Then, when I had a sniff of how the herring were moving, heave out my nets, heavy and damp, and lower the sail and take up the oars and set the boat's course and wait and listen with my hand on the tiller and watch the corks idling on the water and feel the vastness of the sky all about me.

Now and then, I'd look back at the land: the long girdle of the beach and the Whetstone Lighthouse. Even from far out, I could see the lane where my cottage stood and it would always return to my mind then, that my home was empty of my wife, Hannah, and my bed cold. And I'd ask myself, what are you going to do, you poor man, alone as you are, to prepare your children for their lives? And never any answer came to me. And never, day by day and month by month, did I do one thing for them that I hadn't done before the death of Hannah, because no one gave me counsel as to what I *should* do. My daughter, Jenny, cooked our meals and washed our linen and hung it to dry in the sun and the salt wind. She was a dutiful girl. But my son, Pips, he only paid attention to his school lessons one day in three and he stole plums from our neighbours and threw pebbles at their dogs and cats and most of the time was no use to any man.

When I brought the boat in with my catch, Jenny and Pips would bring our old grey mare, Hazel, down to the beach with panniers strapped to her sides. We'd tip the herring into the panniers and while I cleaned the *Mary Jane* and piled up my nets and made everything fast against the tide, the children would lead the horse to the Sheds, where the fish was weighed and sold and we'd get our money wrapped in a scrap of paper. And then we'd go home to the empty cottage and brew tea and put slices of bacon to fry, and I'd wash the sea off my hands and out of my eyes and Pips would run around the table, strewing it with knives and forks and cups and saucers, like an elf strewing a dell with leaves, and Jenny would come after him, straightening everything up. I told them they were good children.

On a summer's morning, when I bring the boat in and we've loaded the horse with the catch and Pips is digging for cockles in the sand, Jenny picks up my brass telescope and puts it to her eye and hunts over the ocean with it. I note the stillness of her back, which, at the age of fifteen, is almost the back of a woman, and I look at her sweet head moving left to right, right to left. And then Pips, he stops digging for cockles and says, 'What can you see, Jen?' But she doesn't answer him and I say, 'Come on, you children, you're not Admiral Nelson. Take Hazel to the Sheds now, and get the catch weighed and paid, then hurry on home.'

And then Jenny, she says quietly, 'Pa, I can see a boat

going down and there's a man in the water and I think he's drowning.'

I snatch the telescope from her hands and put it to my eye and Pips, he's jumping up like a puppy dog and saying, 'Give me the spyglass, Pa, for I'd like to see that: a boat going down and a man in the water!' I cuff his head and say, 'What manner of heartless talk is that?'

In the eye of glass I spy something on the distant swell, where Jenny's pointing, and it looks like driftwood, but she says, 'No, Pa, no that's a bit of the boat, the bow or the keel of it, sticking up above the waves, and you must get back in the *Mary Jane* and hurry now, or the man in the water will be lost.'

'I see no man in the water,' I say.

'He was there,' she says. 'I saw his head above the waves. I could see his mouth, wide open and crying out.'

So we heave the boat down to the water and Pips jumps in and says, 'I'm coming to help you, Pa,' and I notice his cheeks all scarlet with excitement. But Jenny, she stays where she is on the beach with the horse and begins leading her away up to the Sheds as I get the sail up and turn across the wind.

I give Pips the telescope and show him where I saw what I thought was driftwood and we go fast in the offshore breeze, bumping on the wavelets, and he says: 'This is a rotten instrument, Pa. Nothing stays still in it long enough for me to see the drowning man.' I lower the sail and take up the oars and we go round in circles, staring at the water. Then we start to call out to the man, 'Where are you? Where are you?' But no one replies.

'Reckon he be drowned by now,' says Pips.

I say nothing to this, but nudge the tiller with my elbow,

keeping the boat turning and feather the oars to try to steady her in the swell. I don't like the feel of the tide, pulling us out to sea, but we keep on.

We found no drowning man and when we got back to Whetstone, no news came of anyone lost at sea that summer morning.

So then I began asking myself, did Miss Jenny invent the man in the water? Did she want me and Pips out at sea so she could be sure to be on her own, to go where she pleased for that little while? And I longed more than ever to have my wife back at my side so we could wonder about these things together.

From that day, I kept my eye on Jenny. I saw how she carried herself with her eyes downcast and how, when she was ironing sheets or doing the baking, she would sometimes stare out of the window, in a reverie.

I wanted to ask, 'What are you dreaming of? Or who?' And I longed to say to her, 'Don't leave your pa. For God knows, I haven't an ounce of an idea how to do anything in the world except fish for herring, and Pips and I, we'd be no good without you. We'd be like hobgoblins.'

In the middle of a cold night, something woke me and I lay there in the dark listening, imagining I heard Jenny's footsteps going along the lane.

I lit my lamp and got up and went to the room where the two children slept in their wooden beds. There was Pips tucked in with the toy he loved, an old bald bear, pressed against his cheek. And there was Jenny, too, asleep with her arm flung upwards on the pillow. So I turned to go back to my room, but suddenly, as I was at the door, she said, 'Pa, what's wrong?'

'Nothing's wrong,' I said. 'Nothing at all.'

I went out early in the *Mary Jane*, at that hour before the dawn has truly come and when I saw the flash of the Whetstone Lighthouse it was then I remembered what Josiah Green, the keeper of the light, had said to me long ago. Jenny had been eight or nine at that time and pretty as a princess and Josiah had said to me, 'I'll have your daughter for a bride when she's grown, and we'll sail to the West Indies, where I'll make my fortune. And Jenny will have a garden of red lilies and pour tea from a silver teapot.'

I'd said to Josiah, 'You'll be too old, boy, for a girl of mine.'

And he'd said, 'No man with a fortune is ever too old.'

I sat in my boat and stared up at the lighthouse and imagined Josiah keeping watch over the great burning lights and over the gleaming cogs that rotated the glass. I stared until the sun came up.

I say to Jenny, 'Teach me how to bake and how to launder. Teach me everything you do.'

'Why, Pa?' she says.

'Just teach me,' I say.

So she ties an apron round me and gets out a mixing bowl and warms it on the range and weighs flour and salt and shows me how to make a well in this for the stirred yeast and fold it slowly in. Then she covers the bowl with a cloth and tells me, 'Now you leave it alone to sponge for a while, then you beat it and knead it, and then you leave it again to rise . . .'

'Sponge and rise?' I say. 'I don't know what these terms mean . . .'

'No,' Jenny snaps. 'But you will. Or else have no bread.'

When I've kneaded the mix and left it to its rising, Jenny heats up the flat irons and lays a blanket on the table and sets down one of my Sunday shirts and shows me, 'Collar first, then cuffs, then sleeves, then back, then front, then shoulder seams . . .'

'Why is there an order to this?' I ask and she says, 'There's an order to everything. That's what my mother taught me.'

My hands burn and sting, but I try to do what she shows me, to get the shirt smooth, and I see her watching me and then I see the pile of sheets and pillowcases and cloths and petticoats and shawls all waiting to be ironed and I think to myself, How will I do all this drudgery and still keep my livelihood? And I longed to be away from the house, in the *Mary Jane*, alone with my nets and my thoughts.

I turn to Jenny and say, 'Has Josiah Green come courting you?'

She goes to the bread bowl and lifts the cloth and looks to see how far the dough has risen. Then she says, 'Josiah Green is your friend, and a good man.'

'I know,' I say. 'But if he's come courting you, you must tell your pa.'

'I would tell you,' she says.

I look at her and say, 'Have you always told me the truth, Jenny?'

'Yes,' she says. 'Always.'

I am on to the front of the shirt and I know the front is the most important bit, for it's the only place that can be seen, and how could I go to church on Sunday with my shirt looking like a rag? But my iron's gone cool and won't get the creases out. I stare down at my work, helpless to know what to do, and I hear Jenny sigh and she snatches the iron out of my hand and sets down the second one, scalding hot from the range.

I went to visit Josiah Green.

I climbed the nine flights of stairs up to the Whetstone Light Room and my footsteps set up an echo that bounced and flew round the building.

I felt my heart and my lungs complaining and nor did I like the chill darkness and containment of the building and once again what I wanted was to be far out on the ocean, with the sky above me.

Josiah was in a cramped little space, where the cogs of the revolving glass were housed, and his head was close to the machinery, listening to it, just like I listened to the birds and the sea. 'Come on, Josiah,' I said. 'I need to talk to you, friend, and I hope you will be honest with me.'

We went up the iron ladder that led to the platform outside the Light Room and the wind came tearing at us and thrilled me. We held to the little railing that kept us from falling to our deaths and I said, 'Are you courting my girl? Yes or no?'

He was silent a while and I let him be. Then he said, 'I love your Jenny and I'd like to leave this lonely job. I'd like to take her with me to the Caribbean Islands and make my fortune before my fiftieth birthday has come and gone.'

I looked down at the waves beating at the foot of the lighthouse and then I said, 'Does my Jenny love you?'

Josiah shielded his eyes against the glare of the sun. 'The truth of it is,' he said, 'I don't know.'

*   *   *

I go to Jenny in the early evening. New loaves have been baked and all the ironing is freshly done and set in a neat pile.

'Now you must tell your pa,' I say, 'do you love Josiah Green?'

'No,' she says.

I reach out my hand and stroke her dark hair. 'He could take you to the Indies,' I say, 'and you might be a rich woman and grow scarlet lilies and pour your tea from a silver teapot.'

'I know,' she says.

'So tell me again then, if this was to be your future, would you love him then?'

'No,' she says.

Her head, under my hand, is warm and beautiful. I take a breath. In that moment of my breath, I hear the familiar sounds of Pips and his friends playing tag in the lane, as the darkness falls. Then I say to my daughter, 'That morning in summer, when I went chasing after a drowning man, tell me what you saw.'

'I saw a man in the water,' says Jenny.

'Yet there's no body been swept in,' I say, 'and still no report of anyone missing in Whetstone. So tell me the truth, Jenny. Tell me again what you saw.'

She lifts her chin and her dark hair flies as she whips her head away from my caressing hand.

'I saw a man in the water, Pa!' she cries. 'And you can ask me and ask me till the end of time: I saw a man in the water.'

Juliette Gréco's Black Dress

This is a true story about my friend Phoebe's mum. Phoebe told me it during our lunch breaks at the beauty clinic where we both work. These breaks are stingy, so it took a few of them, and Phoebe sometimes said, 'Oh God, I don't know why I'm telling you all this, Karen,' and I said, 'I expect it's because I'm a good listener, like I listen to all the clients' stuff while I'm doing manicures and pedicures,' and Phoebe said, 'Yup, it could be that.'

Phoebe's mum's name was Julie. Her parents lived in an old brick cottage in Surrey, and in the 1950s they scrimped to send her to quite a posh school, near Epsom, where art was taught. Julie was so brilliant at art that the head teacher wrote to her parents and told them that when she was eighteen, they should send her to an art school in Paris, the Académie Something, where she knew the director. I don't know how they afforded this, but they did. Before they let her go, her mother bought her a new tartan skirt and a pale green twinset from Marks & Spencer, and got her hair permed. Phoebe said that, at the time, Julie thought she looked excellent, wearing her twinset and with her dark hair in a demi-wave.

When she got to Paris, she was swept away by the beauty of things.

She walked around in a daze, making sketches of old lamp-posts and stone lintels. At the Académie, she learned to draw naked people and smoke Gauloises. No other girls there had perms or wore twinsets. They had long straight hair and wore matelot jerseys and tight, tapering trousers.

Julie packed away her twinset and stocked up on matelot jerseys from a cheap market stall in Les Halles. Then she went to a hairdresser and got the perm straightened and when that was done, the nice French hairdresser said to her, '*Voilà*. Now you look like Juliette Gréco.'

She found out that Juliette Gréco was a famous singer. But also a *muse*. Jean-Paul Sartre adored her. Jacques Prévert wrote songs for her. Men and women all over France fantasised about her. Handsome Monsieur Fabien at the Académie said she was the most seductive woman he'd ever laid eyes on.

Julie began buying her records. Her favourite song was '*Les Feuilles Mortes*', which was about the way life separates you from people you love. She also studied photographs of Juliette, and she noticed that in every single one of these she was wearing a black dress. Then she read a newspaper interview in which Juliette said that she was adored by everyone in the world except one person and that one person was her mother. Famous as she was, her mother still didn't love her or feel proud of her, so that was why she wore black – as a kind of mourning for her mother's affection.

So then Julie began to think that her own mother didn't love *her* either. She decided that any mother who insisted on perming her daughter's hair had to have jealous feelings about her. She stopped writing letters home. She longed to be somebody's muse. And one day she blew almost all her money on a beautiful black dress.

Phoebe then described how, when Julie put this dress on, she adored the sight of herself so much that she couldn't bear to take it off. So she larded on some black eye make-up and went out into the street like that, and everybody in the street stared and stared at her, and she kept wondering, were these really stares of admiration, or was it just that it was winter and she was walking along in a cocktail dress and narrow little pumpy shoes?

During the Life Class at the Académie, Monsieur Fabien kept looking at her. At the end of the session, he invited her out to a café in St Germain des Près, where he put his suede blouson round her shoulders to stop her shivering in the winter cold. They drank rum and coke. A lot of people in the café gazed at them: at handsome Monsieur Fabien and Julie from Epsom in her Juliette Gréco dress.

He took her back to his studio. Now, she discovered that he wasn't just a teacher of art, but a real artist, with an attic reeking of turpentine and lots of half-finished pictures of naked women standing around among scrunched-up rags on the paint-spattered floor. When he kissed her, she said: 'Monsieur Fabien, I want to be your muse,' and he said, 'OK, *ma belle*. Fuck first. Muse later.'

Julie fell in love with Monsieur Fabien the moment he took her virginity away. She lay in bed with him, looking at her black dress hanging over a chair, and she told Phoebe that at that moment, the whole world became titchy and reduced itself to an attic and a slanty bit of Paris sky, and she thought,

Right, this is where I'm going to stay for ever, and never see Surrey again.

I really liked Julie's story up to here. The stories I have to listen to from the clients are never romantic like this; they're actually quite dull, like nothing ever *happens* in rich women's lives except buying furnishings and paying vet's fees and worrying about Christmas. I was looking forward to the next instalment, but when it came, I felt gutted.

Phoebe said, 'Well, you can guess how it ends, can't you, Karen?' and I said, 'No, I don't want to guess.' And she said, 'The dress got torn.'

'And?'

'He dumped her. She came home. She was miserable for a while. She couldn't eat or make polite conversation. She played '*Les Feuilles Mortes*' over and over on my grandparents' radiogram. I guess she kept imagining Monsieur Fabien with other women, each one thinking she was going to be his muse. She put the torn black dress in a drawer and sometimes looked at it, or held it to her face to breathe in the old scent of turpentine.

'Then my grandmother gave her a talking-to and told her she was being selfish and putting everybody through hell for the sake of some philandering French fool with a dirty floor. So she agreed to go to a local dance, where she met my father, Hugh. And that's the end of it, really. They were married within six months and then she had me. It pretty much ends there.'

'How d'you mean, it ends there?' I said.

'Well, it does,' said Phoebe. 'Nothing more has ever happened to her.'

Our lunch break was finishing and I had an Aromatherapy Massage to prepare for, so I put on my white uniform and tugged back my hair into its tortoiseshell clip and left Phoebe fishing around in her bag for a photograph of her father, Hugh, mowing the lawn of his semi off the Ashtead road.

My Aromatherapy client, Mrs Tyler, seemed nice. She told me a bit about her brilliant job in banking while I worked on her back, which was tanned and smooth, and I caught myself wondering how many lovers had stroked it or touched it with their lips. But I didn't really feel like making polite conversation. All I said to her was, 'Can I ask you something random? Do you by any chance know how much a Eurostar ticket to Paris costs?'

I was using lavender oil, which is astringent, like turps. Mrs Tyler turned her head sideways to breathe in the oil, and a mesh of her dark hair touched my arm.

'I think it varies, Karen,' she said. 'I'm pretty sure it's cheaper in the winter.'

The Housekeeper

Everybody believes that I am an invented person: Mrs Danvers. They say I'm a creation: 'Miss du Maurier's finest creation', in the opinion of many. But I have my own story. I have a history and a soul. I'm a breathing woman.

I first met Miss du Maurier when she came to luncheon with my employer, Lord de Whithers, at Manderville Hall in the summer of 1936. Lord de Whithers married late and would never have expected to outlive his much younger wife, but she died of cancer in the winter of 1935, and since her death Lord de Whithers frequently gives way to those outbursts of ill-temper that afflict heartbroken men. Although these can be wounding, I feel great pity for him and do all that I can to keep Manderville Hall just as the late Lady de Whithers would have wished it to be kept.

Being the housekeeper, I would not normally (or not necessarily) be introduced to the luncheon guests, but Lord de Whithers sent for me on that summer's day to ask me whether, after luncheon, I would be kind enough to take Miss du Maurier – whom he had met by chance at a garden fête – on a guided tour of the house.

'Miss du Maurier is the authoress Daphne du Maurier,' said Lord de Whithers, 'and she seems to think that our beloved Manderville Hall might inspire her to write what I think these days is called a "fiction".'

Miss du Maurier was seated in a brocade-upholstered wing chair. She sat so deep in the chair, holding her small glass of sherry and not moving at all when I entered the room, that the vision I had of her was shadowy, as though only part of her sat in the wing chair, and the rest of her were somewhere else. And – for reasons that I could not fathom at the time – this strange insubstantiality of hers affected me with instantaneous strong feeling, as though I were the one being called upon to bring her to wholeness and to an engagement with the world.

I told Lord de Whithers that I would be delighted to conduct Miss du Maurier upon a tour of the house, but I did not look again at the authoress. I turned and made my way towards the drawing-room door and Lord de Whithers said: 'Thank you so much, Mrs Danowski. I suggest you come back at half past two when I will go for my little rest. You can, of course, include the west wing in your tour, if you wish.'

I closed the drawing-room door quietly, but waited a moment outside it, to hear what Lord de Whithers might say about me. His views upon the world are narrow, and in recent times, the things he says are often uncharitable. He has been heard to disparage my name, even inferring some instability of my character attaching to my Jewish origins. But on this occasion he didn't mention me. All he said to Miss du Maurier was: 'Forgive me for not doing the tour myself, my dear. Since my wife died, I've become prone to melancholy in the afternoons.'

The other thing that people believe about me is that I'm an arsonist – possibly a murderer. For how many people (the butler, the other servants, asleep in their beds) died in the fire that burned down the house Miss du Maurier renamed Manderley? We do not know. The book ends without telling us. All we see are the terrible flames lighting up the sky and the ash blown by the salt wind from the sea. Yet it is strongly inferred that 'Mrs Danvers' (as I was named by the writer) set the fire. Mrs Danvers packed up all her possessions, such as they were, and then she began her jealous burning. As the fire took hold, she slipped away, walking down the azalea walk known as Happy Valley, and was never seen again.

Happy Valley . . .

Miss du Maurier took this name from something I said to her later that day, about the beauty of the azaleas – when they are in bloom and perfuming the air – in the Manderville Hall garden. I said to her: 'When I walk here on a fine spring day, I find that I am completely happy, and I know that this happiness comes from believing – counter to all that I know – that nothing bad will come my way while I am in this place.'

She told me that she understood such a feeling very well, that there were places in the world that felt like sanctuaries. But then she stole these thoughts, just as she stole my life.

My poor life. I live in Padstow in a rented room, with a view of the sea. I earn a small living from a needle-work enterprise.

I have a heart full of memory. I go for walks in the cold of winter, wearing a fur coat that was a gift to me from Miss du Maurier. I hold the coat close around my body.

Manderville Hall, on the south coast of Cornwall, was very large. It had been in the de Whithers family for no less than eight generations, and it was a great sadness to Lord and Lady de Whithers that they had no heir to leave it to. When the time came for His Lordship to die, which might not be far off, the house was supposed to pass to his niece, Miss Adelaide Waverley.

'I do not really like to think about this,' he once said to me, as he and I were going through some of his late wife's books and papers in the morning room. 'Manderville Hall needs to be *inhabited*, as I and my wife inhabited it – with our whole beings. But Adelaide will not do this. She is a careless girl. She could let it all fall to ruin.'

It was not my place to make any comment upon this observation, but I did remember the one visit that Miss Adelaide Waverley had made to Manderville Hall. She brought her own horse in a horse box. She spent most of each day riding about the park. She left her riding clothes strewn about her room, all stinking of leather and sweat, for the maids to pick up. She possessed a screeching laugh, which I found displeasing. When she departed, she left no tips for any of the staff.

I came to the drawing room at half past two, as instructed. Lord de Whithers had already gone to his room, leaving Miss du Maurier alone. She sat on one of the window seats, staring out at the lawns. Her pale hair was lit by the afternoon sun. She turned and smiled at me and I saw that her smile made her beautiful.

'You must think me a wretch,' she said.

'A wretch, madam?'

'To make you do the tour of the house when – I don't know – you might prefer to be sleeping, on this warm afternoon, or making a trip to the village.'

'Oh no,' I said. 'I almost never leave Manderville Hall. I think of it as my home. Even on my days off, I often stay here.'

'Do you? Well, I can understand that. It is one of the loveliest places I've ever seen . . .'

'Lord de Whithers is happy for me to walk in the woods, or on the private beach. There is an old summer-house down on the beach, which nobody uses any more. And I enjoy sitting in there and listening to the sea.'

'Oh, *do* you?' said Miss du Maurier, springing up off the window seat. 'I love the sound of the sea, too. How it sighs and whispers. I've promised myself that before I get too old to want to do it any more, I'll spend a whole night by the sea, lying on the sand and looking at the stars. Have you ever done that?'

'No, madam, I haven't. But I will admit that one night I fell asleep in the beach-house, and when I woke up, I didn't know where in the world I was, but I knew that I was one of the . . . How can I put it without sounding pretentious? I felt that I was one of the *blessed*.'

'One of the blessed?'

'I mean, one of those who can occasionally – and without necessarily wishing to do this – see and feel things very intensely. As I imagine you, as an authoress, might also do.'

She stared at me closely when I said this. Her eyes were large and clever, like the eyes of one who can see into the past and into the future. But her smile had vanished and I had the miserable feeling that I had uttered something impertinent and inappropriate to my position as Lord de Whithers' housekeeper. But then, her look softened and she said: 'Sometimes, strong feeling lays ghastly traps for the soul. Don't you think so? Anyway, let's begin on our tour. Where are you going to take me first?'

She had already seen the library and the drawing room and the dining room and the morning room and the hall, with its fine minstrels' gallery and I didn't think that she necessarily wanted to visit the kitchen or the servants' hall, so I decided to show her the west wing. In my opinion, this was the most beautiful bit of the house, decorated with exquisite taste by the late Lady de Whithers, but hardly inhabited since her death.

Even when she was alive, Lord and Lady de Whithers occupied opposite wings of the house – he in the east and she in the west – like the kings and queens of old who kept each to their own apartments within their palaces.

I led Miss du Maurier up the west staircase and along the wide, carpeted passage to Lady de Whithers' bedroom. In summer, I instructed the maids to keep the curtains closed, so that sunlight would not fade the magnificent French upholstery of the four-poster bed. Thus, the large room seemed dark when we went into it and rather cold. As I stepped to the window, to draw the curtains, I saw Miss du Maurier shiver. She pulled her cashmere cardigan more tightly round her body, and once again I was affected by very strong feeling – this time by a desire to *protect* the authoress, as though some imminent harm was going to come her way.

I let in the sunlight and called her to the window. 'Do come and look at this view, madam,' I said. 'The sweep of the bay is so beautiful from here.'

Miss du Maurier came and stood by me and we gazed out at the sea. She was still trembling and I put my hand gently on her arm.

'Are you cold?' I asked. 'I suppose it is always a little cool in this room.'

'No, no,' she said. 'I'm fine. But there is something so extraordinary about this house – like no other house I've ever been to. It's as if – and I know this is too, too foolish – I've seen it before in some wonderful dream. And in the dream, it didn't belong to Lord de Whithers; it belonged to me.'

That was the first time that she used the word 'belonged'.

I understand now, because of all that she appropriated, how important and how terrible was her use of this word. At the time, however, in Lady de Whithers' bedroom, I made no comment upon it. She walked away from the window and sat down on the bed. She caressed the damask bedspread with her long, sensitive fingers.

'I'm sorry that I never met Lady de Whithers,' she said. 'I feel that she must have been an exceptional woman.'

'Well,' I said, 'she was very beautiful, until she became ill. She wore the most wonderful clothes, bought in Paris. Some of them are still in the wardrobes here. Would you like to see them?'

'Oh,' said Miss du Maurier, 'well, I would. Writers are

terrible, you know, for wanting to peek and pry into things. We never know where inspiration may lie . . .'

I opened one of the wardrobes, which contained a great quantity of winter coats, among them some furs, which, in the long, cold winters at Manderville Hall, had often made me sigh with envy. The only coats that I possessed at that time were made of thin wool or gabardine and I knew that fur alone lends impenetrable warmth to the human frame.

I took out a long mink coat and invited Miss du Maurier to stroke it. Then, I took it off its hanger and Miss du Maurier stood up and I put the coat gently round her shoulders.

'Isn't it lovely?' I said. 'You were cold a moment ago, madam, and now you're not cold any more, are you?'

'No, I'm not. Not a bit cold.' Then she laughed. 'Look at us!' she said. 'We're like naughty children, trying on things that don't belong to us.'

'Yes,' I said, 'I suppose we are.' But then – perhaps because Miss du Maurier looked so strikingly pretty and vulnerable with the heavy fur draped about her shoulders – I ventured to say: 'I know a little about good clothes, for my father was a tailor in Warsaw until the family left for England in nineteen twenty-three.'

'Oh,' she said, 'a tailor! What a beautiful profession. Clothes that are made *just for oneself and for no one else* feel as precious as jewels. Don't you agree? Or like *friends*, even, and when you put them on, it's like slipping your hand in theirs.'

I smiled, in thrall to a sweet remembrance: how, when I was a young child, my father used to make me little dresses out of offcuts of tweed and grey flannel and how my schoolmates envied me these clothes, because they were heavy and lined and warm in our bitter winters. And I allowed myself to sit on the bed – a thing I would not normally ever do – and tell Miss du Maurier about these garments from my past. She stared at me with rapt attention, as though I, and not she, had suddenly become a marvellous teller of stories.

'What a lovely thing,' she said. 'I can just imagine the dresses. Did he put a little lace or velvet on the collars?'

'Yes, sometimes. Or silk, from a linings remnant. For he didn't like waste. He used to say to me: 'When you grow up, you must *take care of things*. And I suppose I never forgot this because here I am, a housekeeper, and this is where I've put my soul – into the care of objects and the well-being of the people they belong to.'

'Well, I am sure that Lord de Whithers values you enormously. And the house is so immaculately ordered. I suppose you might be the best housekeeper of all time!'

She laughed when she said this and with the sudden movement of her body, the fur coat slipped to the floor.

'Oh,' she said, stooping to pick it up, 'I'm sorry. I didn't mean to let it fall. We'd better put the fur away. And perhaps we could go out into the garden, into the sunshine.'

'Yes, of course,' I said, taking the mink coat from her and replacing it on its padded silk coat hanger. 'We can go wherever you like. Would you like to see the summer-house down on the beach?'

'Yes, I would, very much. Is there a kettle there? Could we make a cup of tea?'

What I liked most about descending the steep pathway to the beach was the onrush of sound as one came nearer and nearer to the sea. From the west-facing terrace of Manderville Hall, although the view of the bay was very fine, the *power* of the ocean seemed muted, as though the house, in its lofty position above the steeply sloping lawns, would always dominate it and never be harmed by it.

Then, as you came down towards the sea, you felt the thrill of the harm that it could do. In my time at Manderville Hall, there had been drownings here: bodies which nobody recognised or knew, strangers in our world, whose last trespass had been upon our paradise.

When I told Miss du Maurier about these drownings, she said: 'Oh, how extraordinary! People nobody knew. Somebody must have known them. Did detectives come?'

'Yes, I suppose they did, madam.'

'But none of them ever questioned you?'

'Me? No. I'm only the housekeeper.'

'But you might have seen or heard something.'

'Yes, I might. But I shall tell you what else a housekeeper is, besides being a guardian of objects. A housekeeper is one who sees and hears *everything*, but pretends to know nothing. That is her role in the world, to keep everything closed and shuttered away within her.'

'Oh,' said Miss du Maurier, 'is that really true? What a fascinating thought. And the role of the writer, of course, is to prise open those shuttered and closed places and see what lies inside them. I could be dangerous to you and you would not notice it.'

I did not know what to say to this, so I kept silent. We were standing near the place where the breakers came in and I, who knew the tides, could tell that in a few moments, we would not be safe there. But I didn't move, or suggest that we move; it was as though I was challenging the water to come surging over our feet. It was Miss du Maurier who stepped back, just as a tall wave broke and came rushing upon the dry sand.

'Do let's go into the summer-house and make that cup of tea,' she said. 'And you can tell me about the tailor's shop in Warsaw and why your father chose to leave it. You can tell me what a Polish winter was like. You can tell me who or what you love.'

'Oh, I love no one,' I said quietly. 'I learned early, exactly as you said, that love lays "ghastly traps for the soul".'

I knew that Lord de Whithers would get up from his rest towards half past four and that I should be back at the Hall by then, in case he sent for me. He was a fair but strict employer and seemed to expect the staff to be available to him at all times. It was as though he could not imagine us having any life beyond that of serving his needs.

Normally, I would respect his wishes. I knew that I was very fortunate to have a position in such a substantial house and I never wished to do anything to put my job in jeopardy.

But that afternoon, in the summer-house, I lost all track of time.

Miss du Maurier and I talked for a long while. She lay on the daybed where I had once dreamed away an extraordinary night.

Her head was on a cushion and she fanned out her fair hair till the cushion was almost covered by it. I sat on the hard, wooden floor, faded almost to whiteness by the salt air. We drank tea and smoked cigarettes from Miss du Maurier's silver cigarette case.

And, then, without wishing it, I found myself caught in a vibrant reverie of the past, and I found that I wanted my revelations about this past to come out in a torrent, as though I believed that if they did, I might be liberated from my own history.

I told Miss du Maurier how my mother had died of consumption in the winter of 1923 and that her dying had been horrifying to witness – more horrifying than anything I thought I would ever know – and how, from that terrible day onwards, my father had become inflamed with the idea of getting away from Poland.

'I can well understand that,' said Miss du Maurier. 'If a beloved person dies, it's very hard to stay in the places they occupied.'

'It was not only that,' I said. 'It was because he couldn't conquer his fears for the future. He couldn't deceive himself. He always looked things in the eye and never pretended that what he saw was not really happening.'

'Ah yes,' said Miss du Maurier. 'I think I know what fears you're talking about: the worst that one can imagine.'

I nodded. Then I asked for another cigarette and Miss du Maurier lit it for me, because she saw that my hands were trembling. She gave it to me and I took a long pull of the smoke and felt it stir in my blood and make me bold. And so it was that I poured out the revelation that the Danowski family, along with all the other Jewish families we knew in Warsaw, lived with the understanding that they were despised.

Miss du Maurier sat very still and regarded me with her tender blue eyes. 'Was that how it felt,' she asked, 'that you were despised?'

'Despised. Hated. These are the words. There are no milder ones to convey it. And they – we – we all knew that the day would come when we would be driven away, cast out from everything that was familiar to us, and that all that would survive of us would be our longing and our sorrow. And so my father brought me to England.'

Miss du Maurier said nothing for a moment. I smoked my cigarette. Then she brought her hand to her brow and said: 'Mrs Danowski, I know this is very forward of me, but would you care to do me a charming little favour? I have a slight headache from the sherry I drank with Lord de Whithers at lunchtime. Would you kneel down by me, here, and stroke my forehead? I trespass upon dear women friends sometimes, to ask them to do this for me. They know I suffer fearfully from headaches and this always soothes them and makes them go away. Would you mind terribly? Men cannot do it; their touch is too heavy, you see. Even my husband, though he tries, it is never successful, and I have not been alone with a woman for a long time.'

I do not know exactly what time it was when I kneeled down beside her. I know the tide was in and the sea very loud and almost at our door. But I could not make myself think about anything that afternoon except the person who lay before me, the beautiful Miss du Maurier who had brought forth all the memories I had hardly ever spoken of, but who had also woken in me feelings I had not experienced since I was a teenage girl.

I did as she asked, stubbing out my cigarette, kneeling by her and putting my hand gently on her brow and stroking it. Her skin was smooth and soft and the perfume of her body heady and strong. After some while, I dared to put my face close to hers and whisper in her ear: 'I cannot do this, Miss du Maurier, without wishing to do more . . .'

'More?' she said. 'What more might one do? I expect you may have some wonderful suggestions?'

I could not answer her. I knew in that moment that I was her creature, that she could ask anything of me and I would do it. I felt as though I would be hers for the rest of time.

I put my arms around her and lifted her towards me. She was smiling her heartbreaking smile and did not pull away, but reached up and began to take out pins from my coiffure, so that my thick, dark hair cascaded around my shoulders and fell towards her face.

'Danni,' she whispered. 'Can I call you Danni? For I think, if you spell it with an "i" at the end, that is rather a beautiful name.'

'Call me anything you wish,' I said.

I have never before set down what happened that afternoon in the beach-house. When, in the dusk, we walked out from there, I knew that I was transfigured. I would never again be the person I had been before.

And then we parted. We walked up to the house and she got into her car and drove away from Manderville Hall and I did not know whether I would ever see her again.

As I went into the servants' hall, one of the kitchen maids, Patsy, came in and stared at me with a terrified look, as though she'd seen a ghost.

'Whatever have you done to yourself, Mrs D?' she said.

'Done? I've done nothing,' I replied. 'Get on with your work, Patsy.'

But then I rushed up the back stairs to my room and looked at myself in the small mirror hanging beside my bed. My mouth was bleeding. And I realised I was clutching something in my hand, also spotted with blood. It was a gossamer-soft linen handkerchief with the initials DdM embroidered upon it.

As the days unwound towards September, unvarying in their routine, devoid of any word or any sight of Miss du Maurier, I began to pine like a dog. I cried in my bed. I walked about Manderville Hall with a slow step.

Often, I took out the embroidered handkerchief, which I had tenderly washed by hand in the mildest soap, and held it against my cheek. I considered sending it to Miss du Maurier's house at Fowey. I thought I would send it with some short note asking whether I might be able 'to cure you of a headache when next you suffer in this way'. But pride prevented me from writing.

I knew that I had to wait. I was Miss du Maurier's servant.

I had to wait for her to send word to me.

And then, on one of my days off, a fine September afternoon, I decided to go down to the beach-house. I had not gone there since the afternoon with Miss du Maurier, not wishing to find myself alone in the place where I had been transfigured by another. But something drew me there on this day and I told myself that I might lie on the daybed where I had lain with her and dream my way into a solitary rapture that might still my feelings and let me return to being the person I had been before I laid my hand on her pale brow.

The sun glinted gold on a calm sea and as I neared the little cove, I saw a small motor boat pulled up upon the sand and anchored in the shallow water. I stopped and stared. This was Manderville Hall's private beach and every soul who lived round about knew that they should not trespass there. I considered returning to the house to fetch Lord de Whithers, but I knew that he would be taking his habitual afternoon rest and I had no wish to disturb him. So I went on. People have often observed that, being very tall and dark, I have 'an intimidating presence' and I seldom feel afraid of an encounter — even with strangers who might be in the throes of some wrong-doing. My heart was beating a little fast, but on I went, down and down, rehearsing in my mind a firm but polite invitation to the owner of the motor boat to weigh anchor and depart.

On the dry sand, footsteps were visible, leading from the boat to the door of the beach-house. I stopped for a moment and looked at them, but could deduce nothing from them. Setting back my shoulders and walking with a firm step, I strode to the door and opened it.

Miss du Maurier lay on the daybed. She had covered her body with an old blanket Lady de Whithers had always kept nearby, and she appeared to be fast asleep. One arm reached down towards the floor. Near her hand was an ashtray with several cigarette butts in it, each one tenderly marked with her scarlet lipstick.

I stood quite still and looked at her. No angel in paradise could have appeared more beautiful to me than she appeared at that moment.

Very quietly, I slipped off my coat and kneeled down by

the bed. Miss du Maurier sighed and opened her eyes and saw me and bathed me with her radiant smile.

'Danni,' she whispered. 'Here you are. I came here on your day off last week, but you never appeared. Do you like my little boat? I'm rather good at navigating and using the tides, and luckily it's not very far from—'

I put my hand on her mouth, then put my lips where my hand had been. And I felt, in the next moments, that her yearning for me had been as great as mine had been for her. And we were a long time at this wicked loving of ours, not being able to let go of it, but always searching for more, until we lay exhausted on the bed and the light at the window began to fade.

The motor boat had no running lights. Miss du Maurier at last stood up and adjusted her clothes and told me that she would have to leave, or be drowned in the dark.

'Do not drown, madam,' I said.

She came to me and touched my face. 'I've asked myself if I should resist you,' she said. 'I know that I should. I know that we are terrible sinners. But, God forgive me, Danni, you are too strong to be resisted. So I shall not try.'

So began the great and only love affair of my life.

The beach-house was our hiding place, our refuge, the place where no other soul ever came. On Thursday afternoons (except for those when Miss du Maurier had to go to London on business or attend some military function with her husband), I would come down the steep path at two o'clock and see the boat pulled up on the sand and then I would see my own shadow going before me on the sand as I went to the door and opened it and my beloved called to me.

There was a darkness in it. The darkness made us faint with such great fear that sometimes all we could do was cling to each other and weep and I knew it was a darkness such as my father had felt when he decided to leave his country. He saw what Time might bring, and Miss du Maurier and I saw it. Though she confessed to me that she rejoiced in the 'boy within her' and was only truly happy when she gave that 'boy' his passionate rein, she also knew that the day would come when she would have to bury him again, put him back in what she called his 'box' or his 'coffin'. 'And then, Danni,' she said, 'we will have to part and never see each other again.'

She told me about her soldier husband, whom she admired, but whose embrace she only submitted to and did not like. But she venerated her own married state. 'That,' she said, 'is what the world sees: that I am the wife of Major Browning. And what the world sees must not be obscured. I know you understand.'

I understood. But I didn't wish to talk about this. One day, when Miss du Maurier was describing her life with Major Browning and her pride in his bravery and the sweet solitude he allowed her in which she wrote her books, I had a violent urge to put my hand on her pale neck and tighten its grip. I began talking in Polish. In this remembered language that she could not understand, I told her that I would kill her rather than allow her to leave me. And I heard her laugh. She *laughed at my pain*.

'Danni,' she said, 'sometimes you look as though you

could be very cruel, but of course this is thrilling beyond measure. I shall have to use it.'

A year passed. During that time, I was the fortunate recipient of many gifts from my lover, including a chinchilla coat, which I wear to this day, because I love it so. And, though I'm now cast out from Miss du Maurier's heart, I still remember that only two people in my life truly clothed me with care: my father and Miss du Maurier. And it seems to me that in all the time when I was not clothed by them, I was naked and cold and my flesh knew only suffering.

Towards the end of that year, on a Thursday afternoon in September, when Miss du Maurier and I lay in each other's arms on the daybed, I on my back and she above me, with her breasts and her thighs soft against mine and only the thin blanket covering us, I saw a shadow of a woman approaching the door of the summer-house.

I put my hand on Miss du Maurier's mouth, to prevent her from saying a word. I stared at the door. On came the shadow, silhouetted against the slanting sun. And then we both heard footsteps, firm upon the sand.

The door was locked. We always took this precaution, making the summer-house appear to be as shuttered and empty as it had been after Lady de Whithers' death. And the curtains to the small window were also drawn, giving to our sanctuary a soft and mellow light in which we both, to each other, seemed to be creatures of ravishing beauty. But these curtains were thin and I had never been certain that they fully concealed the interior of the summer-house.

Whoever it was who now stood at the door, rattled the

door handle. Miss du Maurier buried her head in my neck and I held her fast against me and I could feel her frantic heartbeat betraying her fear. The door handle was tried again and the door itself shaken. Then the woman went to the window and tried to see through the drawn curtains. Her head moved this way and that, trying to find a tiny gap in the curtains. There was no gap. (As a housekeeper, I knew exactly how to close curtains and fold one side gently over the other at the centre, so that no gap existed.) But the head kept moving – as though the woman *knew* that something was occurring in the summer-house, and the notion that she could *see us*, even as indistinct figures shrouded in our blanket, made me feel faint, the more so because I now recognised who the woman was: it was Miss Adelaide Waverley, future chatelaine of Manderville Hall.

We could do nothing except lie still and petrified, clinging to each other. Neither of us dared whisper even a word. We were as terrified as soldiers hiding in a shallow bunker from an enemy who was about to blow our lives away. I could feel that Miss du Maurier was on the very edge of breaking down into sobbing and I clamped my arms more tightly around her.

I do not know how long we had to stay like this, cleaving together, aware of Death stalking us round and round. But at last, we heard the footsteps retreating and then fading to silence.

We got up and crept about the place, putting on our clothes.

We did not speak. I pinned up my hair, which was perfumed with my lover's scent.

Later, in the blackest darkness, we walked out and went

towards the boat. I looked up at the sky, to see if the moon was up to guide Miss du Maurier on her sea journey, but there was no moon.

'Take care,' I whispered. I touched her face, but she pulled back from my touch and only looked at me with sorrow and devastation, as though I were some animal she had inadvertently wounded. We pushed the boat out and she got into it and started the motor and drew up the anchor and I stood alone on the beach listening to the ticking sound of the engine and the slap of the water as she pulled further and further out into the bay.

What did I expect?

In my love for her, and with my knowledge of her world, I expected her to leave me for a while. I knew that one Thursday would pass and then another and another and she would not come to the summer-house. But I also expected that, in the end, she would come, that she would not be able to resist, that the 'boy' in her would not forever be confined in his coffin but start to long again for my touch. And so I waited for her. I waited and she did not come. As each week passed, I waited with a fainter and fainter heart.

I began letters to her, but did not send them. I lay in my little room, with my chinchilla coat wrapped around me, and I thought how my life in England, in the service of others more fortunate than me, and for whom I waited endlessly to know their will, had been, in its essence, a mistaken life.

So convinced of this did I become that, in the cold of February, when I at last admitted to myself that Miss du Maurier – in her terror of being discovered with me and of being shamed for this by the world in which we both had to live and breathe – would never return to the summer-house or seek me out anywhere, I went to see Lord de Whithers and told him that I had decided to leave Manderville Hall.

'Leave?' he said. '*Leave?* My dear woman, nobody leaves Manderville Hall unless they're chucked out on their ear. Whatever are you thinking of? Where are you to find better employment in more beautiful surroundings than here?'

'Nowhere, m'lord,' I said. 'I have been very fortunate at Manderville. It is something else.'

'Something else? What d'you mean, Mrs Danowski?'

'Well, sir, it is this. I have a little money saved. I am going to Padstow to set myself up in a small way . . .'

'Set yourself up? What can you possibly be talking about?'

'In a small commercial enterprise. I was taught to sew by my father who, as you know, was a tailor by profession.'

'Yes. A Jew tailor. But I thought you had got beyond all that. I thought we had rescued you from that.'

'Rescued me?'

'From that Jew business. Because I've told you before, it's best to forget all that – especially with the hardening of attitudes in Germany and so forth that we hear about now. Better to meld in. Let me remind and warn you. Far better to meld in here at Manderville, as you have done very well, and just put all that behind you.'

I was standing as straight and tall as I could in the drawing room, but now I felt a little dizzy and had to reach out and hold onto the back of a fragile Louis XVI chair upholstered in blue brocade.

'I understand what you're saying, Lord de Whithers,' I

said, 'but the truth is that I am who I am and I will never be anyone else. Never. And, before it's too late, I would like to try to run an independent life.'

Lord de Whithers began scratching his head. His look was now very severe. 'Independent life!' he scoffed. 'Independent life? Do you know what on earth you're saying? Do you know how much you've been protected here?'

'Yes, I think I do, sir.'

'Well then, how are you going to survive – without Manderville food, without Manderville light, without Manderville money and hot water and allowances for your clothes, not to mention the fresh air that you breathe and the freedom that you have to walk where you will in the park and by the sea and, most importantly, my willingness to overlook you origins? You tell me how.'

My dizziness was now so troubling, I thought that I might fall down in a faint. I clutched at the insubstantial chair. I knew that my voice was almost inaudible as I said: 'I have been told that in Padstow, as in other towns, no doubt, in these times we are living through, there is a return to *mending*. People cannot afford new clothes as they did in the nineteen twenties, so there is a return to having old things made new by needlework. And I am very skilled at this, as your late wife knew. I used to mend Lady de Whithers' underwear and petticoats if they had been inadvertently torn.'

'Torn? *Torn*? What d'you mean? They were never torn. Torn by what or by whom?'

'I don't know, sir. But I am very skilled at what they now call "invisible mending". And I have found a small shop to rent. I will take in old and torn things and try to make them serviceable by my skill.'

Lord de Whithers stared at me for a moment, then picked up his copy of the *Daily Telegraph* and resumed his reading of it.

'What you've told me, Mrs Danowski, is all complete, unadulterated nonsense,' he barked. 'I can't be doing with it. So either you must retract it all or you had better leave as soon as possible.'

The year I left Manderville Hall was 1937.

It was a cold February day, but before my taxi arrived, I went down to the beach and opened the door of the summer-house and went in.

I had cleaned and aired it after that last afternoon with Miss du Maurier, and yet it seemed to me exactly as it had been when we lay together on the daybed, and I longed to take a photograph of it, so that I would never forget it. I imagined myself old, staring at the faded picture and remembering that this place had contained all that I would ever know of love. Then I closed it and locked the door. I looked out at the bay and saw, far out, a small boat making its way round the headland on a calm sea. There were children in the boat and I could hear their laughter, carried towards me by the breeze.

My little enterprise, *Danni's Invisible Mending*, located on Padstow high street, next door to a fish shop, was sufficiently successful to provide me with an income equal to my needs.

I had bought myself a solid and beautiful Singer Sewing Machine, with a foot treadle beneath the ironwork table.

I decided to position myself, with the machine, in the window – so that passers-by could observe for themselves how busy and industrious I was.

Some people entered the shop out of curiosity, to observe my skill close up. And one day the following year, 1938, a well-dressed woman came in and, smiling, said she had mistaken me for waxwork or a mannequin, because I sat so still.

'No, no,' I said. 'I am quite real. And I undertake repair work of all kinds. I've recently acquired an elasticated thread, made in France, with which I can repair corsets and girdles, if that might be your wish.'

This woman now stared at me. She was a tall and beautiful lady with a fox fur draped about her shoulders.

'I'm sorry,' she said, 'but your face is very familiar to me. Where might I have seen you before?'

I put down my work. 'I don't know,' I said. 'For many years I was housekeeper at Manderville Hall and—'

'That's it!' she said. 'We came to a ball at Manderville when Lady de Whithers was alive. I remember you. You glided about everywhere, making sure that everything was just-so. And I said to Lady de Whithers, "Your housekeeper is clearly a marvellously committed person. I don't suppose you'd lend her to me if I ever give a ball?"'

'Ah,' I said. 'And what did Lady de Whithers say?'

'She said, "Certainly not! We rely on her absolutely. Without her, Manderville would descend into disorder and chaos." But now you're here. I expect poor old Lord de With misses you terribly.'

'I don't know, madam. I don't suppose he does.'

'Ah well, things change. Nothing lasts for ever. But they say Manderville Hall has been immortalised in a book, and I was just on my way to the library—'

'Immortalised?'

'That's what I heard. This new novel, *Rebecca*, by Daphne du Maurier. She calls the house "Manderley", but they say that Manderville Hall was really the prime inspiration for the setting. Who knows if that's true?'

I sat very still. A shaft of pale sunlight came through the window and glinted on the black sewing machine. Then I said: 'I met Miss du Maurier once. She came to lunch with Lord de Whithers. I thought she was a very beautiful person.'

The library told me that I would have to wait at least a fortnight to get a copy of *Rebecca*. The book had been hailed as Daphne du Maurier's finest work and it was in great demand.

So I waited. I was not much in the habit of reading, for in all my life's work I'd felt tired at the end of each day and I often fell asleep with a book in my hand. But I wanted to read *Rebecca*. I had the fanciful notion that, by setting the novel at Manderville Hall, Miss du Maurier might, somewhere in the book, contrive to send me a coded message, a message that revealed how strong and true her feelings for me had been.

But then I acquired the book.

My foolish thought about a 'coded message' only betrayed what a naïve person I was in my heart. For I soon enough discovered myself in the novel's horrible mystery. Not 'Danni' who had been loving and tender, but 'Danny', the 'black figure', Mrs Danvers, with vampire's eyes and a white face, like a skull; Mrs Danvers, who is ugly and diseased with jealousy and wears her dark hair piled upon her head; Mrs Danvers who tortures Mr de Winter's young bride by invoking the beauty of his former wife, Rebecca, by opening a wardrobe in her bedroom 'in the west wing' and showing her Rebecca's dresses and furs; Mrs Danvers, who – in her obsession with the drowned and beautiful Rebecca – never ceases to scheme and plot and lay traps for the hapless heroine, and who, at the end of it all, burns down the house and everybody and everything inside it.

I returned the book to the library. It was difficult for me to utter a word about it, but I did manage to tell the librarian that I had not liked it at all.

All of this happened a long time ago, before the war came and destroyed so many lives, and I have to tell myself that I am lucky to be alive and running my little mending business and to be the owner of a chinchilla coat.

But I know that I have been physically affected by Miss du Maurier's decision to make a villain out of me. My skin is very white and dry and the bones of my skull are clearly visible beneath this white skin. I think I am probably frightening to look at, ugly in fact, as ugly as she made me in the book.

I examine my features for signs of evil. I ask myself whether, one day, I shall not take some bitter revenge upon Miss du Maurier, who stole my name and my soul and made me bad. But I doubt that I will, because sometimes I dream that, after I left Manderville Hall, she came once more to the beach.

I dream that she found the summer-house locked and shuttered.

I dream that she tried to peer in through the curtained windows, as Adelaide Waverley had done. I tell myself that she walked up to the house and waited until Lord de

Whithers rose from his afternoon rest and then asked him whether she might see me. And of course Lord de Whithers told her that I was gone – gone without leaving any forwarding address.

I dream that it was this – this knowledge that she would never find me because I did not want to be found – that wounded her so deeply that she decided, in her novel, to turn me into a monster.

These things I dream, lying in my room, listening to the sound of the sea. But I will never know the truth of what she felt. I know only that the novel, *Rebecca*, has now been read by millions of people all over the world. And I am at the heart of it, the evil spirit of Manderley, the jealous destroyer.

Sometimes, I remember what the librarian said when I told him that I disliked the novel.

'You're in a minority,' he sniffed. '*Rebecca* is a triumph, possibly a masterpiece.'

Smithy

His name was Reginald Smith, but people always called him Smithy. And, as he aged, the name 'Reginald' moved away backwards in time and attached itself to a thin boy, once photographed alone on a beach, holding in his hand a miniature Union Jack. At the boy's feet was a sandcastle, surrounded by a frail wall of shells. Beyond the limits of the picture, raged the cold North Sea.

Every day now, through every season, Smithy went for the same walk. He was eighty years old, but an upright man. He walked down to his garden gate and let himself out into the road and trod this road for a quarter of a mile, then turned left and climbed a stile into a green lane, known as Blackthorn End. After a few steps, the quiet of Blackthorn End would gather itself around him. On either side of the path, poplars grew. In front of the poplars were hedges of holly and hawthorn and dog-rose. Beyond the trees, were meadows where horses grazed and these horses would often amble to their wire fence and stare at Smithy, and he would stop and listen to their breathing. Sometimes, in this moment of stillness, he would find himself thinking about Reginald, with his miniature flag, and how, on that same beach,

Reginald had once been lifted onto the back of a pony. He'd
held onto the pony's coarse mane while a man led the animal
up and down under a hot sun. This burning sun had felt so
heavy on Reginald's neck and back, he'd begun to lean
further and further forwards until he lost his footing in the
stirrups and the man had shouted, 'Sit up, boy! Sit up!' and
he'd felt afraid. And afterwards he'd been ill for a while
and lain in a room somewhere, in some unfamiliar room, and
his mother had come and gone with bowls of custard.
'Lovely custard,' she'd said. Come and gone with her lovely
custard and then disappeared for ever. And after that, what?
He couldn't remember exactly. His life just going on, he
supposed: that solitary thing, his life as 'Smithy'.

Though Smithy enjoyed watching and listening to the
horses, he never stopped for long at the top of Blackthorn
End, because he had a task to perform. He'd appointed
himself the guardian of the lane. Every day, he removed
from it anything left behind by other people: chocolate
wrappers, lager cans, cigarette stubs, plastic bottles and
carrier bags. Condoms. The days when there was nothing
to pick up were few. Smithy put all this garbage into a
garden refuse sack and took it home, where he sorted it
according to the council's Recycling Instructions, and then,
tired from his walk, he sat down in an old armchair and
fell asleep. Sometimes, he dreamed he was working once
again at the last job he'd had before his long-delayed retirement, planting trees on motorway verges and cuttings and
embankments: row upon row of thin saplings in green
protective tubing on a vale of earth that seemed, on certain
days, to be as endless and as heartless as the Great Wall of
China. Looking down the line of his fellow workers on this

job, Smithy had once remarked to the man next to him that the group resembled a chain-gang from the American South. The man was black and young and strong. He'd straightened up and stared down at the roaring traffic on the six-lane road and said: 'Are you, like, living in the past, Smithy?'

'Probably,' Smithy had replied, 'but don't worry, lad. I'll be put out to grass soon.'

On a February afternoon, with the horses gone from the meadows and a cold rain falling, Smithy saw something enormous and unfamiliar lying by the dog-rose hedge, halfway along Blackthorn End. Upright and slow, he walked towards it. Its colour was a dull purple and it looked bloated by the winter damp. It was a brocade-covered mattress. Smithy looked down at it. The brocade was torn along one of its edges and, from this rent, an evacuation of grey-white stuffing emerged. Smithy turned and stared at the lane behind him – the bit of Blackthorn End he'd just walked – as though there might be some clue here as to how and why the repulsive mattress had arrived at this spot. He stood absolutely still for some while, shifting his gaze from the lane unravelling behind him to the purple mattress lying there in front of him. He felt sick and troubled. The rain kept falling. He put his hands in the pockets of his tweed coat to try to warm them. Then, instead of completing his walk, he went home.

He hung his damp clothes across the backs of chairs in front of his kitchen range and ran himself a bath. He soaped his body, and then lay there in the bath, watching the steam put a grey bloom on the window. He stared at the tops of his feet, sticking up like mouldy rock-cakes from the cream of scummy water. And he thought how, occasionally in his life, things weren't what they seemed to be – just as his feet were not rock-cakes and nor were the motorway workers part of a chain-gang – and that what he'd imagined to have been a mattress lying in the green lane was, in fact, something else? But what could that 'something' possibly be?

The following day was bright and, as usual, after his lunch of bread and butter and pickled beets, Smithy tugged on his coat and his boots and set out for his walk, with the refuse sack stuffed into his pocket. His lunch felt sour in his stomach. Though he'd never believed in any Saviour of Mankind, he found himself stupidly praying, 'Let that thing not be there.' More than this, he wanted it *never to have been there*. He much preferred to admit that he'd had a moment of senile hallucination than that there should be something so disgusting and out of place lying halfway along his precious Blackthorn End.

Yet there it lay.

Smithy's heart was beating like a tired dog's. Who had put the mattress there – and why and how? There were padlocked gates at each end of the lane, to stop cars driving down it, and only the farmer, Gerry Woolner, had the padlock keys. Someone, then, had lugged it by hand over the stile, then carried it or dragged it eighty or ninety paces. Smithy's gaze returned to these eighty or ninety paces, because he still thought that some answer had to lie on that bit of the lane, yet the lane appeared exactly and precisely as it always did on a winter afternoon, with the sun low in the sky and the grass muddy at its edge and the shadows of the poplars narrow and faint across the path. It was as if the land were saying to Smithy, 'There's no explanation in hedges and trees or stones, boy; the explanation is in you.'

He mumbled aloud that it wasn't his land. He'd never owned any part of Blackthorn End. How, then, could he be expected to take responsibility for it? All right, he was the self-appointed guardian of the place. Out of affection for it, and because he preferred things to be orderly and clean, he tried to keep it litter-free. But a purple mattress was different. It was too large and heavy a thing for him. In childhood, he'd been skinny and prone to fear; now, he was old. And in between these two, there had been only work, a succession of days, the rushing by of traffic on a motorway.

He called Gerry Woolner and Woolner said: 'You still alive, Smithy? Crikey.' Smithy asked Woolner to pick up the mattress on his trailer and take it to the council dump, but Woolner said, no, he wouldn't bother doing that, he'd see to it in the spring, when he could dry the thing out and burn it. Then he told Smithy to keep warm because a cold snap was coming, and hung up.

Smithy didn't know what else he could do, so he lay down on his narrow bed and covered himself with his old green eiderdown.

He felt shivery and full of pain. He would have liked some unobtrusive person to come into his room with a bowl of custard.

He lingered in his room as days and nights came and went.

He saw ice on the window and couldn't bear to move. He heard the roof timbers of his cottage creaking under the pantiles and the wind harrying the sycamore trees. Through his mind tumbled a reckless counting of all the small things he'd tried to achieve in eighty years.

On the fourth or fifth day, Smithy noticed pale sunlight glancing on the eiderdown and he got up and dressed himself and went to the range to get warm, but the range had gone out. So he knew then that what he'd been postponing couldn't be postponed any more.

He went in search of his coat and boots and found them, creased and muddy, under his bed. He put them on, then discovered a pair of old leather mittens balled up among his underwear, and tugged these on and a woollen scarf that snagged against the stubble on his neck. Then, with slow steps, he walked out of his door and down to the garden gate.

The quarter mile along the road seemed to take Smithy a ridiculously long time. He saw that when he reached the stile, the sun had already gone from the lane and was dropping towards the horizon, under a vault of green sky. Smithy tried to walk faster, but his legs were weak and he couldn't make his body move as he wanted it to. The lane, once he reached it, lay all in shadow, but he could see, nevertheless, that the mattress remained there, exactly as it had been.

Smithy felt warm now – hot almost – from the exertions of his walk and he could hear his own breath, like the breath of the horses in the dark. Mustering all his strength, he bent down and took hold of the two cloth handles on the side of the mattress and tugged it towards him. It was far heavier than he'd imagined, but he kept pulling and straining until he got it clear of the grass and onto the rough stones of the path. For a moment, he waited and rested, then, instructing himself to endure, he hauled the mattress upwards till it was standing on its edge. He hoped that, in this position, he'd be able to shuffle sideways with it, step by slow step, till he was back at the stile. Then, he'd let it fall against his body as he heaved himself over the stile, and from his elevated position on the further side of the stile, be able to haul the mattress up onto the cross-post and from there, pull it onto the road. Once on the road, Smithy told himself, the relative smoothness of the tarmac surface would help him. He might be able to drag the mattress behind him like a sled, drag it through the darkness till he reached the cottage gate, and then, when daylight returned, he'd douse it with petrol and burn it and bury the ashes deep.

But Smithy was, as yet, a long way from the road. He managed his sideways shuffling for only a few paces and then the whole weight of the mattress seemed to fall against him, so that he almost toppled backwards, and, to save himself, had to let go of one of the cloth handles, to push the thing away. But his balance was poor. His feet, in the heavy boots, seemed to tangle with each other, and when the mattress tipped away from him, he fell onto it and lay there with his face pressed into the purple brocade.

He remained like this for a moment, inhaling a fusty smell, a smell that was of the earth, but also had about it the stench of human dreams. Then, he pushed hard down with his elbow and with his right knee and eventually managed to turn his body, so that he was lying on his back. He was breathing hard.

Smithy lay there and didn't move. A voice, familiar through time, shouted at him to sit up, sit up! But although, in his exhausted heart, he knew that a stained mattress, heavy with damp, was a fearful thing on which to be lying, what he now began to experience was a comforting stillness of body and mind. He couldn't explain it to himself, but it was almost as though, quite unexpectedly, he'd arrived at some extraordinary place, a place that – perhaps – had been near him all his life, but which he'd never dared to visit.

After a while, Smithy could gauge, by the brightness of the winter stars, that the night would be very cold, and he knew that he should rouse himself and go home. Yet somehow, he didn't feel inclined to do this. He remained where he was on the mattress and began repeating aloud the three syllables of his old name: Reginald. And the saying of his name made him smile and he thought of the boy on the beach, bumping along on the pony, and the roaring of the waves as they came in, and the pity of the flying years.

BlackBerry Winter

It was getting towards Christmas. The day had been bright in London, but by the time Fran reached the house in the wood, the air was freezing.

The house in the wood was her mother's house and her mother's name was Peggy, and Peggy was becoming old and angry and rude. Fran didn't want to be there, but she had no choice. Peggy had broken her right arm, when she tripped over 'some bit of dreadful metal dumped in the wood'. She'd said to Fran: 'It could have been a gin trap! I could have been cut in half.'

She wasn't cut in half, only made helpless and cross by the plaster cast and the pain. She said to Fran the moment she arrived: 'I can't do a thing. I've got no balance. I can't even walk properly. You'll have to take over.'

Fran went to embrace her mother, but Peggy fended her off. 'No, no,' she cried out, 'I can't be touched. You'll crush me.'

So Fran left her and went upstairs to her room, which was the room she'd always had, right from when she was ten years old and the family moved to Norfolk, to the house in the wood. It was cold in here. Fran turned on a little two-bar electric fire. Then she went to the window and looked out and saw the December sun declining behind the oaks and sycamores and putting a light like moonshine on the narrow river that skirted the wood, known as 'The Trib'. Long ago, Fran and her brother James had paddled down The Trib in a canoe and pretended to be Tahitians, and Fran now remembered that pretending to be Tahitians had made them so stupidly happy that it had been difficult, in all the years since then, to come by such gladness again.

Right now, all that Fran could see in her life was a possible *route* to happiness (or what politicians liked to call a *Road Map*), but the truth was that this road map, like so many others in the wider world, had been in place for two years and hadn't yet led to its destination. This destination was to become the wife of her lover, David.

Disappointingly for Fran, David, who was a professor of English and a part-time poet and a person with a velvet voice, remained with the wife he already had, a parliamentary lobbyist called Maeve. He trembled always on the precipice of leaving Maeve, but he did not leave. And it was now Fran's belief that, to make David leap from his present life to a future life with her, something was needed that would make her suddenly stand out in magnificence in his mind. David prized achievement above anything else, and what held Fran back from winning him, she knew, was her own lack of it.

'You're not far off fifty,' Peggy was fond of reminding her, 'and what have you done with your life? Made Christmas decorations out of sacking.'

'Sacking,' Fran had responded, 'is an honest and lovely fabric, but you're not being honest, Mother. I'm a working partner in a successful gift shop, which happens to specialise in homecrafts.'

'Well,' said Peggy, 'if you want to glorify a bit of sewing, that's up to you.'

Fran unpacked her clothes and put them in her old wardrobe, which used to creak and grumble in the night, like something alive. Then, she sat down on the single bed and took out her BlackBerry and emailed David. She told him that she almost wished Peggy had been sliced in half by the gin trap; she told him that the moonshine on The Trib had made her long to be a Tahitian again; she told him that her love for him was as dark and familiar as the wood. When she signed off and contemplated her evening alone with Peggy and the TV, she experienced thirty seconds of wanting to be dead.

In the night, came a harsh winter storm, blowing out of nowhere, tormenting the trees, sending a month's rainfall in six hours to swell The Trib till it flooded over and swept the debris of the wood down into Peggy's garden.

Tired from her drive from London, Fran slept so deeply that she didn't hear the storm, nor her mother crying out from her bed. Then, she was woken by something beating on her shoulder, and it was Peggy's walking stick pounding her, and she saw Peggy as a huge shape in the dark, like the shape of a horse and rider that had come into the room.

The electricity was out. Fran got up and groped for her dressing gown. She helped Peggy into the single bed, still warm from her own body, and covered her gently, as she might have covered a child. Then she went down to the kitchen to find candles and a torch. She stumbled about in the dark, shivering, violently confused by the arrangement of the kitchen units and the arrangement of her life. She yearned for David.

She found two candles in silver candle-holders and lit these and carried them up to Peggy, who turned her terrified face towards them and said: 'Not those! They belong in the dining room.'

Fran set down the candles and said nothing. She took an old blanket from the wardrobe and covered herself with this and sat in a chair, and they waited for morning. By Fran's chair was a bookcase and Fran took out a book at random and saw that it was called *The Circus in the Attic and Other Stories* by Robert Penn Warren, published in 1947, and she said, 'I'm going to read to you, Mother. It'll calm your nerves and help time to pass.'

'Not necessarily,' said Peggy. 'Not unless you read very well. Reading aloud is a lot more difficult than sewing.'

Fran ignored this and said: 'This is a story called *Blackberry Winter*. Are you listening?'

'I suppose so,' said Peggy. 'I have no choice.'

'Right. Here's the story: *It was getting into June and past eight o'clock in the morning but there was a fire – even if it wasn't a big fire, just a fire of chunks – on the hearth of the big stone fireplace—*'

'Chunks of what?' interrupted Peggy. 'Chunks of *what*?'

'Peat,' said Fran. 'That's my guess.'

The morning revealed the devastation.

Rotting leaves, moss, beech-nuts, toadstools, broken branches, tangles of briars and stones had been swept out of the wood by the swollen Trib and were piled up like trash all over Peggy's lawns and flower beds. In between the piles, were pools of water. The Trib flowed on in its new wide path. The wind had died.

Fran didn't want her mother to see this. The only thing, animate or inanimate, Peggy loved was her garden. Fran told her to stay put in the bed, but she refused. She had to be helped to the window and she stood there, leaning on the stick and cursing.

'Where's Thomas?' she said at last. 'Where the hell is he? Go and get him and tell him to start putting everything straight. The sight of this will kill me.'

Thomas lived alone in a bungalow beyond the wood, and, since losing his wife, had scraped a living tending other people's gardens. But he was old now, and as stubborn as Peggy and forgetful and sad.

When he opened his door to Fran, he was wearing his pyjamas. In his mouth was a thin cigarette. On his kitchen table was a colander and a muddy stem of home-grown Brussels sprouts.

He lit a small gas burner and made Fran a cup of tea. Then, he started picking off the sprouts and said: 'Listen to me, Miss Fran, and don't take umbrage. Your ma, she'll be the death of me. Crikey, she will. The miz'ry she give me, you wouldn't believe.'

'I would believe,' said Fran.

'I know why you've come – to ask me to put everything right. Your ma wants all that muck swept back into the wood. But some things can't get back to where they were. Crikey, no. So you tell her this: it's beyond me, Miss Fran. I know we've got Christmas soon, but I can't help that. I'm an old man. You tell your ma Nature's done her job and that's the end of it.'

'So you won't be coming any more, Thomas? Is that what you're saying?'

'No, I won't be coming any more. I'm saying it. That storm talked to me loud and plain.'

Fran walked back slowly through the wood. Pale sunlight fell in thin cascades along her path and the air felt suddenly warm, like spring air, when the winter has come and gone. She felt tired, strangely peaceful, content to drift. When her BlackBerry bleeped, she was startled, and her heart began to beat faster, as it always did when she saw that there was an email from David.

Are you OK up there? he wrote. *What a fantastic storm! Replicated here at home when Maeve found your poem on my BlackBerry. Never mind. I think it has the makings of a good poem. What d'you say to becoming a two-poet household? I love you. David.*

Fran sat down on the grey roots of a beech tree. It seemed to her that few moments of her life had been as beautiful as this one.

She sat without moving for a long time, imagining all the future Christmas Days she would spend with David, walking by the Thames, visiting friends, drinking mulled wine or champagne, exchanging presents at twilight. Then she scrolled to her Sent Messages on her BlackBerry and stared at the mail she'd sent to David the previous evening, describing the moonshine on The Trib, her longing to be a Tahitian again and her love for him 'as dark and familiar as the wood'. And she saw that, as occasionally happened, the BlackBerry had broken up her lines in peculiar places, so that what had been prose had suddenly, fraudulently, taken on the density and seeming economy of a poem.

Fran laughed. Perhaps, she thought, if you live with someone you love, everything becomes easy and accessible to you – even writing poetry. She replied to David's mail with the one word, *Yes*. Then she walked back to the house in the wood and made breakfast for Peggy on an old camping stove, whose blue flame threatened always to flicker and die, but never did.

While she spooned eggs into Peggy's mouth, she told her that Thomas was too ill to work today, but that she, Fran, would spend the day clearing the garden and that by evening, everything would be better.

'Don't be so stupid,' said Peggy. 'You can't do it. You don't know a thing about gardens. I'll wait for Thomas.'

'Thomas isn't coming back,' said Fran.

'Of course he's coming back.'

'No,' said Fran. 'He's not. The storm talked to him. He's made up his mind.'

Lucy and Gaston

Southwold Beach, Suffolk, England, June 1976

When the others decide to go swimming, Lucy stays in her deckchair. She watches them run towards the ocean – husband, daughter, friends. They're the dearest people in the world to her.

The day is hot and Lucy's head is sweating under her straw hat. Lucy's daughter, Hannah, tries to persuade her to come with them to the water, 'just as far as the edge, Mum, just to paddle and cool off'. So she gets up from her deckchair, wondering whether, this time, in this affectionate company, she'll be able to bear it and not shrink from it any more: the chill of the sea. But then, she raises her head and sees it complete, the vast and heartless, shining bay, and she sits down again and says to Hannah, 'No, sorry, darling. I'm not ready.'

Hannah, who is an almost-beautiful young woman of thirty-two, takes Lucy's hand in hers. As the others begin a little joyful race towards the breaking waves, she says gently, 'Do you think you ever will be ready?'

'I don't know,' says Lucy. 'I keep thinking something will happen, and then I won't feel it any more and I'll be OK.

But that day doesn't seem to come. I'm fifty-six and it still hasn't come. I know it's pathetic. I really am sorry.'

Hannah kisses the hand she was holding and returns it tenderly to her mother's side. 'You don't need to be sorry. Nobody minds. It's just you we're thinking about.'

'I know. And on a day like this, in this heat, it's ridiculous, but there we are.'

Lucy tries to light a cigarette. Her hand holding the lighter shakes. The lighter flame is snuffed out by the breeze. Hannah calmly takes everything, lights the cigarette and gives it to Lucy and when Lucy has inhaled a long draught of it, she says: 'I had a dream about him last night.'

'About Dad?'

'That dream I have sometimes. Mermaids, or young women like mermaids, swim down to him. He's lying there on the seabed. Absolutely just as beautiful as he was. And the women, or mermaids or whatever they are, start chattering to each other, saying, "Hey, look at this man. So sweet in his uniform. Isn't he a darling?"

'And they cluster round Dad. They stroke him. They don't kiss him. It's not erotic, really. They just stroke him till all the creases in his uniform are gone and his hair – you remember his blond hair in the photographs? – is all smoothed down and tidy. Then, one of them says, "we'd better go. He's not ours." And they swim away.'

'I think that's quite a lovely dream, Mum,' says Hannah. 'And they were right: he wasn't theirs. He was yours.'

'Well, yes, just for the briefest time. Just long enough to give me you.'

The two women are quiet. Lucy smokes. Hannah looks to where her stepfather, Ray, and his friends, Peter and

Monica, are now making their way through the low breakers, jumping like children. Along the beach comes a man on an old bicycle, selling iced Coca-Cola from a little cart drawn after the bike.

'Darling,' says Lucy, 'that would be lovely. A Coke. Wouldn't it?'

The farm of La Charité, south of Caen, France, June 1976

Gaston eats his lunch in the shade of a holm-oak plantation. His thirty-year-old son, Paul, is with him. They drink from a stone bottle of cider and feel contented with the fine summer day and with the world. Gaston looks up at Paul, to where sunlight catches the smooth, tanned skin of his cheek, and says: 'You know you've got your grandfather's good looks. Lucky for you. They skipped a generation with me, but you got them.'

Paul says nothing to this. He's heard it many times before and he doesn't need his father to tell him he's handsome. Girls tell him without saying a word. He bets he's already had far more girls than Gaston ever dreamed of. Girls feast on Paul, as though he were made of honey. He changes the subject. He says, 'Have you thought any more about my suggestion for the drainage of the wet-meadow, Papa? You know we should plant the trees before the autumn rains.'

But Gaston is still preoccupied with the resemblance of his son to his own father, killed on the road not far from where they sit in the beautiful oak shade. He chews his sandwich and says with his mouth full, 'Sometimes he'd look at me, your grandfather, your dear Pappi, Antoine, whom you never knew. He'd stare at me with that amused look he had, and say: "You've got a funny old mug, Gaston. But never mind. With boys, it's the heart that counts and you've got a good heart. Lucky you're not a girl, eh?" He used to say that from time to time: "Lucky you're not a girl!"'

Paul smiles. This, too, he's heard before.

'I've calculated,' Paul says, 'that we could plant thirty willows, leaving plenty of space in between for growth to full maturity. Thirty willows would drink that meadow dry and all the autumn flood problems would be solved.'

'He talked about it once: about willow trees. Pappi talked about it. Never did it, though. Killed on the road to Caen before he could buy the saplings . . .'

Paul looks over to Gaston. Sometimes – and now is one of those times – he seems much older than his fifty years. He appears to Paul like an old man, choking up with half-remembered things, as though there were a great struggle going on inside him to find, in among all that was half-remembered, those moments which had been absolute and true.

And nobody helps him do this by encouraging him to say what is on his mind. Paul's mother, Solange, lives her life in the corners of rooms, furtive in her gestures, stepping from hearth to table so silently, it's as if she were wearing cloth shoes. Before Gaston met and married her, she'd wanted to be a nun. Perhaps she's never stopped wanting to be a nun? Perhaps silence was what she longed for, and still longs for, in the world? But she took pity on Gaston – so alone in 1944, so terrified to find himself an orphan at nineteen. He had clung to Solange and couldn't bear to let her go. In the nights, they'd both screamed, like children in pain.

Pity for Gaston's memory-cluttered mind suddenly chokes Paul, and he says: 'Talk to me some more about Pappi. Was he still handsome when he died?'

'Oh yes,' says Gaston. 'That's for sure. He was my age, or older. But I can see him walking home up the lane, muddy from his day in the fields, tired too, I reckon, but he didn't let that show. He was a fine man. I worshipped him. I used to say to myself, I'd do anything to get his love. I'd imagine all kinds of madcap things, like becoming a war hero, to make him proud of me. I used to think there wasn't anything I wouldn't do, if he asked me. Not a single thing on earth. I was ready to commit a crime. *Anything*. And I did.'

'You did what?'

'No, I mean I *was*. I was ready to do anything for Pappi. I went on and on thinking, or believing, that what I did, I did *for his sake*. To make him proud. You see?'

'He'd be proud of how you've kept the farm going. Proud of everything at La Charité.'

'You think so?'

'Yes. It's ship-shape. It pays a good living . . .'

'Good enough for you and me. But you'll never be rich.'

Gaston lapses into silence, finishes his lunch and then lights a Gitane. The flattish cigarette still adheres miraculously to his lips as he says suddenly, 'I'm not keen on this idea you've got for planting willows.'

'Why not?'

'Too expensive, son.'

'We could do it over two seasons.'

'No. It's not worth the labour. What's a bit of flood water

in October? I like that meadow as it is, as it's always been. Let's leave it alone.'

RAF Base, Tangmere, Sussex, England, May 1944

Everybody knew that the D-Day landings in Normandy were going to come soon and that the RAF pilots would then be in combat over France.

Lucy's friend Patricia had said to her: 'The thing I think is going to be most important for them is that when they come back from a sortie . . . from facing German flak and all that awfulness . . . I think it's going to be really important that we look beautiful for them. Don't you agree, Lucy?'

Lucy went and stared at herself in the mirror. She had no idea whether she was beautiful or not. She had blue eyes and mousy hair. Her mother had never said she was pretty. But then, when she'd met Geoffrey, one of the most handsome men she'd ever laid eyes on, he'd told her she was lovely. That was the word he'd used: *lovely. My lovely Lucy.*

With wartime restrictions, they couldn't have what Lucy's mother termed 'a proper wedding'. But they had made their vows in church and Lucy had worn a little white velvet hat and carried a posy of lily of the valley, and Geoffrey had looked a dish in his RAF uniform, and Lucy had believed she was the most fortunate young woman in the world. Later, in the cool March night, when they were making love, Lucy thought, Now he must never leave me. Now, he is inside me for ever, part of my being. I shall never let him go.

They talked, in a sweet, companionable way, about their future. They wanted children and a house of their own with a garden, where these children could play. They agreed about everything. Their dreams were identical. And when, in May 1944, Lucy told Geoffrey she was pregnant, he did a little dance of happiness.

'Darling,' he said, 'that is pure heaven! We're going to have a great life.'

Of course, they had to talk about the war and what was going to happen after the Normandy Landings. Geoffrey was flying Typhoons. He said, 'The Typhoons are incredibly strong and impressive, but actually, I loved my old Spitfire. I could stand on the ground and reach up and pat the cockpit, like you pat a horse, but the Typhoon dwarfs me. Climbing into it is a feat of mountaineering. You can get to feel that your plane doesn't think much of you.'

'Oh darling,' said Lucy, 'let me go and talk to your silly old plane, then. I'll tell it you're the best pilot in England!'

So even that – that talking about the war and the battle to come, leavened as it was by little jokes and expressions of tenderness – was never as painful as it might have been. Nothing, thought Lucy, will ever be really painful again, as long as Geoffrey and I are together, as long as he loves me.

Yet now, her face in the mirror, touched up by a tiny dab of rouge, because the pregnancy made her pale, reflected back at Lucy something she didn't want to see; it reflected fear.

The farm of La Charité, south of Caen, France, May 1944

At eighteen, Gaston shared the burden of all the farm work with his father, Antoine.

It was just the two of them, now. Gaston's mother had

been shot while visiting a relative in Caen on the day the Germans marched into the city. Her body was carried back to La Charité on a hay cart.

Though Gaston mourned his mother, the thing which terrified him most was the idea that he could lose his father. For he saw that his father was an exceptional man: strong, handsome, hard-working and kind. He is, thought Gaston, the rock on which my life rests. If anything or anyone takes him away, I'm going to be helpless.

He began to watch over him.

Instead of getting up at five thirty to start the milking, he rose at five o'clock, so that Antoine wouldn't have to sit so long on the hard milking stool. He took down his mother's old recipe book and taught himself how to make nourishing *daubes*, *cassoulets* and *crêpes*, to make sure his father had a good diet. Instead of letting Antoine go alone to sell their surplus produce at the market, he insisted on accompanying him – just in case 'something bad' happened on the road. In this occupied land, it was impossible to predict how things might change from week to week, or even from hour to hour.

Word had reached La Charité that there was going to be an invasion soon, from across La Manche. The news went round that it was going to be massive and that the Germans would be driven out of France in a matter of weeks.

Gaston and Antoine talked about the 'liberators' who were going to come: de Gaulle's brave army, of course, but also British, American, Canadian, Australian and who knew what other nationalities. They tried to imagine this vast army massing in England somewhere, but it was difficult to see it, difficult to believe that it would actually arrive. And what would the Germans do, when or if it did arrive? Would they burn the farms? Would they kill everyone and everything in their pathway as they retreated?

'What we have to do,' said Antoine, 'is to stay alert. There may be fighting all around us. We have to be careful and hold our nerve, so that we're not caught in a trap, like fools. And dust off your rosary, Gaston. God can't be on the German side any more.'

RAF Base, Tangmere, Sussex, England, June 1944

Lucy had been taken to see the Typhoons. She had touched the fuselage of one with her small, white hand. On the 6th of June, she said to Geoffrey, 'Is it going to get very terrible now, darling?'

'No, no. You mustn't worry. The guns will barely catch our shirt-tails!' Geoffrey reassured her. 'We're just going to give those ill-mannered panzers a lesson they'll never forget.'

Lucy went to find her friend and said: 'I'm so frightened, Patricia. I want to be strong for Geoffrey. I don't want to feel terrified like this. I want to be like Queen Eleanor of Aquitaine. Is there a knack to it?'

'Yes,' said Patricia. 'I think there is. What I do, whenever Simon goes out on a mission, I imagine he's gone to the bookies.'

'The bookies?'

'Yes. You try it, Lucy. Imagine Geoffrey's just popped out to put a little bet on the two-thirty at Newbury. Try to see him there, at the bookies' window, with all the fug round him that's in those places, and those old geezers you see there, keeping their trousers up with string and laying their last ha'pennies on the gee-gees.'

'Gosh,' said Lucy. 'Does that work?'

'Yup. If your imagination's good enough. You have to be able to truly *imagine* things. I mean, I can actually see Simon walking out of the bookies' shop and sauntering home, cool and calm, with nothing to worry about except, will his horse win at Newbury? If he's late and it gets dark, then you've got to pretend he's gone into a pub and had a pint and then another pint or a whisky or something. But he's quite safe, OK? Simon's safe. Geoffrey's safe. They won't be hurt. They won't die. And soon enough, they'll come walking in the door.'

The next time Geoffrey flew, Lucy wrote to her mother: *I'm trying to imagine Geoffrey's gone to the bookies. My friend, Patricia says this should be easy. You just have to picture it. The trouble is I'm not sure I've ever been in a bookies' shop. So I can't quite decide what it would be like. What I think I'm going to have to do is to believe Geoffrey's at his club in London (where I haven't ever been, either, but I can somehow imagine it better, with palms in pots and waiters in tailcoats et cetera) and then he's going to get a train home and walk in the door, clutching some potted meat he's bought at Fortnum's.*

She paused here in her letter because she knew something was troubling her, and then she realised what it was: evening was coming on and Geoffrey hadn't returned.

She patted her hair, drew herself up taller in the chair, because she knew that Queen Eleanor had been tall – tall and strong and never giving up or giving in.

She resumed her letter. *The thing is, Mummy*, she wrote, *whatever trick stops me from being afraid I'm going to use.*

I've told myself that if I never give in to fear, then no harm will come to Geoffrey.

The farm of La Charité, south of Caen, France, June 1976

The weather was so fine and warm now that it was difficult to believe summer would ever end and autumn arrive, with its winds and floods. But arrive it would. The previous year, the floods had crept almost to the house, and so Paul was determined to have one last try at persuading Gaston to start planting willows in the back meadow that bordered the stream.

One hot afternoon, while Gaston was taking his siesta, Paul fetched a pick and a shovel from the barn and walked to the back meadow and began to dig. What he wanted to show his father was that, even now, when no rain had fallen for two or three weeks, this land was boggy and the water-table still so high that, when the river broke its bank, it was unable to absorb much water at all, putting the house at risk from flood damage. The statistics on drainage by willow plantation were very good; the trees would certainly solve the problem. Paul just couldn't understand why Gaston was being so obstinate about this.

The ground was hard at first. Paul had to cut away the layer of thick summer grass, then smash into the earth with the heavy pick. But no more than a half a metre down, the soil darkened and softened. Paul decided to widen the hole, so that he could stand in it and keep shovelling out the earth. He reasoned that when Gaston saw how relatively easy it was to dig in this meadow, he would relent and order the trees. Paul worked out he would be able to plant four or five saplings a day. In a week, the whole task could be completed.

Bringing the pick hard down again, to make the hole bigger, Paul suddenly felt a jarring pain in his arm. The pick had hit a stone.

He nursed his arm for a moment and took a drink of water, and wiped the sweat from his neck. Then, he took the shovel and began to scrape carefully across and round the stone, to see how large it was.

The sun was still high, and as Paul stood up to rest, he saw it glinting on the stone. Except that the stone was not a stone. It was something that looked as though it were made of some kind of glass or Perspex. He couldn't think what this could be, unless, long ago, there had been a green-house or cold frames out here, which had been allowed to fall down and lie buried in the earth, but he could never remember any such structure and Gaston was not a man to let anything fall to ruin.

Paul tapped at the glass gently with the pick. He expected it to crack, but it didn't. Scraping away more soil, he unearthed a rusty metal bar, holding the glass structure in place and at the end of the bar was a handle. Paul stared at this. Clearing debris and stones from it, he put his hand into it and pulled upwards, but nothing moved. Whatever it was he'd found was clamped shut by time and weather.

He sat down beside it and smoked a cigarette. The sun went in and when he looked again at the strange structure, he seemed to see it afresh and formed a new idea of what it might be: it was the canopy that covered the cockpit of a plane.

Lucy and Gaston

RAF Base, Tangmere, Sussex, England, June 1944

Lucy sat very still, listening to the eight o'clock news.

She'd tried to eat some supper: a slice of tinned ham and a baked potato. But it had been impossible to eat. She tipped the food away.

The BBC newsreader told her that fighting in Northern France was still very heavy. German resistance was proving 'stronger than expected' and Allied progress was slow. 'Hopes,' said the newsreader, 'of liberating the beleaguered city of Caen have been temporarily deferred.'

Lucy switched off the wireless and went and lay down on her bed and put her hand on her belly, where the baby lay safe and nourished inside her. There was still plenty of light in the sky – enough, Lucy thought, to allow the pilots to find their way home. Geoffrey would still have fuel left. There was no need to worry about him yet . . .

She set herself to imagining Geoffrey in his club, sitting in an over-stuffed leather chair, comfortable and happy, smoking a cheroot, listening to the musical ticking of a mantelpiece clock, letting just a little more time go by until he got up and said goodnight to the people he knew there and walked out into the darkness and then home through her front door.

But now, with a swoon of terror, she knew he wasn't going to come home. He was never going to come home. On this day, the 16th of June 1944, he had died.

Lucy got up and ran to Patricia's house and beat on the door. Simon opened it and Lucy fell into Simon's arms. 'He's gone!' she cried out. 'I know it! I feel it! Geoffrey's gone, Simon!'

She broke down and sobbed and Patricia came and put her arms round her and round Simon. They let her cry for a long time, then they sat her down on a sofa and Simon gave her a glass of brandy. He kneeled by her and said: 'We were going to come and see you, but we didn't because there's still hope, Lucy. We've seen this before: planes limping home . . . after we'd almost given up. And Geoffrey's a brilliant flyer. We know he was still alive at nineteen hundred hours. He was in the Caen–Falaise area. He'd been hit in the tail but he radioed in that he still had buoyancy and had a good chance of making it across the Channel . . .'

Lucy stared at her friends.

Still alive at nineteen hundred hours.

Now, it was nearly nine o'clock and she could see it all as clearly as though she had been watching a motion picture: the burning Typhoon goes into the sea. It sinks down the fathoms, turning over and over, and Geoffrey's body falls out of the open cockpit and begins its own slow descent, with his arms outstretched.

How deep was the sea? How many minutes did it take for the body to reach the ocean floor and lie still, among the starfish?

The farm of La Charité, south of Caen, France, June 1944

Hoeing peas in the field which bordered the Caen road, Gaston heard the plane and looked up.

The sight of the Typhoon in the distance thrilled him. They'd been seen in the skies for ten days now. The pilots, British and American, flying low, would wave at the French farmers in the fields. The waves said: *It's all right. We're on your side. You've got nothing to fear from us. The liberation of France is coming!*

This one was still quite far away. It banked and turned and at the top of the turn, the engine seemed to stutter for a moment, but then down it came again and began to approach the boundary of La Charité, and Gaston could now see anti-aircraft shells exploding in the sky. The Boche were firing at the plane.

Gaston leaned on his hoe and stared up. He wanted to wave at the beleaguered plane – *I'm on your side!* – but he knew he was too far away, as yet, to be seen by the pilot. He took off his cap.

Then, at the corner of his vision, he saw something coming towards him down the Caen road, and he didn't recognise at first what this was, because the heat in the air made far-off things shimmer and break apart. Then, he recognised it as the pony-cart Antoine had driven out in earlier, to take tomatoes and marrows to their neighbour, poor Madame Marzan, who could no longer care for her own vegetable plot.

Gaston raised his cap, to wave to his father in the pony-cart, to wave to the British pilot. Though the roar of the Typhoon's engine afflicted him, he thought optimistically of the time that was coming, when the war would be over, when the Germans would be gone and all would return to a sweet quiet at La Charité, leaving him and his father alone to work and prosper. And he longed for this – for the skies to be empty, for his heart to be still.

Again, he heard gunfire. The plane seemed to bounce and shudder, as though the pilot might have lost control of it.

More shells exploded in the air. Gaston threw down his hoe, jumped the shallow ditch and stepped onto the road. The plane dropped lower and began to follow the line of the road. Then, from under its wings, bright flashes appeared. The plane was firing its guns.

Gaston gaped. The attack on the Typhoon was clearly being mounted from behind it but now, the pilot was strafing the road ahead. Fountains of earth and stones burst upwards as the shells hit. With no thought for his own safety, Gaston bolted towards his father in the pony-cart. He could hear the horse whinnying in terror. Then, he saw Antoine climb out of the cart and try to run towards the ditch, but he didn't reach the ditch. Bits of the road rose up and danced, momentarily, around Antoine and flung him on his face.

As Gaston stumbled on towards his father, the plane banked again and turned and flew westwards, heading for the sea.

Southwold Beach, Suffolk, England, June 1976

The light drains from the sky and the sea appears grey and flat, but the air is still warm.

Lucy and Ray's friends, Peter and Monica, own a beach hut and are preparing a simple supper for them and for Hannah, who sit on the hut's little veranda and sip white wine.

Ray says to Lucy, 'You know, I've never known the sea so warm here. Today would have been an ideal day for you to try it.'

'I'm sure it would,' says Lucy.

'I mean,' says Ray, 'it honestly barely felt cold for a moment. I know you always think it's going to be freezing, but today it wasn't.'

'Perhaps I'll try it next time,' says Lucy.

'Yeah, but you *won't*,' insists Ray. 'There'll always be some reason why you can't get near it. And it's a bit mad . . . after all this time.'

'It doesn't matter, Ray,' says Hannah. 'It doesn't matter if Mum never goes into the sea again in her whole life.'

'Well, it doesn't *matter*, in any significant sense of the word. It just strikes me as a bit bizarre, because I think Mum could conquer this, if she tried.'

'She does try.'

'She doesn't. She just sits there. She could put a toe in the water, just a toe, to see what it felt like, but she won't even do that.'

'No,' says Lucy. 'Ray's right. I don't try. I'm still waiting.'

'Waiting?' says Ray. 'Waiting for what?'

'Just waiting.'

'I don't know what you mean. Waiting for Geoffrey to come back from the dead, or what?'

'That's a horrible thing to say,' says Hannah.

'Yes, it is,' says Ray. 'I'm sorry. I just get . . . annoyed with it all sometimes. Things should be *over* when they're over, but I've lived with this for twenty years.'

Silence falls on the little veranda and there are only the sounds of Peter and Monica making the supper, talking quietly to each other. Lucy lights a cigarette and says: 'I know I've said this before, but I do sometimes think that something will come, that something will happen . . . I mean, you hear about this, about people being cured of their phobias and fears, don't you? I've read about it: people who are afraid of things for years and years and then a day comes and they realise, they're not terrified any more. They can face it, whatever it is.'

'I expect it's because they've spent some time with a psychiatrist, who has helped them to conquer stuff. And I don't know why you've always refused to do this.'

'What can a psychiatrist tell me, Ray? I'm afraid of the sea – repelled by it – because Geoffrey's plane went down into it and his body has lain there, unburied, for thirty-two years, and I know that if I went swimming, I'd feel as though I was treading on Geoffrey's face. How can anything a psychiatrist says alter that simple fact?'

Ray turns away. Lucy sips her wine. The sighing of the sea suddenly seems louder than before. After a moment, Peter comes through with a dish of crudités, sliced salami and olives.

'Fodder,' he says. 'More coming. All rather simple. Pretend you're in France.'

The farm of La Charité, south of Caen, France, June 1976

By the time Gaston wakes from his siesta and goes looking for his son, Paul has unearthed the entire canopy of the plane's cockpit.

Sweating in the afternoon sun, he crouches down and touches the glass, then tries to wipe it clear of the earth that clings to it. Below the glass, he can now see a lumpen shape, and he thinks that this is the shape of the dead pilot, bone and dust now, but somehow held together by his helmet and his flying jacket.

What he feels is a mingling of shock and thrill.

He looks up and sees Gaston coming towards him. He watches his father's face. Gaston says nothing and Paul says nothing. Gaston comes and stands near his son, looking down at the plane in the earth. Then, he buries his face in his hands. 'No!' he cries. '*No!*'

Paul leads him away. They sit down in the kitchen. Paul finds a bottle of Calvados and pours a shot for Gaston. He waits in silence a long while. Gaston drinks the Calvados and stares out at the room, as though the room might be a place he'd never visited before.

Eventually, he begins to talk. His voice is choked and quiet.

'That day in June,' he says, 'the day Pappi died on the road, I carried Pappi's body home in my arms. I laid him out here, on the table, and he was still warm and blood was still leaking from his wounds. I could do nothing. All I did was kiss his face. His face hadn't been touched. The wounds were to his spine.

'I stroked his hair. I howled like a fox.

'Later, when the sun was beginning to go down, around eight o'clock, I left him and went out to get a breath of air, and to try to think what I could do. But I couldn't think of anything to do. I was alone now. And I was all muddled and conflicted in my head, because Pappi had been killed, not by the Germans, but by a Typhoon – by a British pilot, who was meant to be on our side. And I thought, The world is finished for me now.'

Gaston holds out his glass and Paul refills it with Calvados.

Tears begin to roll down Gaston's cheeks as he says: 'I've kept the damn thing a secret for all this time, because of that. Because of my anger. Because, after that day, I've never been happy and calm in my mind again. I know it was wrong of me. That pilot should have had a proper burial, with honours. He was as brave as the next man, and I knew that. With the flak coming at him, he was confused, that's all. He mistook Pappi's cart for a German jeep, or some damn enemy truck. But I couldn't forgive him. I've never forgiven him. I did what I did and that's the end of it.'

Gaston weeps. Paul lays his hand on his father's bowed head.

'Tell me what happened next, Papa,' he says gently.

Gaston fumbles for a handkerchief, blows his nose and says: 'It was when I went out to get that breath of air, around eight, that I heard the plane again – the Typhoon. I looked up and there it was, that murdering plane, and it was coming towards La Charité again, but this time it was on fire.

'I cried out. It was coming lower and lower all the time and I thought it was going to take out the house and Pappi's body in the kitchen – everything.

'I shouted and screamed at it. I swore blue murder at the air. If I'd had a gun with me, I would have fired it, to make sure the pilot who'd killed Pappi paid with his life.

'But it didn't touch the house. It sailed over it, with flames streaming behind, like a comet's tail. Then it fell. It just plunged into the ground, in the middle of the water-meadow. It went into that muddy earth, and the impact was so great that the earth took it and seemed to swallow it up. The flames were snuffed out. Everything ended for it in that last fall – for the pilot and for the plane. There was a little smoke, not much, some fragments of blackened metal. The field swallowed it all.'

Solange comes home from her visit to Caen and piles her shopping on the kitchen table. When she looks at the faces of her husband and son, her hand flies up to the silver crucifix she wears round her neck.

'What's happened?' she asks. Yet Solange's voice is so quiet that the question almost isn't there.

Lucy and Ray's house, Westleton, Suffolk, June 1976

Ray takes the call from the French Embassy in London. The Chargé d'Affaires is both formal and apologetic. In elegant terms, he outlines the strange circumstances: the rediscovery of the Typhoon, the dating of the crash, the identification of the pilot, the remorse of the farmer, in whose field the plane lay buried for so long. The French State, he says, wishes – in the near future – to hold some commemoration ceremony for a brave British serviceman.

Ray thanks him for his courtesy. He sits down and calls Lucy to his side and takes her hand and says: 'They think they've found Geoffrey. He didn't go down into the sea. He went down into a field south of Caen.'

Lucy is mute. Her brain feels as though somebody had thrown a black cloth over it. She stares at Ray.

'No,' she says, after a while. 'He told Control he was heading for the Channel.'

'Yes, heading for it,' says Ray, 'but he didn't make it. His plane fell into a field and apparently the impact was so great, the earth just closed up around it.'

Lucy reaches for a cigarette and Ray lights it for her.

'I don't know what to do . . .' she says.

'Well,' says Ray, 'the French are offering to pay for a funeral in Normandy – with full military honours. You may want to go to this. Hannah and I will be with you, of course. You can invite as many people as you like. Geoffrey's RAF friends? Simon and what-was-her-name? The French just need a little time to make the arrangements.'

Lucy smokes. She raises her head and looks out of the window at the fine summer afternoon and she thinks, It would have been an afternoon like this, with a clear sky and the birds singing in the hawthorn, and there he fell and rested, and the grass grew over him and the seasons came and went and the frost hardened the earth around him and sealed him in.

'How do they definitely know it's Geoffrey?' she asked.

Ray cleared his throat. 'Erm . . . his plane, Lucy. His flying jacket. Papers . . .'

'Yes,' she says. 'Yes, of course. Those things just . . . endure . . .'

'Do you think you can bear to go to Normandy, to see him buried – the remains, I mean? They say he'll lie alongside some of the RAF men he knew.'

'I want to see him buried,' says Lucy. 'I want him to have a proper coffin . . . and a flag draped on it. Geoffrey loved the flag. But there's one thing I don't understand, Ray. Didn't anybody see the plane go down? Why didn't someone dig Geoffrey out?'

Ray gets up and begins to pace around the room. He wishes Hannah were here to help him with this moment.

'One man knew,' he says quietly. 'His name is Gaston.

Apparently Geoffrey's guns killed Gaston's father by mistake on the Caen road. So he let Geoffrey and the plane just lie there, swallowed up by the field. He thought nobody would ever find them. He feels remorse now, but none at the time. I suppose that's how it was in nineteen forty-four.'

The British Cemetery at Bayeux, north-west of Caen, France, July 1976

The short service is conducted by a French priest, assisted by an English rector from the Protestant church in Bayeux. The Mayor of Bayeux and Deputy Mayor attend, as do the Mayor of Caen and his wife. A small contingent from a French regimental band accompany the hymn-singing and then play an old English wartime song, hastily learned: 'We'll Meet Again'. A bright sun shines on the thousand white gravestones of Bayeux. A local photographer walks quietly around, taking pictures.

There are other French people there, some in Army uniform, and Lucy has no idea who they are or why they've joined the gathering, to bury a long-dead English pilot. She looks round the faces, but recognises no one aside from the few old friends who have come with her and Ray from England.

She has been handed a rose, to throw into the coffin, once it's been lowered into the ground. She and Hannah walk side by side to the grave's edge to throw in their flowers, then they cling together as they walk away. Lucy watches other people approach the grave and let the roses fall. It's done, in every case, with reverence and precision. Each mourner walks to

the grave, throws in his flower, inclines his head, and with-
draws. The band begin their slow rendering of 'We'll Meet
Again'.

Then, one man, aged sixty or so, Lucy guesses, and dressed
in a Sunday suit, comes forward. He isn't carrying a rose, but
a bouquet of wild meadow flowers. He is weeping. He stands,
looking down into the grave. Then he kneels and reaches
down and places his flowers on the coffin. And, at once, Lucy
knows who this is.

When the ceremony is over, Lucy makes her way towards
this man. She touches his arm. '*Vous êtes* Gaston,' she says.
'*Je suis* Lucy.'

Gaston bows to her. Then he raises his hands in a gesture
that says, *What has happened is inexpressible in words.*

Yet Lucy wants there to be some words. In her halting
French, she tells Gaston that she is sorry, very, very sorry, that
Gaston's father was killed by her husband. 'If he had known
. . .' she stammers, 'he would not have fired the guns. I know
he would not have fired.'

'I believe that, too,' says Gaston. 'I believe it now. But
when I saw my father fall, in the middle of a summer afternoon . . .'

They stand, face to face. Gaston clutches Lucy's hand.
Then, he says, 'I hope you can forgive me, Lucy. You lost your
husband, the father of your daughter . . .'

This is brave of Gaston. Lucy sees that the man is still
fighting back tears, and she reassures him that he is forgiven.
She wants to say that the image of Geoffrey lying in the earth
in Gaston's field is preferable to the one she has lived with
for thirty-two years, of his drowned body decaying on the
cold ocean bed, but she knows her French will tangle on this

complicated sentence, so she only says again: 'I understand why you did what you did. I understand it.'

They clasp each other's hands. The feel of Gaston's rough hand holding tight to hers is strangely comforting. There is something eternal in it. And at the edge of their vision, they are aware of Hannah and Paul standing quietly and talking together and Gaston looks over at them and says: 'We are fortunate, Lucy, that our young people are untouched. See how beautiful they are?'

'Yes,' says Lucy, 'they are.' But she knows the encounter must end now; Gaston wouldn't be able to bear another minute of it. She nods to Gaston and turns to leave, but as she turns, she says: 'Gaston, you said your father died "in the middle of the afternoon". Can you remember what time it was?'

Gaston shakes his head. 'All I know is, the sun was still very high. It made mirages on the road. I'd say it was about four o'clock – the time you have your English tea!'

'Thank you, Gaston,' says Lucy. 'Thank you.'

He bows. She walks away. She is holding the Union Jack that she has been given, neatly folded, that was draped over the coffin while it stood at the graveside. She can smell the earth in the rough fabric, earth and dust and sunlight.

Later, in the comfortable hotel that has been provided for the family, Lucy lies awake as Ray sleeps and snores.

In her mind, she writes a letter to a friend she hasn't seen for a long time.

Dear Patricia, says Lucy's letter. *I know that we muddle everything with time, but certain things remain absolutely clear, don't they? One of these things is Simon saying, on the evening of the day Geoffrey died*, He was still alive at nineteen hundred hours.

I've heard it in my mind all my life: He was still alive at nineteen hundred hours. *And it must have been some time after that that he crashed in Gaston's field.*

Patricia, Gaston says his father died 'in the middle of the afternoon', but Simon and Geoffrey didn't go out on that sortie until about five fifteen, did they? I remember that, for once, the Typhoons had been stood down at Tangmere all that morning. Geoffrey and I had been sunbathing on our porch.

But then the call came from Control. Renewed German tank activity reported near Caen. So they left the base at five fifteen, which is six fifteen French time. Then they had to form up over North Weald and sweep from there.

They couldn't have been in the area before five forty-five at the earliest, which is six forty-five, French time.

So you see my thinking? I may be wrong, but I don't think I am. Can you check to see whether Simon remembers exactly what time they went out? I'm glad I said nothing to Gaston, because this would have made everything worse for him, but, whoever killed his father on the Caen road, I think it wasn't Geoffrey. I think it's plain and simple: it was another British or American pilot, in another Typhoon, not him.

Southwold Beach, Suffolk, England, August 1976

Here they are again, eating supper on Peter and Monica's beach-hut veranda.

During the hot afternoon, Lucy sat, as usual, in her deck-chair, while the others went swimming. She resisted Ray's entreaties to join them. She told him she was perfectly happy just to enjoy the sun. She reminded him that summer would soon be at an end.

But now, as Monica makes coffee, Lucy gets up and walks in the dark to the sea. Nobody stops her or tries to follow her. She removes her clothes and makes a neat pile of them on the wet sand. A rising moon shines on her naked body.

She braves the breakers calmly, longing for the buoyancy of deep water, to lift her and let her feel, just for a moment, the gravity of the world drop away.

She swims strongly, with a feeling of wonder at her own strength and power. Then she hears Ray calling to her and she turns again towards the shore.

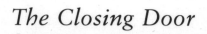

The Closing Door

The children assembled at the station barrier.

Their trunks had been sent on ahead of them, so what they had with them were small suitcases, as though they might have been going away for the weekend. But the youngest of the children was ten years old, and it was from the violent weeping of this one girl that it was possible to imagine the long stretch of boarding school time to which the waiting train would carry them.

She was a stumpy little person, optimistically named Patience. The elastic of her grey school hat dug into her dimpled chin. Her mother, Marjorie, held her close and the hat was knocked to the back of her head, revealing a disorderly festoon of brown curls. Marjorie pressed her mouth to these curls, kissing them and trying at the same time to whisper words of courage, but it was very difficult for her. She felt herself to be embarking on a furiously misguided enterprise. It was the early autumn of 1954. She had surely not nurtured and fed her War Baby and single-handedly kept her from all harm and depredation in order to surrender her to this expensive school . . .

'Why do I have to go? *Why?*' wailed Patience.

'Darling,' said the mother, 'I hate it, too. Hate it as much as you do. What am I going to do when I get home and you're not there?'

But this was the wrong thing to say, absolutely wrong. It was what she felt, but should never have said, for it only brought on a new Niagara of tears in Patience. For now, not only was the child going to suffer the loss of her mother; she was also going to have to imagine this mother in distress, crying probably, sitting by the gas fire with a cup of tea and weeping, forgetting to make herself any supper, forgetting everything but this awful separation . . .

What Marjorie should have said, but could not say, was that her parents-in-law had insisted upon Patience going to what they called a 'reputable school'. They had not thought any of the London day schools were reputable enough. Children only learned to become responsible adults, they believed, if you sent them away from home. No matter if these children suffered a bit. Who in the world had not suffered? And who, indeed, more than they, who had lost their only son, Timothy, in the last week of the war?

'Tim would have wanted it,' they'd told Marjorie kindly but firmly. 'Tim despised mollycoddling. Tim would have insisted upon it. He would have wanted us to pay the fees, and we will. And you know, Marjorie dear, Tim was a very wise young man. He was almost always right.'

But she couldn't lay the responsibility for the separation on them, couldn't alienate Patience from her grandparents, because it wasn't fair on them. She was all that remained to them of Timothy. She even resembled him, with the same chunky body and disobedient hair. Marjorie saw how much they loved to stroke Patience's curls, remembering their son.

They yearned to be as proud of Patience as they had been of him, and they believed, somehow, that boarding school was the key to bringing this about.

In the group of children and parents who surrounded her, Marjorie now sensed a movement. The ticket barrier had been opened and the moment was coming when all the girls would have to get on the train.

She had paid no heed to any of these people. They were nothing to her. But now she looked round at them, to see how they were managing this moment. She saw, with a feeling of relief, that there was a little crying going on among the other children. One of them, a tall, slender girl of twelve or thirteen, carrying a new lacrosse stick, had pressed the net basket of the stick over her face and was sobbing into that, while a tall man, evidently her father, helplessly patted her shoulder.

'Come on, old thing,' she heard this father say, 'think of midnight feasts and all that malarkey. Think of being Captain of Junior Lax! And half-term will be here in a jiffy.'

'I miss Jasper!' cried the girl.

'I know you do. But we'll take good care of him. Mummy will take him for a walk every morning.'

So then, thought Marjorie, if it's hard for these two, then probably it's hard for everybody, except that for most of them there might be 'Mummy and Daddy' and not just 'Mum' as Patience called her.

Patience had never known 'Daddy'. She had often been shown a black-and-white photograph of him, wearing his Irish Guards uniform, holding her in his arms in 1944: tiny Patience, swaddled in a white lace shawl, clasped in Daddy's broad-fingered hands. He had been smiling for the camera – the anxious smile of the proud father, proud soldier – but that was the last picture ever taken of him.

Since then, for Patience, there had only been Mum: Mum alone in her small flat with her part-time job in a bridal shop, Mum who had never seen anything of the world, Mum who saved string and borrowed her books from Boots' Library, Mum who loved her daughter more than life.

And it was coming nearer, nearer, the moment when Marjorie would have to unwind Patience's arms from round her waist and lead her forwards to the barrier. She tried to stand a bit more upright, but the weight of Patience clinging to her was implacable, as though she had been roped to the ground. And she thought, I am bent like an old person, bent down by the gravity of love.

'Come on, angel,' she said, as firmly as she could. 'I'm going to come with you as far as the ticket man. But then you're going to have to be brave and get on the train. Everybody else is going now. See? You can't be left behind.'

'I want to be left behind!' screamed Patience. And now she raised one of her determined little fists and hit Marjorie on the shoulder. 'I hate you for making me go!' she cried out. 'I hate you. I hate you!'

Marjorie knew that this now risked to become what Tim would have called 'a scene', and that the other parents would pity her, or even despise her, for not crushing it the minute it started, so, with surprising strength, she grabbed Patience by the fist that had struck her and turned the sobbing child round to face the trains and the great vaulted station roof above them, still black from the years of war.

'Patience,' she said, 'nothing you do or say is going to change the fact that you are going away to school. You are going to learn Latin and Greek and do chemistry experiments and act in plays and read Shakespeare and run round a huge park in the sunshine. You are going to be happy there. I'm going to write to you every day. *Every day*. But now you're going to say goodbye to me. Here's your train ticket. You are going to say goodbye to me now.'

Patience's crying ceased quite suddenly. She looked shocked, as though Marjorie had slapped her. She stood still and let her face be wiped with a handkerchief. She was shuddering and pale, with eyes puffy and red, but Marjorie knew that now she would find the courage to board the train.

Marjorie kissed her on both cheeks, set her hat gently back on her curls, mortified to notice how the wretched elastic cut into the flesh of her chin, and trying to ease it with her finger, but with her heart beating in relief that, at last, the child was attempting to master her grief.

'Well done,' she said. 'Well done, Patience.'

Then she watched her go, joining the cluster of grey-uniformed children walking to this new piece of their lives and trying not to look back, but looking back all the same and waving and then suddenly running on. She saw that the ticket puncher at the barrier was trying to laugh and joke with the boarding school girls, and she thought, Acts of kindness are not rare. We still live in austere times, but people have not exhausted their reserves of compassion.

She stood quite still until she could no longer see Patience.

In fact she hadn't been able to catch sight of her for a long moment because two women, two mothers of departing girls, their arms linked together, had barged in front of her

and were waving and calling out to their girls: 'Bye, darlings!
Bye! Bysey-bye!'

Something about these women – their expensive suits,
perhaps, their gloves and small velvet hats, their ridiculous
Bysey-byes, or was it their seeming gladness of heart? –
awoke in Marjorie a feeling of instant dislike. She wanted
to push by them, elbow them out of her way, trample on
their feet, even, so that she might catch a last glimpse of
Patience climbing onto the train or straining out of a
window. But they somehow prevented her. They had taken
up a position and would not be moved from it. Marjorie
was forced to stand where she was, unable to see anything.
Then a whistle was blown and the train's great engine hissed
into life and it was gone, and Patience was gone.

When the train could no longer be seen, the women
hugged each other, laughing delightedly.

'Right,' said one, 'now we can get on with life!'

'What a blessed relief!' said the other.

They turned and walked past Marjorie. She saw that
one of them was dazzlingly pretty, with great blue eyes like
Bette Davis. The other looked plain by comparison, but had
a beautiful slim figure like Wallis Simpson, and you got from
them the idea that they complemented each other, and knew
it, and now, freed from their children, they were going to
walk together back into lives they believed to be wonderful.

They went out of the station and walked towards the
Number 11 bus stop. Marjorie followed. To get home to
North London, she would have taken the tube, but the
thought of going home – to sit alone and imagine Patience
arriving in a cold dormitory and unpacking her trunk and
putting her new tartan rug on some hard, iron bed

– dismayed her. She preferred to shadow these strangers. She wanted to observe what life it was they were going to get on with.

They sat on the top deck of the bus, at the very front, looking down in fascination on the scurry of the suited City men. They took off their little velvet hats and shook out their shiny hair.

Marjorie sat near the back, pretending to gaze out of the window, but in fact barely letting her eyes stray from the women, who were now smoking cigarettes jammed into long black cigarette holders. She couldn't hear what they were saying to each other, but they reminded Marjorie of people at a party, laughing, waving their cigarettes about, having a good time.

Marjorie began to wonder if their children, freed from them and now being carried through the Hertfordshire countryside, were also laughing. She tried to imagine them: 'Little Bette', 'Little Wallis'. Laughing as they sped back towards their dormitory nights, their cold classrooms, their thin food.

Or was the lost and scented presence of these mothers already making them sad? Did they suspect, or even *know*, that, as soon as the train had gone, they would rush back to the grown-up world with such terrible alacrity?

On crawled the bus, going towards Victoria and the river. These were not parts of London Marjorie often visited. Nothing much ever seemed to lead her south or west. All she'd known for ten years was staying in one place and caring for Patience and working in the bridal shop. On work days, Patience would come to the shop after school and sit quietly in one of the fitting cubicles, reading her book, or else help with pinning and measuring, while the brides stood on little stools, staring at themselves, trying on veils, their eyes brimming with tears of hope.

She wondered how much further the women would travel. And when they got off at last, what would she do? She was miles from Muswell Hill. The September afternoon was already shading to evening. Perhaps she should get off at Victoria Station and begin her long tube ride home? For what right did she have to sit on a bus, passing judgement on strangers?

But she did not get off. She thought, If I see where they live, then, perhaps, I will know. Then, I will get some picture of the life their children prevent them from living. I will understand what it is – by loving Patience so desperately – I've missed and might one day have.

As the bus approached Sloane Square, the women stubbed out their cigarettes and got up and came swaying along towards her, smelling of expensive perfume and of all the smoke they had inhaled. The great blue eyes of Bette stared at her for a moment, and she imagined her whispering to Wallis, 'Wasn't that the woman with the caterwauling child at the station? What's she doing on our bus?' But they went down the stairs and walked away. They did not look up.

Marjorie jumped off the bus just as it was pulling away. She stumbled, but didn't fall. Keeping her distance, dreading to be seen for the busy-body she was, Marjorie followed Bette and Wallis to a square of tall red-brick houses, arranged around private gardens. Bette had a key to one of the houses and the two women went in and the black front door was shut.

Marjorie stood some distance away, in the shadow of a lilac tree that hung over the railings of the gardens. She stared at the closed door.

After ten or fifteen minutes, a taxi stopped, not in front of Bette's house, but just opposite to where Marjorie was standing. A man wearing a City suit got out. He didn't pay the cab driver, but just walked hastily away. Marjorie pressed herself deeper into the shade of the lilac tree. The taxi drove on, and as it passed her, Marjorie could just glimpse the silhouette of a young woman, visible in the rear window.

Now, she saw the man ring the bell of Bette's house. He looked anxiously behind him, as though to make sure that the taxi had gone. Then the door was opened and Marjorie saw Wallis, whose husband this man must be, throw her arms round his neck and draw him inside the house.

'Darling!' she heard her say. 'Darling, come in!'

Then the door closed once more.

Marjorie stared at the door until the darkness shrouded it. Lights came on in the house and she looked up at these, but could see no one at any of the windows. So here, she thought, is where this has to end – with the closing of a door. How much more did I imagine I was ever going to know?

Yet she felt that she had seen something important, something that might end in ruin.

She imagined Wallis, ten or eleven years ago, wearing her bridal gown, standing on a little plinth, while seam-stresses crawled on the floor, tucking and pinning. She imagined her trying on different veils and, as she laid them over her shiny hair, dreaming of her marvellous future with this man, this man in his City suit, with a safe job and a beautiful income.

But now, it was all beginning to slip away. She wasn't pretty enough for him, not as pretty as her friend Bette, not as young and pretty as the girl in the taxi. Today, freed from her child or children, she had imagined she was moving back into the selfish, grown-up life she loved, but, unknown to her, that life had turned its back and was moving away from her.

It was late now. Marjorie left the square and walked until she found a telephone box. She counted out some money and fed it into the slot – almost all the coins she had in her purse – hoping it would be enough.

She had the number of the school scribbled down on a piece of paper. She dialled it and pressed Button A when a voice answered. She asked to speak to Patience. But it was the school secretary who had picked up the telephone and this severe woman informed Marjorie curtly that calls from parents were not allowed, except in emergencies.

'This is an emergency,' said Marjorie. 'I'm ringing from a coin box and I have only limited money. My daughter was very, very upset when she got on the train. I need to know that she is all right. So please go and find her as quickly as you can.'

She was told to wait. Time passed and it got very dark in the box, dark and cold. Marjorie emptied her purse and found one more shilling in it.

At last, a subdued voice said: 'Mum? Why are you ringing from a phone box? Where are you?'

Hearing this little voice, far away, and with only a shilling of time left to her, Marjorie felt exhausted, on the very edge of collapse. She wanted to say, 'I don't know where I am. I'm miles from anywhere familiar to me. I don't know what I'm meant to do now.'

Instead, she said brightly: 'I'm fine. I just went on a little walk, to clear my head. I wanted to know you're all right. Are you all right?'

'Yes. I put my new rug on my bed, like you told me to.'

'Good girl,' said Marjorie. ' Is the dorm OK?'

'Yes.'

'Good. That's what I wanted to know. Oh, and one more thing I wanted to say: I love you very much.'

'I love you, too, Mum,' said Patience. 'But I'm trying not to think about you. It's better if I don't.'

'I understand, darling,' said Marjorie. 'I completely understand. That's very sensible of you. What matters now is getting on with your life.'

21st-Century Juliet

4th March

My thirtieth birthday. Oh well.

Home to Capell House. Mummy and Daddy give a dinner party for me. Before dinner, Daddy takes me aside and makes a big thing of saying he wanted to lay on fireworks for me, but was 'absolutely overthrown' to discover they cost £1,200 a minute.

The Hon. Peregrine Paris, flower of the county, turns up. Not invited by *me*, the toffee-nosed twat. Mummy drinks about five litres of champagne and crucifies me by braying, over the pudding: 'Perry, I just can't understand why you and Juliet have never got together!' Perry went scarlet. Quite sweet, that. But mainly, I wanted to fall off the edge of the planet.

5th March

Long walk with Daddy and the new lurchers, Housey and Montague.

Daddy suddenly grim. Says he didn't want to burden me

with this, but the family finances are in dire shape and he and Mummy may have to sell Capell House. Shocking to see Daddy so miserable. He says: 'Juliet, I just dread what could happen, dread going to the bloody wall. I'd rather the earth swallowed me.'

Montague starts chasing sheep and we have to hare all over the place trying to get him back on the lead. On the way home, Daddy says: 'By the way, what are your thoughts about Perry Paris?'

'I don't have any thoughts,' I reply.

Then Daddy starts on about how much Perry likes me and how he's the richest person in Wiltshire, etc etc. I tell Daddy straight off that imagining Peregrine Paris as a son-in-law is complete fantasy. Then find myself remembering that I'm thirty (shit) and no one has asked me to marry them yet and I'm getting fed up working in PR.

7th March

Back to Fulham and the flat and work. Sometimes it feels awesomely bad slaving away for a lewd Aussie philistine like Jimmy Anselme. His head is a complete *globe* of ephemera. His new thing is to refer to himself as 'Nursey', because (quoth he) he 'massages the egos of the rich and famous'. And this stupid 'Nursey' thing's caught on. Jimmy's referred to like that in the tabloids now.

Feel desolate about the idea of losing Capell House. Like all my childhood would be snatched away . . . Nursey catches me daydreaming and says: 'focus up, Jule.'

Meet Mummy for lunch. She bangs on about Harrods being staffed by 'ignorant immigrants, who don't know how to direct you to the escalator'. Claims Daddy says they all should be sent packing to where they came from because they're skewing the economy.

8ᵗʰ March

Woken at dawn by horrendous *thump, thump, thump*. Lawrence downstairs has got builders in. God knows what he's having done: probably getting some clever heat lamps connected, so he can grow shag by artificial light.

Sometimes, I envy Lawrence his hippie flake existence. He just seems to exist on yoga and weed. Don't think he even *knows the way* to Waitrose.

11ᵗʰ March

Wake at six thirty again. Lawrence's builders jabbering in the garden, in Moldavian, or something. How can anyone jabber that fucking early?

Open my bedroom window and yell at them to shut up.

Long day with Nursey. Perry's featured in the new *Hello!*, lurching out of some posh revels. Reveal to Nurse that the Hon. PP is supposedly thinking of marrying me, and Nurse goes: 'Strewth! Go to, babe. He's number twenty-nine on the Rich List.'

Take a vodka onto the roof terrace when I get home. Then look down and see a face staring up at me. One of the Moldavians. He's sitting in Lawrence's cannabis patch, smoking. He's covered in white dust. Call down I'm sorry I yelled at him this morning. Then, wow. He just smiles at me with this incredibly amazingly sexy smile. On impulse I raise my vodka glass, like I'm inviting him up. Minutes later, he's ringing my bell. I ask him to take his muddy shoes off. When they come off, his socks have holes in them. Suddenly feel I'm a neurotic, house-proud bitch. Pour him a huge vodka.

Talk for quite a long time. He keeps staring at me. The strangeness of him totally does my head in. Find myself longing to touch him. He leaves when my phone rings: Perry asking me out to dinner on the 22ⁿᵈ. (I say yes, but my thoughts aren't exactly on it.)

16ᵗʰ March

Writing this at work. Nursey's in New York, so I can skive. Got to get down what happened last night.

Well. I did something completely mad, rash and sudden but totally wonderful. Feel dazed when I think about it. I went to bed with the Moldavian builder.

Whole new thing for me. Seriously new, even though I've slept with about forty-six people. I mean, I've never had a lover like that. EVER. Now, I can't think of anything else. I just want him back, now, now, now.

His name's Roméo. Pronounced Ro-*may*-o. As in Alfa. I've nicknamed him 'Mayo'. Want to spread him all over me.

17ᵗʰ March

Mayo and I make love for eight hours. Voicemail clicks in while we're exchanging lovers' faithless vows: Perry confirming dinner next week. (Guess he's been wondering if I was going to cancel.)

18ᵗʰ March

Think I'm in trouble. Think I've fallen in love with Roméo.
   Just didn't know sex could be like that.

19ᵗʰ March

Keep hoping I'll come to my senses, but I can't seem to. Phone cousin Tibs and ask him to come round. Have to tell somebody before I go completely insane. Tibs says he'll come on Thursday. He's off to some bloody Formula One race in Verona.
   Starting to panic about Wednesday. The thought of sitting through dinner with Perry Paris is unreal. What in the world are we going to talk about?

20ᵗʰ March

Keep bursting into tears. Exhaustion from my mad nights. And confusion.

Roméo tells me he loves me. I know it's all violently insane, but I seem to be hooked.

Mummy phones. She's heard I'm having dinner with Perry. Reminds me that he owns three houses and five polo ponies. Hear Daddy in the background, sending love across the mad barking of Housey and Montague and sounding horribly cheered up.

22nd March

Dinner with Perry.

Out it all comes. He's loved me from afar. (Classic Perry word, that: *afar*!) Can't get me out of his head. Would like to spend the rest of his life with me.

I'm cold as a tomb. Just can't think what to say or how to deal with this.

Tell Perry I'll 'think about it'. (Is this lame and cowardly, *or what*?) Let him kiss me goodnight, then hate myself for doing this.

Now, I'm in bed, weeping.

23rd March

Tell Mayo I love him. He says he was told there was no sun in England, but I'm his sun. His English is definitely improving.

Have an awful dream about Mummy bashing immigrant sales people in Harrods and calling them 'the enemy'.

24ᵗʰ March

Cook supper for Cousin Tibs. I adore the bastard like the brother I never had. We get smashed on the (four) bottles of Corvo he's brought and I tell him about Mayo and about Perry's declaration. Relief to get everything out in the open. And Tibs is really sweet and on my side and agrees with me that good sex is awesomely rare and that Perry Paris is verging on being a pillock.

But then Tibs tells me he's heard Capell House is *definitely* going to have to be sold. Says Daddy got 'burned' by some fool's paradise of an offshore investment.

Our mood goes down. We sit and slug the Corvo, feeling totally sad and useless.

Very late and pissed, we hear Lawrence chanting below, in the garden.

7ᵗʰ April

The other two guys working with Mayo on the downstairs flat are called Beno and Mercut. Mayo brings them up to the roof terrace after work, to introduce them to me. Beno looks daggers at everyone. Mercut is nicer and speaks a sweet, weird kind of English. He says: 'Roméo tell us he going marry you. Is this thing true, Juliet? True or a dream?'

'A dream,' I say.

Perry calls to ask me out again next week. Says he'll take me to Claridge's.

10th April

Force myself to go to Capell House, even though I'd rather spend the weekend with Roméo.

Mummy starts crying while we're planting out sweet peas. Says piteously she may not be at C. House to see them flower. Says she's just praying for 'something to come along and save us'.

12th April

Dinner at Claridge's with Perry. In the taxi going home, he sticks his hand up my skirt. I come right away. (I guess my body's been re-programmed by Mayo.) So then Perry thinks he's the world's best lover and that I must be crazy about him. Going down the Old Brompton Road, he proposes.

I tell him this is all too sudden and that I need more time. But I take him to bed – just to *see*, just to imagine what it would be like to be the wife of the Hon. Peregrine Paris and own nine cars and a Constable. Make myself feel sexy by thinking about my love, my heart's passion, Roméo. Perry says: 'God, Juliet, you can be a tigress.'

I can't stand it when people add 'ess' on to the ends of words, to make them female.

Shove Perry out at 2 a.m.

13th April

No sleep last night.

When I phone in sick, Nursey says: 'Oh come on, Jule.

Do keep up, lamb; have you forgotten we've got the Valentios arriving from Rome?'

Tell him I can't move my limbs, which is virtually true. Perry Paris is 6' 2" and weighs a ton.

Sleep till midday, then phone Tibs.

He slopes round and we sink a few vodkas with the curtains drawn, to hide us from the outside world. Tell Tibs my life is in a complete muddle. After the third or fourth vodka he says: 'Listen, Jule, I understand you like your bit of rough, but we're all fucking broke, so why don't you haul PP into the family and he'll save the whole shebang?'

We sit on the floor, laughing till we feel sick.

14ᵗʰ April

Mayo asks me to marry him. (Marriage proposals are like buses, I guess. You get none for thirty years, then two come along at once.)

His proposal is really touching and old-fashioned. He goes down on one knee. He says he will work hard 'all his life' for me. He's so adorable and sexy and mine and irresistible that I say 'yes' – as a kind of dare. He dances round the flat. Then we make love for about four hours.

What am I *doing*?

15ᵗʰ April

Nurse in a foul mood. Says I expect everyone to be at my beck and call, which, coming from him – saucy, bloody wind-up merchant – is just totally unfair. Sometimes, I hate Australians. They're so sarky and sure of themselves. And he treats his assistant, Peter, like a serf.

16ᵗʰ April

Mayo brings me a gold ring. It's cheap and ugly and weighs nothing.

But I put it on my third finger etc. As I do this, I feel a kind of dread go right through me.

Beno and Mercut are making an incredible amount of noise downstairs. Sounds like Lawrence's back wall is being felled – with or without his permission. Roméo laughs and says his friends are jealous because he's marrying an English girl, so he can get legal status.

Legal status?

Oh shit. Why don't I *ever* seem to see the totality of any situation?

17ᵗʰ April

Perry keeps phoning. Says he wants an answer to his proposal, which is fair enough, considering what he's offering me in the way of real estate, fine furniture and annual income.

I (stupidly) tell him I've got things to sort out. 'What things?' he snaps.

I tell him I'm in trouble at work, which is sort of true. Nursey is being foul to me. Says to me today: 'Why don't you just marry that loaded throwback of yours, lambkin, and stop cluttering up the job market?'

20th April

I'm getting in a muddle with Mayo's ring – taking it on and off. Now, I seem to have lost it. Shit. Pray it's in my desk drawer at work. Also, my period hasn't arrived . . .

22nd April

Momentous day. Dinner with Perry. Decide to simplify my life and marry him.

I don't love him. But tell myself I probably will in the future, when I'm living in Upper Grosvenor Street with a Filipino housemaid and a permanent chef and my own chauffeur at the door.

23rd April

BIG celebrations at Capell House. Mummy and Daddy beside themselves with joy and relief. Perry comes over with the ring: vast heirloom of an emerald surrounded by diamonds, but it's far too big for my finger.

I've noticed Perry's got sausagey hands, and so had all the Paris ancestors, judging from this. But he's going to get it cut down to size for me. And I guess I can live with sausages.

Still no period.

Roméo leaves a message on my mobile saying he's looking at the stars and thinking about me.

(I've found his tragic ring. Now I'm on the verge of having to wear two different engagement rings on different days and at different times . . .)

Date set for my wedding to Perry: the fatal day is 14ᵗʰ September.

24ᵗʰ April

Daddy and I play badminton in the rain. He loses. He says: 'Juliet, nothing can touch me now that you're engaged to Perry Paris. Through all my days, nights, hours, work-time and play-time I've hoped for something like this for you. Hand on heart.'

28ᵗʰ April

Nursey gives me the day off.

Mummy and I have lunch in Harvey Nicks, then hit the bridal departments across Knightsbridge and the West End.

Mummy acts blithe, but I can't help noticing the dresses *start* at 3k.

We have to put on white gloves just to touch them. We have our own personal assistant in each shop. In Liberty when I put on a veil, Mummy starts sobbing and so do I. For different reasons.

Tibs phones. He's heard the joyful news. Says to me: 'Good decision, Jule. Sensible coz. Now you'd better get that other matter wrapped up and out of your life.'

Spend the night with Roméo. Want it never to be morning.

Iˢᵗ May

Nursey takes me out for a drink. He's nice at first, then he says: 'I suppose it's your fucking wedding and your girl-brain's turning on the fifteen fucking ways to fold a table napkin, but if you don't focus up, Juliet, I'm going to have to sack you.'

'Sack away,' I say. 'You were never loyal to anyone, Nurse, so why start now?'

3ʳᵈ May

Call in sick. Nursey sacks me.

Oh well.

Feel so confused and rotten about myself, I call Tibs. Promises he'll come round tomorrow evening.

4ᵗʰ May

Worst day of my life so far . . .

Tibs arrives at six, high as well as drunk. Immediately starts calling down to Mayo, Beno and Mercut: 'Which one of you illegal fucking migrants is screwing my cousin?'

WHY did I ask Tibs to come round? Why? WHY?

Beno, Mercut and Mayo come up to the flat and start

screaming at Tibs in Moldavian. Tibs calls them 'fucking illegal scum'. Jesus Christ. I yell at them all to calm down. Then one of them (I seriously don't know which one) pushes Tibs and he falls backwards down the stairs

5th May

Couldn't go on with the diary yesterday . . .

Tibs is in hospital. He's on life support. I heard his head hit the bottom step.

Roméo has vanished. He and Mercut and Beno just disappeared moments after Tibs fell.

Can't stop crying. The suddenness of things. AWFUL, AWFUL. All my fault. *Everything.*

6th May

Police come round. Really hard for me to lie to the law, I'm so well brought-up. But I had to say it was an accident. Told the police Tibs was 'a bit drunk on vodka' and just fell. Didn't mention Mayo or the others. Now I've committed perjury or whatever. And if they finger-print my room, they'll find Roméo's body fluid all over the sheets.

Keep calling and calling Roméo on his mobile, but get the voicemail saying: 'Roméo mobile 'ere. Give me your voice again.' Breaks my heart, this message. But he's gone. They've all gone. Of course they have.

Go to see Lawrence, to see if he knows anything. Says he'll try to find out where Mayo and the others are.

Tibs's 'accident' all over the papers. (Luckily they do seem to think it was an accident.) Also pic of me and Perry and the news that *Hello!* is interested to cover our September wedding. Can't bear to think about Tibs.

Perry and Daddy come up to London. They think I'm just crying for Tibs, but of course I'm crying for the whole fucking mess. I hang on to Daddy and weep and tell him I'm sorry. He keeps saying: 'Not your fault, angel. Not your fault.' If only he knew . . .

Long for Perry to leave, but he doesn't. He's brought the size-adjusted engagement ring. Now, it's on my finger, but I don't exactly love it. I keep thinking about Mayo's little gold ring. Situation so weird and awful and full of lies. Feel I really do love Roméo and not Perry. But if I break it off with Perry and say I'm marrying a (probably illegal) Moldavian builder who may have fatally wounded Tibs, Mummy and Daddy could quite literally die.

7ᵗʰ May

Go to see Tibs on his life support. Poor baby. This sight is so terrible, I can't believe I'm looking at it.

Still nothing from Mayo. And now his mobile is 'no longer in service'.

Guess he's fled away for ever.

Cry for five hours.

8th May

Tibs died in the night. My fault. My fault. My fucking fault!

Uncle Mart and Aunt Helena out of their minds with grief.

I tell Mummy we've got to postpone the wedding. She guts me by saying: 'No, Juliet. No need to make everything worse than it is.'

I tell her I really *want* to postpone it, but she says, 'No, don't be selfish, darling. Think of other people.'

Oh God. Feel Mummy's just casting me away, like she knows I'm responsible for the whole tragedy . . .

Terrible dreams about darling Tibs and fears about more terror to come. Wish I could go to sleep and wake up to find everything had just *been a dream*.

14th May

Tibs's funeral. I wail for him. The only 'brother' I had or will ever have. And he could be such an awesome laugh.

The sadness of Uncle M and Aunt H too hard to bear. If they knew I was to blame, they'd slay me with a fish-gutting knife. Feel I want to confess to them, but a voice in me won't let me do it.

Forgot to wear Perry's ring to the funeral. He looked beadily at my naked hand. I said the emerald was too big to fit under my black gloves. Told him later I couldn't sleep with him until I got over mourning Tibs. He said that was 'a bit bloody steep'. Drove back to London at about 90mph. Don't care if I die.

18ᵗʰ May

No diary for ages. Too wretched to write it.

I get a visit from Lawrence to tell me Mayo got in touch with him. Roméo and the others are being deported as illegal immigrants. They're in a deportation 'hostel' called Mantua House, in Dover. Mayo says he wants to see me to ask my forgiveness for Tibs. Lawrence reminds me I could save Roméo from deportation by going through with a marriage.

I break down like a baby and say to Lawrence: 'What am I going to do? Tell me what to do.' We go into his flat and he rolls me a joint to calm me down. Then he says abstractedly: 'it really is all a bit baleful.'

So much for hippie counsel.

19ᵗʰ May

Feel horribly alone. Keep imagining Tibs's body under the earth.

20ᵗʰ May

Drag myself into the car and drive to Dover. Dull sky. No sun.

Mantua House a desolate shit-hole. Like a prison. Smells of sickness and death. Can't stop shivering all the time I'm there.

Mayo lies on a hard bunk in a dark room. His mouth is dry when I kiss it.

Says to me; 'How come, with all that happen, you still so fair?' The things he says, the words he chooses, just get to me sometimes. I tell him I know he didn't mean to kill Tibs. He drinks a sip of water and says: 'I drink to you, my love.'

I try to stop crying, because I have to be honest with him at last. I owe it to everyone. I just can't marry him. So I tell him it's impossible, that we're too *alienated*. I remind him we come from different worlds. I return his ring and tell him to forget me.

He barely moves or reacts. He looks terribly ill. He tells me his life is over. While he's talking, I feel my period start. Blood begins to run down my thighs.

30ᵗʰ May

Diary more or less abandoned.

Spend all my money on *stuff* from Lawrence. And not just spliffs.

I miss Tibs like mad. And I miss my lover more than I can bear to admit.

I think his absence will follow me all through my life.

14ᵗʰ September

My wedding day.

Daddy's face shines with joy as he leads me down the aisle. Is he happy for me, or merely happy about not losing Capell House?

I'm far too thin for my dress. When I get into it, it just hangs on me like a shroud.